Law in the
Sociological Enterprise

Law in the Sociological Enterprise

A Reconstruction

Lisa J. McIntyre

WASHINGTON STATE UNIVERSITY

Westview Press

BOULDER • SAN FRANCISCO • OXFORD

Published in 1994 in the United States of America by Westview Press, Inc., 5500 Central Avenue, Boulder, Colorado 80301-2877, and in the United Kingdom by Westview Press, 36 Lonsdale Road, Summertown, Oxford OX2 7EW

Library of Congress Cataloging-in-Publication Data
McIntyre, Lisa J.
    Law in the sociological enterprise : a reconstruction / by Lisa J. McIntyre
    p. cm.
    Includes bibliographical references and index.
    ISBN 0-8133-1948-X (hc.) — ISBN 0-8133-1949-8 (pbk.)
    1. Sociological jurisprudence. I. Title.
K376.M33   1994
340'.115—dc20

                                                                    93-6418
                                                                        CIP

Printed and bound in the United States of America

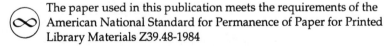

The paper used in this publication meets the requirements of the American National Standard for Permanence of Paper for Printed Library Materials Z39.48-1984

10   9   8   7   6   5   4   3   2   1

Contents

The Impact of Law on the Workplace
in the Late Twentieth Century, 202

Figures

Foreword

Despite successful challenges to the sterility of legal formalism, neither legal realists nor students of sociological jurisprudence have developed a satisfactory "theory of the distinctively legal" (Selznick 1968, 51). Using the powerful metaphor of law as a type of contract characteristic of civil, as distinguished from communal, society, Lisa McIntyre here advances such a framework, if not a fully developed theory. Her analysis of the law and social relationships, and of the consequences for those who are legally recognized as Persons (and for those who are not), is informed by both legal scholarship and sociological research, and it in turn informs both.

Because Persons have access to law, law transforms their resources. This transformation, McIntyre argues, is the essence of the distinctively legal. Her argument is grounded in the richness of historical scholarship as well as in research that probes recent social changes and contemporary conditions.

Individuals, groups, and organizations all use the law and react to it. Law is both enabling and constraining, and McIntyre examines its constitutive effects, especially its legitimating effects, as well as the manner in which law reflects "minimally acceptable values" as "a guardian at its outer limits." McIntyre thus also theorizes the complex—and often oversimplified—relationships between morals and law. She shows, for example, how law provides "legitimating formulas" for changes in relationships between Persons, for challenges by Nonpersons to their exclusions from the civil domain, and thus for expansion of that domain.

Understandably, McIntyre does not address all of the knotty problems related to the causes and consequences of expansion of the civil domain. In Part Two, however, the conceptual and historically illustrated apparatus of Part One is applied to the family and to the workplace—two of the most fundamental areas of American institutional life. In her discussion of family life and work life, she makes bold briefly to suggest the nature of future legal issues in these domains.

McIntyre acknowledges that the distinctions between Persons and Nonpersons and between the civil and communal domains "in and of themselves probably add little to our understanding of social things." But, she argues, understanding social institutions and processes in modern—particularly Western—societies requires knowledge of law's role. Her book provides a framework for theoretical and empirical inquiry into the nature of that role.

In her concluding chapter, McIntyre notes that an increase in litigation "signals . . . renegotiation of social expectations and the civil contract." Moreover, the effects of litigation and the threat of litigation reflect the importance of law in challenging—and in many cases modifying—inequities of power, and especially access to the levers of power, within the civil domain. They reflect also the untidy and often vexing problems of democracy and pluralism under conditions of uncertainty and risk that are attributable to increasing technological complexity and social interdependence.

McIntyre's book thus is both a challenge and an invitation, not only to sociologists but to all who would understand social life and the critical role law plays in it. The challenge is to extend and test ideas that are here set forth; the invitation is to make the study of law in society the mutually fruitful enterprise it can become.

James F. Short, Jr.

Acknowledgments

Writing this book turned out to be more of an odyssey than a straightforward enterprise. Fortunately, at hand were colleagues and friends willing to assist me in my quest to make some sociological sense of legal materials. Many of the debts I incurred were big ones: Robert Meier's encouragement, mentoring, and friendship got me started on this project. Donald Levine's comments, as always, kept me on track. Cindy Price bravely volunteered her students as guinea pigs and used an early version of this manuscript in her senior seminar.

When it came to coping with my way of doing scholarly stuff, my colleagues at Washington State University have proved far more tolerant than either I or they expected. Several took the time to read this book as it evolved: Marilyn Ihinger-Tallman, Irv Tallman, Mark Stafford, Joe DeMartini, Charles Tittle, Louis Gray, Armand Mauss, Lewis Carter, and Valerie Jenness. Thanks especially to Professor James Short—his guidance helped me successfully navigate the special perils facing the untenured in the academy.

Students in my undergraduate "law and society" classes and graduate sociology of law classes played important roles in the writing of this book. Their skepticism about the importance of law and sociology and their annoyingly penetrating questions about law-as-contract helped to hone my thinking. Thanks also must be given to Leslie Atkins, Ginna Babcock, Debra Henderson and Shawna Huggins for their careful bibliographic work and to Tammy Small for her editorial assistance. Katherine Streckfus, a talented copy editor, lassoed many of my wandering sentences, and Shena Redmond, project editor from Westview Press, guided this book into print. Finally, Judy Stone helped me to keep hold of my sanity during the years of writing.

Lisa J. McIntyre

The Civil Contract Perspective

This book was written to help sociologists and other social scientists further their understanding of society and interpersonal relationships and the role that law plays in these. The idea that law is important in society is hardly a new one. Comte, Spencer, Tönnies, Marx, Durkheim, and Weber would have been hard-pressed to conceive of a sociology that did not pay careful attention to law; each found the study of law to be an important source of sociological insight. To them it was clear that law had emerged in the nineteenth century as one of the fundamental elements of modern society. Therefore, the study of law was a necessary part of the sociological enterprise.

From Durkheim's perspective, for example, the law represented not only a "visible symbol" of social solidarity (1933, 64) but a crystallization of and objective point of reference to a social life otherwise "perpetually in the process of transformation and incapable of being mentally fixed by an observer" (1938, 45). Law figured even more prominently in Weber's project—his emphasis on power and authority and the way these were played out against the economic and normative structure of society made the study of law an imperative (1978). Similarly, Spencer, Tönnies, and Marx found law to be inextricably intertwined with the social fabric.

Notwithstanding these auspicious beginnings, by no feat of imagination can one pretend that law is anything like a fundamental concept in the field of sociology today. The situation seems paradoxical: As law has come to play an increasingly central role in society, it has come to be relegated to an increasingly peripheral role in sociology. The peripheral role of sociolegal studies is, I think, a barrier standing in the way of the success of the sociological enterprise.

I anticipate that any assertion that "ignoring law in sociology is a serious problem" is one that would be greeted with surprise (if not disdain) by many readers. It is telling, I think, that many sociologists generally think of "the law" as a particularly relevant variable only in such fields as criminology.[1] It is, of course, the rare criminologist who dares to study crime and criminals without at least making reference to criminal law. A criminology that did not attend to the role of law would—at best—be considered silly: After all, *crime* and *criminal* are concepts that only make sense with reference to law. Given the pervasiveness of law and its effects in American society, it is no less foolish to try to understand and explain, for example, the nature of family without knowledge of the law of domestic relations (marriage, divorce, custody). For many purposes, the nature of family can no more be explained without reference to law than the nature of crime can be, for it is law that decides which sorts of domestic arrangements are to be given the special protections and resources accorded "families" in this society. As I will show in Chapter 7, even something as legally mundane as a zoning ordinance can have an impact on family lifestyle (e.g., who can live with whom).

Similarly, it is difficult to truly understand the workings of modern formal organizations while ignoring antitrust law, which determines, among other things, what sorts of deals businesses can strike. As I will show in Chapter 8, understanding the nature of workplace relationships in this society means understanding, among other things, the nature of labor law and employment law. Likewise, a comprehensive study of medicine and health care delivery systems must make reference to the law of torts. And it is not only with respect to serious areas of life that law intrudes. In American society, the law even plays a significant and determining role in both professional and amateur sports (Fotiades 1989) and in leisure-time activities (the clubs people join, the recreational facilities they frequent, and the like).

My convictions about the importance of law in sociology developed as I was doing research in the Public Defender's Office of Cook County, Illinois. I began that work by trying to resolve a contradiction. There was, on the one hand, a widely held belief that public defenders were mere cogs in the wheels of a bureaucratic justice system: Lawyers who owed their jobs to a system bent on convicting defendants were thereby disabled from defending their clients. One political scientist put it this way:

> It is rather frightening to realize that the very same institution that is attempting to convict the defendant is also paying the salaries of those who are theoretically doing their utmost to refute these charges and

---

1. Most introductory textbooks in sociology, for example, confine mention of law (if they mention it at all) to chapters on crime and deviancy.

win an acquittal. The obvious question in the minds of many disillusioned individuals convicted of crimes after being defended by a public defender is how far his lawyer was willing to go in pushing his client's case if such an aggressive posture jeopardizes his future employment by angering other criminal justice actors. (Wice 1983, 4. For the classic statements of this position, see Sudnow 1965 and Blumberg 1967)

The consensus in scholarly circles was that public defenders could not defend because they were not allowed to defend. But, on the other hand, a great deal of empirical research had failed to find any difference in terms of outcomes for clients represented in court by public defenders and those represented by privately retained counsel (see, e.g., Wheeler and Wheeler 1980).

The contradiction between the analytic perspective and empirical findings was resolved, in part, by the discovery that public defenders were not "mere employees" subject to the whims of their employers, the judges. Public defenders, even those who owed their jobs to the most prosecution-minded judges, had a resource that had gone unnoticed by many social scientists. What resource? The law; more specifically, the Sixth Amendment requirement that those accused of crimes receive a competent defense. This constitutional mandate is a weapon wielded by public defenders. Judges cannot place too many restrictions on aggressive public defenders without putting their own reputations and even their judicial jobs in jeopardy. One lawyer told me of a case in which he had taken a trial court judge to the state supreme court, where he sought and received a writ of mandamus—a ruling telling the judge to follow the law properly (McIntyre 1987).

In retrospect, the fact that many sociologists had overlooked law as a resource for public defenders is astonishing. Then it occurred to me: If scholars had overlooked, or at least underestimated the importance of law in the courtroom—an environment in which law's influence seems especially patent—it was likely that similar oversights were occurring in other social arenas. Given the centrality of law in today's society, such oversights may be undermining sociologists' ability to understand social dynamics outside the courtroom to the same extent they were undermining their ability to understand social dynamics inside the courtroom.

There are some who would disagree with my suggestion that we need to reconstruct law's place in sociology. First, some would suggest to the contrary that law is no longer of any great importance in society and therefore of little consequence to the social scientist. In the minds of some, in postmodern society law has been rendered impotent by new foci of power, specifically, the nonjuridical disciplines (e.g., medicine, psychiatry, criminology). Foucault's work (see Gordon 1980) is said to have shown the inadequacy of the "classical understanding of power [that] turned on the notions of sovereignty and law" (Taylor 1986, 75):

> Foucault's thesis is that, while we have not ceased talking and thinking in terms of this model, we actually live in relations of power which are quite different, and which cannot be properly described in its terms. What is wielded through modern technologies of control is something quite different, in that it is not concerned with law but with normalization. . . . In fact, what has happened is a kind of infiltration of the process of law itself by this quite alien species of control. Criminals are more and more treated as "cases" to be "rehabilitated" and brought back to normal. (Taylor 1986, 75)

I disagree. Even if one ignores the diminishing enthusiasm for rehabilitation of prisoners, and the growing stress on punishment in penal law, law is still a very important factor in society. Although Foucault seemed to suggest a diminution of law's importance, it is more plausible, as Carol Smart has argued so cogently, "to posit a move in the opposite direction." In other words, it is more likely that there has been an increase in the importance of law. As Smart noted, this increase is witnessed by "the growing legalization of everyday life from the moment of conception (i.e., increasing foetal rights) through to the legal definition of death (i.e., brain death or 'body' death). It may be that law is colonized in some instances, but in others law may be extending its influence" (Smart 1989, 8).

Second, some might object that the law on the books is too far removed from the reality of everyday life for most people and thus that little can be won by looking at law. This critique is the more intriguing one, for on the face of it, it does seem that most people live out their lives without having much occasion to journey into the world of courts and lawyers. Yet, it is foolish to believe that any one of us can remain untouched by it. The very ubiquity of law has led us to take it for granted. Many of the more intimate details of life are entwined with legal concerns. For example, marital choices are constrained at least to some degree by state laws defining "incest," just as in former times they often were constrained by state laws defining "race." Likewise, parental custody of children is constrained by what the law says about parental fitness. Though generally speaking, parents enroll their children in school, their educational choices too are regulated by the law. If people grow unhappy with their marriages and/or their children, the law limits what they can do to remedy the situation.

Does the playground at the local park have a slide, swings and monkey bars? If not, that's perhaps because the potential for lawsuits growing out of playground injuries pushes up the cost of insurance. Even a simple legal issue can affect how neighborhood children play together and change the dynamics of neighborhood life. The message is that the law intrudes in ways that people generally do not think about because they have come to take these things for granted. Taking law for granted is a mistake—as I hope to show in this book.

At the same time, for all the attention I think law deserves from sociologists, I do not think that it should be conceived of as an "engine of action" (Coleman 1988, S96). Instead, to push that metaphor to its limit (but, I hope, not beyond), in the train of social life law is better thought of as a coal car, for law is an important resource or form of social capital. Looking at law is no substitute for gathering other sorts of data. But an understanding of the law can complement and strengthen one's understanding of social life.

In sum, law is related to most facets of social life in contemporary society, and because of the nature of this relationship, understanding law's role and influence is critical to understanding social groups and their operations. As sociologists, we cannot afford to be sanguine about our lack of knowledge about law.

Part One: Theoretical Considerations

In Part One (Chapters 1-6), I will propose a way for sociologists to begin to think about law. My goal will be less to offer or defend a particular definition of law than to articulate a sociologically relevant perspective on law. More specifically, to paraphrase sociologist Arthur Stinchcombe (1968, 3), the conception of law I seek here is one that will strengthen the capacity of sociologists to invent explanations about the nature of society and social interaction.

One crucial difficulty with making systematic use of law in sociology is that the importance of law varies. In some societies, law is of small consequence; in others (especially modern ones), it is a fundamental force. Even within a particular society law usually affects different people in different relationships differently. Some people have no access to law or are constrained by it; for others, law is a great resource and source of empowerment. The perspective I wish to develop is one that will allow sociologists not only to take these differences into account but, indeed, perhaps to even begin to explain them.

The sociological view of law that I will develop in this book is based on the idea of *law as civil contract*. In Chapter 1 I will suggest that law is best viewed as a contract that essentially articulates *expectations* about the basic rights and duties of *certain individuals* in *certain types of relationships*. Of course, the idea of law as contract is hardly a new one, but as I will discuss in Chapter 1, my use of this concept is different from its use by the early "contractarians."

In subsequent chapters, by drawing upon the idea of law as civil contract, I will explore the nature of the interdependency of law and society, or (as some might see it) law's intrusion into society. There is perhaps no need to "argue the general interdependence of law and society" (Selznick 1959, 115). But if this fact is to be more than a benign truism, it must be acknowledged that the interdependency between the legal and social arenas can exist in varying degrees and be manifested differently in different societies and at different times. My goal in Chapters 2-6 is to use the civil contract idea to develop a vocabulary, and a framework within which to use that vocabulary, that will better equip sociologists to study the nature and scope of this interdependence. The focus of these chapters will be three of the important dimensions of the civil contract: Persons, relationships, and expectations.

To begin the exploration of the important dimensions of law in society, in Chapter 2 I will address the issue of who is and who is not party to the civil contract; who is, in other words, a *Person* or a *Nonperson* in the eyes of the law. In brief, the critical difference is that whereas Persons have access to the resources provided by law, Nonpersons do not. Other effects of law on Persons and Nonpersons will be identified in Chapter 3, where I will discuss the nature of the Nonperson's existence in society.

The distinction between Persons and Nonpersons suggests the existence of two analytically, though not empirically, distinct spheres or arenas of action within society. I will call these the *civil domain* and the *communal domain*. Generally speaking, the crux of this distinction is that relationships in the civil domain are ones into which the law can intrude and/or ones in which law can be invoked by Persons. Relations in the civil domain, then, are subject to law. The communal domain, in contrast, embodies those relationships and parts of society in which law has no place. The communal domain, in short, is that part of society that is "lawless" (though certainly not "normless").

In Chapter 4, I will take a preliminary look at the relationship between the civil and the communal domains. Why is the civil domain (i.e., the reach of law) greater in some societies than in others? What causes the civil domain to grow larger (or smaller) relative to the whole of society itself? In other words, what causes the law to become more or less intrusive in society?

In Chapters 5 and 6 the focus shifts, moving from visible structures (persons and relationships) to ideas and expectations. What is the relationship between social expectations (i.e., norms) and legal ones (i.e., law)? Can law be an autonomous and creative force in society or does it simply mirror social values and norms?

Part Two: Applications

I will begin the second part of this work by admitting that I have left many questions unanswered. One question is, of course, To what degree will including law in sociology assist practitioners in building sociological understandings and theory? In response, I offer two illustrations of how using the civil contract perspective might help to augment sociologists' understanding of important aspects of U.S. society. In Chapter 7, I will examine law in the development of the family, and in Chapter 8, I will examine the impact of law on working life.

Chapter 9 concludes the work with a summary of the law as contract perspective and some final remarks.

*   *   *

Throughout this book, although the emphasis is on law, the goal is to construct a perspective on law that will augment our understanding of society. That, after all, is the nature of the sociological enterprise.

The reader should thus be warned: This work is not an attempt to refashion the sociology of law per se, and it is not written for a sociology of law audience. For this reason, I have avoided as much as possible the "sociology of law" jargon. My objective is to make law more accessible to sociologists who study other social things by sensitizing them to the kinds of questions that all sociologists ought to be asking about the role of law in society.

1

A Sociological
Conception of Law

Twenty-five years ago, Paul Bohannan observed that "more scholarship has probably gone into defining and explaining the concept of 'law' than into any other concept still in central use in the social sciences" (1968, 73). Figure 1.1 illustrates the variety of these definitions. Noted legal scholar H.L.A. Hart found the persistence of definitional attempts in studies of law to be unique among the academic and professional disciplines:

> No vast literature is dedicated to answering the questions "What is chemistry?" or "What is medicine?", as it is to the question "What is law?" A few lines on the opening page of an elementary textbook is all that the student of these sciences is asked to consider; and the answers he is given are of a very different kind from those tendered to the student of law. No one has thought it illuminating or important to insist that medicine is "what doctors do about illnesses", or "a prediction of what doctors will do", or to declare that what is ordinarily recognized as a characteristic, central part of chemistry, say the study of acids, is not really part of chemistry at all. Yet, in the case of law, things which at first sight look as strange as these have often been said, and not only said but urged with eloquence and passion. (1961, 1)

There would be little profit earned by reviewing these definitions in depth; the point is simply that the number and range of definitions in use prove that law has been a difficult concept to pin down. In fact, some would argue that it is impossible to conceive of law in a way that is satisfactory for sociological purposes, that is, in a way that

Law is defined as a formal means of social control that involves the use of rules that are interpreted, and are enforceable by the courts of a political community.
F. James Davis 1962.

We shall unite in viewing as law that body of principle and dogma in which a reasonable measure of probability may be predicted as the basis for judgement in pending or in future controversies.
Benjamin Cardozo 1924.

A social norm is legal if its neglect or infraction is regularly met, in threat or in fact, by the application of physical force by an individaul or group possessing the socially recognized privilege of so acting.
E. Adamson Hoebel 1954.

An order will be called law if it is externally guaranteed by the probability that coercion (physical or psychological), to bring about conformity or avenge violation, will be applied by a staff of people holding themselves specially ready for that purpose.
Max Weber 1978.

Law is "command of the sovereign."
H.L.A. Hart 1961.

The prophecies of what the courts do in fact, and nothing more pretentious, are what I mean by the Law.
Oliver Wendell Holmes 1897.

Law, in its most general and comprehensive sense, signifies a rule of action. . . . It is that rule of action which is prescribed by some superior, and which the inferior is bound to obey.
William Blackstone 1769.

Law is the result of the configurations of obligations which makes it impossible for the native to shirk his responsibility without suffering for it in the future.
Bronislaw Malinowski 1926.

Law consists of behaviors, situations, and conditions for making, interpreting, and applying legal rules which are backed by the state's legitimate coercive apparatus for enforcement.
Stephen Vago 1988.

Law is governmental social control. It is, in other words, the normative life of a state and its citizens, such as legislation, litigation and adjudication.
Donald Black 1976.

[Law is the] tool of the dominant class [that] ends by maintaining the dominance of that class. Law serves the powerful over the weak; it promotes the war of the powerful against the powerless. Moreover, law is used by the state (and its elitist government) to promote and protect itself. . . . (Law is) nothing other than official oppression.
Richard Quinney 1972.

FIGURE 1.1 Some definitions of law

would allow law to play an important role in building social theory.[1] For example, political scientist Malcolm Feeley has argued that law is probably *not* so "distinctive a social phenomena [*sic*] that it can serve as a *core* concept in the development of general social theory" (emphasis added).[2] He said,

> In different cultures and at different times, law performs different functions and is entwined in different ways with other forms of social control and methods of dispute settlement. What may be regulated by law at one time or in one setting may very well be controlled by informal peer group pressure, selfhelp, or other authoritative institutions in another. Law, unlike kinship, language, or power, does not seem to be a fundamental phenomenon. Unlike these other phenomena law is not ubiquitous, and its nature varies; hence it does not capture a constant, identifiable activity, process, or set of relationships around which basic social theory is likely to be formed. (1976, 501)

---

1. This problem of definition turns out not to be as unique as Hart thought. As Donald N. Levine pointed out in *The Flight From Ambiguity* (1985), there are many fundamental concepts whose definitions are ambiguous at best: "Heinz Eulau offers a characteristic expression of the pathos of ambiguity when he writes that '"elite," like so many other concepts in the lexicon of the social sciences, has become an all-purpose term with so many cognitive and affective meanings and uses that one might well wish to banish it from serious social-scientific discourse.' Reviewing a book that sets forth no fewer than 108 distinct interpretations of the concept of equality, Brian Barry observes: 'The whole idea of equality is a mess—probably the term should be scrapped.' Similarly, Richard Schacht concludes a book-length examination of ambiguities linked with 'alienation' by suggesting that scholars might do well to stop using the term. Aubrey Lewis cites a number of psychoanalysts who want their colleagues to get rid of the ambiguous word 'anxiety,' and David Martin argues that sociologists of religion should simply abandon the concept of 'secularization'" (16).

2. A different assessment has been given by James S. Coleman. "One might even argue," he said, "that law, as a set of rules having a high degree of internal consistency, as well as principles behind those rules, has as strong a claim to constitute social theory as does any alternative body of principles offered up by sociologists" (1986, 1313). In his recently published opus, *Foundations of Social Theory*, for example, Coleman uses the law of agency as a guide to understanding modern "disjoint" authority relations (1990, Chapter 7).

This assessment seems to exaggerate law's "specialness." For example, it may be said of kinship systems too that their nature varies and that the concept of kinship hence does not "capture a constant, identifiable activity, process, or set of relationships." Notwithstanding this similarity between kinship systems and law, however, there is no gainsaying the fact that kinship is a fundamental social concept.

Although no one definition of law (or kinship, for that matter) will be useful for all purposes, sociologists can still ask a fundamental question: What sort of conception of law is useful for scholars interested in explaining the role of law in social relationships? Although Durkheim never really defined law per se, his analysis of crime (in *The Division of Labor in Society*, 1933) teaches an important lesson: It is not especially helpful to specify or define law in terms of its contents or functions, for these vary from society to society. The implication is that such questions as "What is law?" and "How are we to conceive of law?" must be answered in terms of law's *form*.

Law is a social form—that is, a kind of social relationship with a particular structure—just as kinship is a social form; and just as kinship is distinguished from other forms of sociation by its structure rather than by its contents, what distinguishes law from other social things (norms, rules, social control, power, and so on) is its structure or form.

The idea that law is a form of interaction is at least implicit in many extant definitions of law (e.g., law as command of the sovereign, law as an expression of the dominant classes' power). But many of these conceptions of law are not as helpful as they might be to sociologists because they tend to be tied (if not riveted) to particular ideological and functional conceptions of the law—each of which has its own specific ax to grind. As anthropologist Clifford Geertz pointed out, depending upon their particular orientation, functionalists see law "as a clever device to keep people from tearing one another limb from limb, advance the interests of the dominant classes, defend the rights of the weak against the predations of the strong, or render social life a bit more predictable at its fuzzy edges" (Geertz 1983, 232). Yes, law does perform these functions—at various times, in various places, and in various ways. But these definitions of law do not capture its essence; they do not capture what Selznick would term the "distinctively legal" (1968). More important, they do not make law very accessible to sociologists wishing to use law in explaining other social phenomena.

The Idea of Contract

Underlying the present view of law is the idea of "contract"; for the law is here seen as simply *a type of contract*—albeit one writ large. To justify and make clear my use of the idea of law as contract, I first need to explicate the concept of contract in the usual (legal) sense.

This is hardly a difficult task, for even in the legal sense, the idea of contract is not at all obscure. In this day and age contracts are familiar features of everyday life. A contract is basically an enforceable promise about what is owed to and by people who have entered into some sort of exchange relationship with one another. Contracts specify in more or less detail expectations about the rights and duties of the contracting parties. In U.S. society today, legal contracts range from the simple deal finalized with a handshake (or even a nod of the head) to elaborate bargains documented by multipage texts.

Contracts may be familiar features of everyday life, but of course not every relationship is contractual. Under what circumstances do people make contracts? Many writers have stressed that contracts are necessary in situations in which trust is lacking, either because there is *distrust* or because the people contemplating a relationship do not know one another well enough to trust or to presume shared understandings and expectations (Reuschemeyer 1973, 7; Brown 1938, 14). In such cases, a contract provides an opportunity to spell things out and acts as a point of reference should dispute arise. However, historical and cross-cultural evidence emphasizes that contracts are used even when trust is present. In such situations, contracts are not used to define or specify expectations of performance, but rather to publicly *affirm* or to reiterate values and expectations that are deeply and sincerely shared. In other words, when people trust one another, their contracts are apt to be fairly vague. When they do not trust one another, their contracts are apt to include a great deal of specificity (i.e., fine print).

Marriage contracts provide a good illustration of the relationship between contractual precision and trust. When trust is high, that is, when people presume (1) mutual expectations and (2) good faith on the part of their contracting partners (as they probably do when allowed to choose their partners and marry for love) the marriage contract is typically quite vague (e.g., filled with promises to "love, honor, and cherish") and neither party feels much need to include any "fine print" or detail. The contract serves more as a ritual (that is, public) affirmation of the prospective partners' intentions; to *affirm* jointly held values and expectations rather than to specify rights and responsibilities. In contrast, when trust is low or absent, that is, when people are not quite so sure of mutuality and/or good faith, the marriage contract is quite specific (as it tends to be in cultures in which marriages are arranged).

It might be argued that it is not the existence of trust between principals but the *complexity* of the proposed deal that determines the specificity of the contract. On the face of it, this claim seems quite reasonable. The more contingencies that must be provided for, the more things need to be detailed in the contract. Yet, in a real sense, "complexity" depends upon mutuality of expectations and good faith. To return to the example of marriage, it is difficult to imagine any relationship that is more complex and in which one faces more potential contingencies. Yet, marriage contracts can be quite simple: When two individuals believe themselves to be of the same mind, anticipated complexities disappear.

The existence of a contract, then, need not indicate distrust or lack of trust. Indeed, the very willingness to contract requires a certain degree of trust (Shapiro 1987). The presence or absence of trust, shared expectations and values, and so on, has less bearing on the likelihood of a contractual arrangement than on the precision with which the contract spells out rights and duties. Other things being equal, when trust is high, contracts will be vague; in other words, the specificity of the contract will be negatively related to the amount of trust between those in the contracting relationship. Among lawyers, it is often said that a successful contract requires a "meeting of the minds"; that all parties to the contract should have a common understanding of their respective obligations. Clearly, when people presume that they share understandings, this meeting of the minds seems easier to achieve than when distrust exists. In fact, when trust is high, parties to a contract may assume (sometimes, inaccurately) that they have reached agreement even when of all the details have not been spelled out.

Although an absence of contractual precision should be a fairly reliable indication that trust exists, the existence of precision is not such a reliable indication that trust does not exist. Exceptions arise especially in situations where people who trust one another a great deal nonetheless rely—out of habit or tradition, or owing to pressure from less trusting interested third parties (e.g., family members, lawyers)—on standard contract forms (which may be quite elaborate and complex). Antenuptial agreements, for example, traditionally were instigated by parents wishing to protect themselves and their offspring from possibly spendthrift spouses (Barber 1983).

A legal contract is much more than a promise: It is an enforceable promise. What sets a contract apart from a mere promise is the fact that, by definition, the contracting process is one that gives a third party a role in the relationship. Therefore, even though a contract may be between *A* and *B*, once the bargain is sealed, the state and its power to enforce the contract become part of the package.

Because they spell out legally enforceable rights and duties, contracts in effect *create* law. Indeed, the Twelve Tables of ancient Rome are said to have contained the provision, "As a man shall declare in a legal transaction, so shall the law be" *(Cum nexum faciet mancipum que, uti lingua nuncupassit, ita jus esto)*.[3] Contractees thus not only engage in "norm-making" (Shapiro 1987, 632), they engage in *law-making*. As Durkheim put it, "Every contract thus supposes that behind the parties implicated in it there is society very ready to intervene in order to gain respect for the engagements which have been made" (1933, 114).[4] In other words, the ability to make contracts gives ordinary citizens a kind of legislative power insofar as the contract not only specifies their respective rights and duties but gives each party access to the sovereign's enforcement apparatus in the event the other breaches his or her contractual obligations (Fuller and Eisenberg 1981, 82).

In essence, contracts transform the nature of the resources held by those who sign them. Say that Albert and Bill have a contract that spells out each man's rights and duties in the relationship. If Albert breaches the contract and in so doing injures Bill, then Bill can call upon the power of the state to effect some sort of remedy. Thus, even if the injured party (Bill) is the proverbial ninety-pound weakling personally holding fewer resources (having less power) than Albert, Bill is actually *stronger* than Albert because he can invoke the power of the sovereign in order to force Albert to hold up his end of the bargain. Bill is "in the right." At the heart of the contracting process is a transformation of resources for persons who are party to the contract. The basic nature of this transformation can be summed up by the phrase "right makes might."

To make the example less abstract, let's assume that Albert is the president of the multimillion-dollar Acme Food Canning Company.

---

3. The Twelve Tables are the earliest known Roman code of law (451-450 B.C.) (Nicolas 1962, 15).

4. Although Durkheim here calls the power that contractees can invoke "society," it is more accurate (I think) to use the label "the state," for it is clear that Durkheim was speaking of "legal" contracts and not merely of promises between individuals. In Durkheim's early work, the distinction between society and state was not very important, although it would become so later (see, for example, Durkheim's "Two Laws of Penal Evolution" [1901] 1978).

Bill is a small truck farmer. President Albert contracts with Farmer
Bill to purchase his entire crop of apples at the end of the growing
season. This year, there's a bumper crop of apples and the Acme
Canning Company can't use all the apples it has contracted to buy, so
President Albert reneges on his deal with Farmer Bill. This causes an
injury to Farmer Bill who was counting on selling his crop to Acme but is
now left with bushels and bushels of rotting apples. Still, even though
Farmer Bill is just a "little guy," he can invoke the law to force
President Albert and his company to uphold their end of bargain.
Right makes might.[5]

Most of the time the state is a silent rather than an active partner
in the contract relationship. Although its presence in the background
may well discourage President Albert or Farmer Bill from breaching
their contract, its power is in reality invoked only at times when the
relationship is in crisis. And, in fact, the presence of a crisis (breach) is
no guarantee that the state's power will be invoked (it is apparently
commonplace, for example, for businesses to avoid suit in cases of breach
of contract; they simply take their losses and cease to do business with
the offending party) (Macaulay 1963).

Yet, however much the sovereign entity may appear to remain in
the background of a relationship, it is not an altogether indifferent
partner. As Durkheim so aptly pointed out, "Everything in the contract
is not contractual. Wherever a contract exists, it is submitted to
regulation which is the work of society and not that of individuals"
(1933, 211). Or, as Weber noted, "in no legal order is freedom of contract
unlimited in the sense that the law would place its guarantees of
coercion at the disposal of all and every agreement regardless of its
terms" (1978, 668). The state, then, places limits on the range of
contracts it will enforce; the law will not allow itself to be invoked to
enforce "unlawful" or "unconscionable" contracts.[6] Thus, although the

---

5. A cynic might respond that my example is something of a fairy tale and
that President Albert would send Acme's lawyers into court and make the
litigation too costly for Farmer Bill to pursue. This scenario is certainly
possible; having the law "on one's side" is no guarantee that one will get what
one is owed. However, at this point I think that we can agree that the chances
of getting what one is owed are better when the law is on one's side than when it
is not. The more realistic critique of my example is that President Albert—
knowing full well what the law says about contracts—would never dare breach
the contract in the first place.

6. An *unconscionable contract* is one that no reasonable person would
accept as fair and honest.

"Mob" may employ "contract" killers, such contracts, of course, will not be enforced by the state. To cite a less extreme example, it can also be noted that modern U.S. law is not likely to enforce a contract to purchase a freezer on time between an unscrupulous appliance retailer and a naive consumer for five times the freezer's retail value. These days, such a contract is judged to be unconscionable. Similarly, most courts have held that prenuptial agreements in which one party agrees not to contest a divorce should the other party wish one are unenforceable. As a rule, asking someone to waive his or her legal rights is contrary to public policy. Thus, not all contracts are legal and enforceable. In fact, Weber suggested, "A legal order can indeed be characterized by the agreements which it does or does not enforce" (1978, 668).

The state may play out its role in the contractual relationship in a more or less overt fashion. To take an example from the Anglo-American legal past, in return for playing its role the state at one time routinely demanded its share of the deal—as when it required that all those entering into contractual relations pay to have their contracts marked with the official state seal or have an official stamp affixed (the notorious stamp tax that got the American colonists so excited was a result of this sort of arrangement). There was even a time when the state required that it not only approve some contracts in advance but have them in its possession before they became enforceable. Blackstone[7] conjectured that it was this holding of contracts that ultimately led to the naming of England's infamous "Starr Chambers":

> It is well known that, before the banishment of the Jews under Edward I, their contracts and obligations were denominated in our ancient records *starra or starrs,* from a corruption of the Hebrew word, *shetár,* a covenant. These starrs, by an ordinance of Richard the first, preserved by Hoveden, were commanded to be enrolled and deposited in chests under three keys in certain places; one, and the most considerable of which was in the King's exchequer at

---

7. Sir William Blackstone (1723-1780). From 1753 to 1758 Blackstone lectured at Oxford University on English law—the first such lectures ever given in a University. His major work was *Commentaries on the Laws of England.* Legal Historian Charles Rembar noted that the *Commentaries* "had particular force in the new United States, where the law was part of a frontier culture starved of reading matter. The *Commentaries* pervaded not only the thought of lawyers but the lay idea of law as well, so durably that in American films in the 1940s the guardhouse lawyer is called 'Blackstone' by his buddies" (Rembar 1980, 46).

Westminster; and no starr was allowed to be valid; unless it were found in some of the said depositories. The room at the exchequer, where the chests containing these starrs were kept, was probably called the starr-chamber. ([1769] 1979, 4:263n)

Law as Civil Contract

The concept of contract is important because law is viewed as itself a type of contract, namely, a *civil contract*. Law is the articulation (again, in more or less detail) of expectations about the rights and duties of the parties to the contract. It is a contract about certain minimally acceptable behaviors or "oughts." When these expectations are breached (or are seen as having been breached by one of the parties), the injured party is entitled (though not required) to invoke the power of the sovereign in order to effect some sort of remedy.[8]

One might be tempted to cite various mandatory reporting clauses in the criminal law as exceptions to this rule that says a person is "not required to invoke the sovereign power," but it would be wrong to do so. Sociologists have long observed that the criminal law acts as if it were a "contract" between sovereign and subject/citizen rather than among citizens themselves. Hence, the "injured party" in a criminal action is technically the sovereign and not the literal victim. The option to proceed in criminal cases in modern U.S. law resides with the sovereign's representative (e.g., the police or a prosecutor).[9] Of course, in what Weber would call a "rationalized" legal system, the sovereign's use of its option to ignore rule breaking is sharply circumscribed, but the option nonetheless does exist (as demonstrated by the existence of such concepts as police and prosecutorial discretion).

The fact that the "victim" of a breach of the civil contract is "entitled but not required" to invoke the sovereign's power suggests an important difference between what happens in response to *law*

---

8. This is not to say that law only operates in the breach; how it does more is something discussed in Chapters 5 and 6.

9. See *Linda R.S. v. Richard D.*, 410 U.S. 614 (1973). In the United States, rare exceptions do exist—a few states have statutory provisions that might be used by private citizens to "challenge prosecutorial inactions," or decisions not to prosecute. It is possible that, with the rise of victims' rights groups, the number of jurisdictions allowing such challenges could rise, but this development does not seem likely in view of the constitutional difficulties it would create (Green 1988, 488n).

breaking as opposed to what follows *violation of a social norm.* Contrast the situations facing Abby and Betty:

> Abby, a college student, has breached a legal contract in which she agreed to pay the owner of an apartment building $400 per month in rent. When Abby doesn't pay, the owner may choose, on the one hand, to invoke legal machinery and begin eviction proceedings. On the other hand, the owner may choose to give Abby extra time to pay the rent. Further, even after eviction proceedings have begun, the owner may relent and give Abby a chance to pay up her rent and stay in the apartment. The choice of what to do is entirely up to the owner of the building.

> Betty, a college student, has breached the norm that one must not tell ethnic jokes. The student to whom Betty told an ethnic joke is shocked and appalled and tells several others what Betty said. As a result, Betty is shunned by all other college students for being insensitive. Once the news of Betty's norm-violating behavior is public, it can't be rescinded and the shaming stopped.

The primary difference is this: In order for a legal response to occur, the law *must* be invoked—legal action doesn't just happen. Once invoked, it can be consciously rescinded or stopped prior to the administration of a sanction. Hence, the owner of Abby's building has control over what happens to Abby. This is not true of a social response to norm violation. The victim of a violation of a nonlegal norm may wish to ignore the infraction, but if it is discovered, once informal sanctions (e.g., stigmatization) are set in motion, the victim (or any other individual, for that matter) has little control over the process. Thus, once Betty's faux pas becomes known, it is likely that no one can consciously stop the sanctioning process.

The reason parties have less control in norm-violating cases than in law-breaking cases is that breaches of social expectations "victimize" the social group rather amorphously; there can be no control over the response because there is no agency of control. Legal sanctions, in contrast, involve a certain amount of machinery (even if only primitive), and machinery can be switched on and off.

Durkheim made a similar observation in his discussion of the difference between the sanctions that grow out of penal (i.e., criminal) law and those that emanate from "purely moral rules" or norms:

> [Sanctions coming from penal law] consist essentially in suffering, or at least a loss, inflicted on the [perpetrator]. They make demands on his fortune, or on his honor, or on his life, or on his liberty, and deprive him of something he enjoys .... It is true that those [sanctions] which

are attached to rules which are purely moral have the same character, only they are distributed in a diffuse manner, by everybody indiscriminately, whereas those in penal law are applied through the intermediary of a definite organ; they are organized. (1933, 69)

Elements of the Civil Contract

Any contract, including the civil contract, creates legal obligations on the part of those who are party to it. The word "obligation" is derived from Latin *(obligato)* and originally referred to a "sealed bond." In the legal sense, contract-as-obligation refers to a bond between persons which confers upon them certain legal advantages and disadvantages (see Scruton 1982).

Wesley Newcomb Hohfeld (1923) wrote about these legal advantages and disadvantages in his discussion about "jural" or legal relationships.[10] He noted that in the abstract, there are four legal advantages and four legal disadvantages:

Legal Advantages

Right: an affirmative claim on another

Privilege: a liberty, or freedom from the claim of someone else

Power: affirmative control over a given legal relationship

Immunity: freedom from legal power or control in a legal relationship

Legal Disadvantages

Duty: that which the law requires to be done or forborne by a specific person

No right: incapacity to make a claim against another

Liability: a condition in which one's legal relationship is subject to the control of another (children are typically liable to control of parents)

---

10. Wesley Newcomb Hohfeld (1879-1918) taught law at Stanford and Yale. He is remembered best for his analysis of basic legal concepts and his insistence that terms in legal discourse be used with precision.

Disability: incapacity to alter a legal relationship

There are a number of ways in which these advantages and disadvantages can be arrayed to show the dynamics of "jural relations." For the purpose at hand, the most relevant array is what Hohfeld called "jural correlatives." Jural correlatives have to do with how legal advantages and disadvantages are arranged between two parties. The possible jural correlatives are sketched in Figure 1.2.

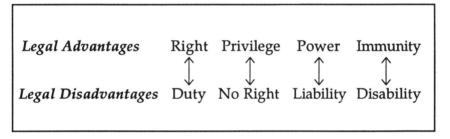

FIGURE 1.2 Hohfeld's jural correlatives

Arrayed this way, legal advantages and disadvantages are called "correlatives" because the existence of any particular *advantage* on the part of one party necessarily implies the existence of a specific legal *disadvantage* on the part of the second party.

Let's say that two people—Bob and Andy—are in a legal relationship. According to the first correlative, if one has the *right*, the other must have a *duty*. Thus, if Bob has the right to a big piece of cake, Andy has the duty to give it to him. If Andy has no duty, then Bob has no right. According to the second correlative, if Bob has a *privilege* or the freedom to walk across the yard, then Andy has *no right* to stop him. Likewise, if Criminal Bob has the privilege not to confess to a crime, then Officer Andy has no right to compel Bob to confess. Third, if Bob has legal *power* in a relationship, that is the same as saying that Andy is *liable* to that power. If Judge Bob has the legal power to increase Andy's child support payments, then Andy is liable for those increased payments. Finally, if Bob has *immunity* to something, then Andy cannot do—or is *disabled*—from doing anything about that. So, if Bob is a diplomat and Andy is a prosecutor, Andy is disabled from prosecuting Bob because he has diplomatic immunity.

Many people tend to think of law in terms of social control, and for this reason they generally stress the legal disadvantages that the civil contract confers. The typical understanding of law, in other words, tends to stress the "thou shalt not . . ." side of the civil contract. What is helpful about Hohfeld's conception is that it stresses the extent to which every legal disadvantage necessarily implies a legal advantage. The civil contract is thus as much about resources as it is about constraints.

Look more closely at the idea of legal advantages. Note that, for example, a right is defined as an "affirmative claim on another." This definition stresses the fact that legal advantages only manifest themselves in relationships. For example, landlords' rights exist against tenants' duties; workers' rights exist against employers' duties; students' rights exist with respect to teachers' duties. The same is true with respect to legal disadvantages; they are only manifested in relationships.

One can describe legal advantages and disadvantages this way, and in fact, most discussions of such things stress the interpersonal relationship aspect. But a different perspective helps to capture the "sociological" flavor of rights. Defining rights not as claims against another person, but as *an affirmative claim against the sovereign or state* emphasizes the public aspect of rights. In this sense, a "right against another person" is a kind of ticket that entitles the holder of that right to invoke the law, that is, the power of the state, to make sure that right gets fulfilled or that others do their duty. Thus, a person's right not to be battered by his or her spouse is, in this sense, a right to compel the police to provide protection. One's right to private property not only implies that no one else has a right to trespass on it or steal it but can be invoked as a claim on the state to protect property owner's interests against trespassers, thieves, and claim jumpers. Children have a right to food, and their parents have a duty to provide that food. If they do not, the child can invoke the power of the state to compel the parents to provide it somehow. In this sense, all rights have a public aspect to them. No legal advantage supplies protection in and of itself, but rather allows citizens to call upon the power of the sovereign.

This ability to call upon the power of the sovereign is the benefit of law or of the civil contract. Just because it is written somewhere that someone has a right doesn't mean he or she will receive it. As Hobbes ([1651] 1962, 129) said, "Covenants without swords are but words." In order for a covenant to hold, the power of the sovereign or state must exist somewhere back in the relationship.

At the same time, the bearer of a right or any other legal advantage must assert it for it to be realized. Sometimes, what matters is not whether someone has a right, but whether or not he or she asserts it. If one asserts a right, then the state or the sovereign has the duty to make sure that right is respected. What is important to note is the fact that, under most circumstances, one's use of any legal advantage is optional. Thus, all citizens have a right to vote, but they don't have to use it; people have the privilege of not having to incriminate themselves, but they may confess if they wish; and so on. Similarly, your legal disadvantages may be invoked at someone else's whim: For example, in the United States a police officer has no right to require someone to incriminate him or herself, but unless the suspect invokes the privilege against self-incrimination, the police officer can ask!

This public aspect of rights is important. The law as civil contract idea emphasizes much the same way as the ordinary legal contract does—that *law transforms the resources* of those who have access to it. In essence, law makes the state or civil apparatus what social psychological exchange theorists might call the *nth* party in certain kinds of relations. As Weber pointed out, "Every [legal] right is thus a source of power of which even a hitherto entirely powerless person may become possessed" (1978, 667).

The idea of law as a civil contract provides a key to understanding law's impact on society; it is exactly this transformation of personal resources, coupled with the victim's control over these resources, that forms the essence of the "distinctively legal."

Civil Contract and Society

The idea of a contract writ large is hardly a new one; in fact, the notion of "social contract" is one that dominated political philosophy for generations and has been more recently reinvoked by Rawls (1971). My view of the civil contract is quite different, however, from that put forth by social contract theorists. The most important difference has to do with assumptions about *who* is party to the contract.

The original contractarians (Hobbes, Locke, Rousseau, etc.) maintained that each person who lived within a particular society was party to its social contract. Thomas Hobbes spoke of the social contract as a "covenant of every man with every man" ([1651] 1962, 132); Jean Jacques Rousseau argued that the terms of the social contract "reduce themselves . . . to a single stipulation, namely: the total alienation of the whole community of each associate, together with every last one of his rights. . . . Each gives himself to everybody" (1762, 19). The social contract, they argued, was what bound the entire society together because it articulated the rights and duties of *each* of a society's members (except when, as in the theories of Hobbes and Rousseau, the sovereign was exempted).

It is difficult to sustain such a vision of law's place in society because, as Durkheim said (for a different reason) of Rousseau's social contract theory, "It has no relation to the facts. The observer does not meet it along his road, so to speak" (1933, 202). Not all individuals in any society stand in the same relation to the law. "Discrimination," as Donald Black asserted, "is ubiquitous" (1989, 21). It is more accurate, then, to say that the law functions as if it were a contract *only for a subset of society*—namely, those persons who are parties to the contract.

For purposes of clarity, one can separate any society into at least two analytically separate constituent domains: civil and communal. As I explore in great detail in the chapters that follow (and illustrate graphically in Figure 2.1), each of these domains has two ingredients: actors and relationships. More specifically, the civil domain includes people who are parties to the contract and *some* of their relationships with one another—those relationships that are recognized as valid (or are "cognizable") by the law/civil contract. The rest of society makes up the *communal domain*—which includes people who are not parties to the civil contract as well as all relations that are extralegal. So, for example, relations between friends—which include no legally enforceable advantages or disadvantages—exist in the communal domain; relations between business partners—to the extent that these comprise advantages or disadvantages that are legally enforceable— exist in the civil domain. (Of course, this is an analytic distinction rather than an empirical one. The two individuals involved may be friends as well as business partners. Hence, part of their overall relationship is communal [the friendship] and part of it is civil [the business partnership].)[11]

The Problem of Consent

The existence of two domains in society—the civil and the communal—suggests a resolution (for present purposes, at least) to a

---

11. One hesitates to muddy the waters at this point, but it must be noted that some societies have more than two domains. For example, as I will discuss in Chapter 7, in England people longed served—in essence—two sovereign powers: the state and the church. As a result, relationships in society may have been subject to two sorts of laws: secular (or common) law and church (or ecclesiastical) law.

problem that plagued seventeenth- and eighteenth-century contractarians (Hobbes, Locke, Rousseau, etc.), that is, the issue of "consent." Many of those who opposed social contract theory charged that it was flawed in that there was (and could be) no consent to the social contract by all the people living under its jurisdiction. This problem was seen as a fatal flaw in that a contract without consent was no contract at all.

Locke (among others) attempted to resolve the problem by distinguishing between "tacit" and "express" consent. Simply put, tacit consent to the social contract was assumed on the part of anyone who accepted the protection of the sovereign: "Every Man, that hath any Possession, or Enjoyment of any part of the Dominions of any Government, doth thereby give his *tacit Consent*, and is as far forth obliged to Obedience to the Laws of that Government during such Enjoyment, as any one under it" ([1678] 1963, 2: ¶119).

Locke argued that remaining under the protection of a sovereign makes one subject to its power and obligated to follow its rules. If someone objects to this, he said, all he or she need do is to leave the dominion of that sovereign, for "he is at liberty to go and incorporate himself into any other Commonwealth, or to agree with others to begin a new one, *in vacuis locis*, in any part of the World, they can find free and unpossessed" (¶121). (Locke's position brings to mind the ubiquitous bumper sticker: My country, love it or leave it.)

Critics responded that Locke's "solution" to the problem of consent was no solution at all and that it merely camouflaged the problem. David Hume, in his essay, "Of the Original Contract," reacted to Locke's idea by saying, "It may be answered that such an implied consent can only have place where a man imagines that the matter depends on his choice." Yet, it was preposterous, Hume suggested, to imagine that many people really did have a choice: "Can we seriously say that a poor peasant or partizan has a free choice to leave his country, when he knows no foreign language or manners, and lives from day to day, by small wages which he acquires? We may as well assert, that a man, by remaining in a vessel, freely consents to the dominion of the master; though he was carried on board while asleep, and must leap into the ocean, and perish, the moment he leaves her" (Hume [1748] 1965, 263).

What makes tacit consent difficult to accept as the equivalent of express consent is that it seems unlikely that each human being living in society, if asked, would actually consent to the social contract. It is one thing to argue that "staying" implies consent when exiting is merely inconvenient, but quite another when exiting means great loss and possibly even death. Thus, it makes little intuitive sense to say that the slave who remains by his master's side without attempting to escape is "tacitly consenting" to his enslavement. At the same time, the functional equivalence of tacit and express consent is not—in all instances—an absurd notion. For some (for example, those with the resources to leave, or to make their complaints heard [Hirschman 1970]), staying obviously is tantamount to consenting to the contract. For example, it does make sense to assert that the college student who stays in a course where she is subjected to an incredibly heavy workload may not like this fact but by not dropping the course is giving tacit consent to the course workload.

Moreover, because the civil and communal domains are distinct, a stronger case can be made for the validity of tacit consent qua consent: One need not argue that *everyone* in society consents to the contract; if the civil domain is not coterminous with society, then it is possible to exit (or be excluded from) the civil domain without leaving society. Such is the existence of the outlaw. Exclusion is also characteristic of others who "drop out"—hippies, Gypsies, and, more recently, many *Sannyasin* (as the followers of Bhagwan Shree Rajneesh were called). It is also characteristic of South African whites who marry blacks. The situation of black people in South Africa under apartheid also illustrates the fact that in many societies there are groups of people who live in society without ever having been included in the civil domain. This is, after all, the nature of the nonenfranchised person's existence. As I will suggest in Chapter 2, to live in a society and yet be excluded from its civil domain is to live in "occupied territory."

Of course, withholding one's consent from the civil contract and dropping out are not without costs—possibly extreme costs. And it is likely that these costs do prevent some people from exercising the option to exit. The college student mentioned above, for example, may feel that she can't drop the course because it is required for students in her major. But does the existence of exit costs necessarily mean that staying (and thus giving tacit consent) is a result of other than "free will"?

No. In the first place, the distinction between free will and duress is not so easily made.

As Justice Holmes has said, it is characteristic of duress that the victim makes a choice, in accordance with his own self-interest, between two evils. But a similar motivation underlies the ordinary contractual transaction. We speak of a contract as being "voluntary," the result of "free will," but it is easy to forget that a will exercises its freedom only in selecting one of several courses of action. I agree to pay ten cents for a loaf of bread, not because I want to give the baker ten cents, but because that's the only way I can get the bread. I am choosing between alternatives, giving up the dime or doing without the bread. If my will were [sic] completely unrestrained, I should certainly prefer to get the bread and also keep the money. My freedom is simply the opportunity to decide whether I will give up the ten cents, or do without the bread—to choose one of two courses, neither of which is entirely satisfactory. (Dalzell [1942] 1979, 238)

Arguably, one *always* has a choice. Sociologist Georg Simmel put it this way: "Even in the most oppressive and cruel cases of subordination there is still a considerable measure of personal freedom. We merely do not become aware of it, because its manifestation would entail sacrifices which we usually never think of taking upon ourselves" (1950, 182).

Simmel's point is well taken—there is always a choice. But all choices are not equal. My sense, for example, is that most people would see the choice confronting the overworked college student as a situation in which the individual may exercise a reasonable degree of choice. In contrast, most people would probably judge that the slave who must choose between servitude or death is being coerced. Similarly, "10 cents or no loaf of bread" is a reasonable choice but "your money or your life" signifies duress. The distinction that must be made, I think, is not really a distinction between free will and duress or coercion. The distinction that must be made is between being forced to make *reasonable* and *unreasonable* choices.

This is by no means an easy distinction to make. The difficulty in distinguishing between reasonable and unreasonable turns on the fact that what is perceived to be reasonable may change a great deal over time.[12] As I will discuss further in Chapter 8, 150 years ago having to choose between using an unsafe piece of equipment at work and losing one's job was considered a reasonable choice to have to make, as was

---

12. John Dawson's (1947) discussion of the history of meanings applied to the concept of "economic duress" illustrates this inconstancy quite vividly. Although today many scholars still consider "consent" to be the cornerstone of contract, the concept is less important now than it was 100 years ago. The perceived importance of consent in making a contract legitimate was a product of the times in which the theory of contracts emerged. As P. S. Atiyah noted, that was a period in which "the idea of freedom had reached its highest point": "The classical model of contract grew up in the shadow of a number of intellectual movements which stressed the importance of free choice and consent as the origin of legal and moral obligations alike. It is unnecessary here to do more than point to the obvious sources of the legal ideal of freedom of contract—the classical economists, the Benthamite utilitarians, the radical politicians calling for democracy, and, perhaps more generally, liberalism and all that it stood for" (1981, 7).

being required (decades later) to sign a "yellow dog contract" as a condition of employment.[13] Today these choices would be considered (in most cases) unreasonable, and laws are in place to protect workers from having to make such decisions.[14] In a similar fashion, looking back we judge the "choice" given African American citizens seeking public transportation in the 1950s (i.e., sit in the back of the bus or don't ride the bus) to have been an unreasonable one. At the time, however, many believed it was a reasonable choice for society to impose.

For a more contemporary illustration consider the following:

> Dr. X happens to notice that the foot of C, a minor child, is swollen and blue. Dr. X inquires and finds that an injury occurred over a week ago and the foot is broken. However, C's parents have refused to do anything about the injury and when Dr. X asks permission to treat the foot, they refuse. Dr. X treats the foot anyway. Despite the recalcitrance of the parents, the good doctor is entitled to payment for the reasonable value of the services rendered. This result is based on the quasi-contract and the duty of the parent to care for a child. (Schaber and Rohwer 1984, 111)

Is the "choice" being forced on C's parents a reasonable one? Most people probably would respond that, given the circumstances, it is, but it too is a variety of the "your money or your life" demand.

The distinction between reasonable and unreasonable choices is only a matter of degree. The line dividing the two is an issue that is determined by the civil contract (law) as well as by normative (social or extralegal) expectations.

"Social Contract" Tests Legitimacy, "Civil Contract" Illuminates Dynamics

The intent here is not to suggest theoretic resolution of matters of long-standing debate in political philosophy. For one thing, the goal of the political philosophers who use the idea of *social contract* is quite different from the goal underlying the use of *civil contract* in the present work. Classical and contemporary contract theorists use "social

---

13. Yellow dog contracts required employees to promise not to join unions. No longer legal in the United States, these contracts are discussed in more detail in Chapter 8.

14. Many provisions of the Occupational Safety and Health Act, for example, serve this purpose.

contract" as a device to justify the imposition of sovereign power upon an entire society, or at least to test the legitimacy of such power. The validity of their use of this concept rests firmly on the requirement that all members (or, at least, all adult members?) consent. As Don Herzog noted in his examination of consent theory, such theories include, "briefly, any political, moral, legal, or social theory that casts society as a collection of free individuals and then seeks to explain or justify outcomes by appealing to their voluntary actions, especially choice or consent" (1989, 1). The validity of the contract metaphor as it is used here, in contrast, does not depend upon the premise that *all* people in society consent to the contract. To the contrary, the point is that only *some* people consent; that only some people in society are parties to the contract. In the present context, the object of the contract metaphor is to help illuminate (not legitimate) the nature and dynamics of the law and society relationship, and clearly, just as not everyone stands in the same relation to the law, not everyone consents to the same degree. In fact, in many societies most people do not consent at all.

2

Law and Social Relationships

The law is first and foremost about relationships for it is only within the context of relationships that the transformation of personal resources made possible by law can occur. But the law does not influence or intrude into all social relationships to the same degree. Some relationships involve no legal advantages or disadvantages, others are packed with them. Two concepts form a basis for understanding the extent to which law is a factor in society:

- First, individuals in society are differentially eligible for the potential transformation of resources that the law provides.

- Second, even for eligible individuals the transformation of resources that the law affords may be invoked only in certain types of relationships.

Persons and Nonpersons

In most societies different individuals have different access to the transformation of resources that the law provides. Within a particular society it may be that the sovereign responds to the claims of some people injured by breaches of the civil contract, but ignores injuries done to others. This reflects the fact that not all individuals are equal parties to the civil contract. To put it more starkly, not all individuals who live within a society are fully "Persons" in the legal sense. Legal Persons are those who have "standing" in the eyes of the law, that is, people who have no special legal disabilities and who have full power to invoke and marshal the resources of sovereign protection. Before I explain this conception of Person in more detail, a few explanations of terminology would be helpful.

First, as noted in the previous chapter, "legal disability" denotes a lack of legal power to do something. The term can be used in both a general and a specific sense. In the general sense, for example, people are typically disabled from selling property to which they do not have title. In other words, people cannot sell or otherwise dispose of property they do not own. I will be using the term in a more narrow sense to refer to disabilities peculiar to certain categories of individuals. In many jurisdictions, for example, children are legally disabled from, inter alia, signing contracts, purchasing liquor, having sex, and smoking cigarettes (see, Davis and Schwartz 1987; Rodman, Lewis and Griffith 1984). Individuals convicted of serious crimes may be disabled from voting, holding public office, entering into certain types of contractual arrangements, obtaining professional licenses or bonding and even insurance and pensions (Grant, LeCornu, Pickens, Rivkin and Vinson 1970).

Second, in law "standing" has a highly technical meaning having to do with whether a litigant has a cognizable interest in a dispute such that he or she can bring it into court. That is, one only has standing in a controversy if one has a concrete, personal stake in the outcome of the case. I am using the word in a broader sense to imply that one has the capacity (or ability) to invoke the law. In this sense, standing is the opposite of legal disability.

In many respects, the concept of standing connotes "political" (or legal) power as this idea is used in the colloquial sense, or at least access to such power. I have used the alternative phrasing ("standing") in hopes that it will free us to inspect, in a more sociological way, the impact of having access to the transformation of resources that law provides. Like the classical contract theorists, most students of political power have concerned themselves with (and limited themselves to) the relationship between individual and sovereign; yet, there is a great deal to be learned from an examination of relationships between individuals and groups of individuals, even though these relationships may be mediated by the state (Schwartz 1978, 4-5).

Some might object to any suggestion that Personhood is an artifact of the civil contract, that is, to the idea that Persons are not born but made by the civil domain (see, for example, Noonan, 1984). To make sense of this, however, one need only reflect on the fact that not until the thirteenth century did the word "person" arrive at its present meaning. It is derived from the Latin *"Persona,"* which originally meant a mask worn by an actor. It later came to refer to a character in a play or a part acted by a player (Williams 1983, 232). I am using

Person, in the late Latin (c. A.D. 160-600) sense, to refer to the mantle or mask that is assumed by (or put onto) an individual to allow him or her to be recognized by the law. In many legal systems, the mask of Personhood may be worn by both natural persons and artificial ones (e.g., incorporated groups).

Corporations as Persons

The use of the phrase "incorporated group," as opposed to just "group," is an important clue to the fact that we are talking about something legal, for incorporation is a legal thing. Although people have acted collectively at least since the first group of people banded together to kill a saber-toothed tiger (or an elephant, or whatever), the incorporated group per se is a relatively recent human invention. The word "corporate," comes from the Latin word *"corpus,"* meaning "body." Incorporated groups are groups that (from the legal perspective) are viewed not as a sum of individuals but as having one body. Incorporated groups are legal or juristic Persons. In other words (in the old Latin sense), incorporated groups are those groups that wear the mask of Personhood. How did this idea come about?

Until the thirteenth century, the law did not find it necessary to think of a group of humans as having a unitary body, for it responded to all groups as simple aggregates of humans.[1] Then things changed. In the thirteenth century, the King of England took the revolutionary step of issuing charters to towns. Cambridge, England, for example, was issued one of those early charters. What the charter meant was that in the eyes of the law, a new "Person" had come on the scene; like a human Person, a town could own toll roads and other sorts of property, sell or rent its property, have a treasury, and enter into contracts. A charter also meant that towns could come into courts as litigants—that towns could sue and be sued.

But to make all this possible, the law had to invent a new concept—a new sort of entity that was not identical to any particular human being but was just as distinct, having its own rights, resources, and interests. This notion of group-as-Person might seem quite simple from a twentieth-century perspective. In the 1990s, becoming a corporation is hardly an exotic thing. One simply fills out a form and

---

1. For the history of corporations I have drawn heavily from James Coleman's provocative book *Power and the Structure of Society* (1974), Chapter 1.

pays a fee. In return, one is awarded "articles of incorporation" and can begin acting as a corporate being. But 600 years ago the process was anything but simple; it was both complex and quite revolutionary. At first it was not clear how this corporate entity was to be treated or thought of by the law. But rather than make up a whole new category, the law simply created a legal fiction—the juristic Person. The corporation was given a legal mask of Person in the eyes of the law.

English towns and villages were not the only entities that could become legal Persons distinct from the individuals who made up the group. Churches, especially on the continent of Europe, also acquired this status. Local churches were originally established and given lands and money by a landowning patron. After they were established, churches often drifted from their original patrons and moved into a sort of legal limbo. As they attempted to contract to buy and sell land, or obtain the services of local tradespersons, a puzzling question arose: Who was it that was party to the contract?

The obvious thing was to say that it was the priest. But this answer presented difficulties. Priests might be moved from parish to parish; worse, priests would die. Who then would inherit church property? Church members were understandably reluctant to give their churches to the priests. But if the priest could not sign contracts himself, who was the party to the contract? Who was buying and selling the land or hiring the tradespersons? For a time, the courts dealt with this problem in a bizarre fashion: If a church was named "St. Peter's Church," then St. Peter was viewed as the owner of the church (never mind that St. Peter had been dead for more than a millennium).

And so, as in the case of towns, the law began to recognize that the church was not owned by St. Peter but was itself a distinct entity or Person before the law. Churches, like towns, could enter into contracts and become involved in disputes. These Persons, in other words, could act and be acted upon even though they had no physical bodies.

Ultimately, as things turned out, the law did not just recognize these forms of actions, these new legal Persons; it helped them out as well. At one point in history, the family was the group most involved in business together. Legally, families were not regarded as a group, as everyone in the family was legally embodied in, or came under the umbrella of, the Person of the male head of household—he signed the contracts, and was liable for debts, and so on. Because of this arrangement, the family group presented no problems to the law.

As economic enterprise began to outgrow the family it became useful for several unrelated persons to join together to carry out business. Most people would be reluctant, however, to join with a bunch of nonfamily members and become personally liable for their possibly outrageous debts and silly contracts. A way needed to be found for people to protect themselves from the liabilities that joint enterprise might bring. Because the economic well-being of the country seemed to depend upon getting people together to do business, English lawmakers invented the doctrine of "limited liability" and applied it to corporations. Under this doctrine, corporate debts and liabilities could be traced back to individual members of the corporations, but they were stopped before reaching everything the individual owned. For example, the doctrine of limited liability meant that if a corporation owed someone a million pounds a member of the corporation was only liable for some amount not exceeding the extent of his or her original investment. Thus, if the corporation member had only invested ten shillings in the corporation, that was all he or she could lose if the corporation went bankrupt. It was this notion of limited liability that probably made possible the growth of the great English trading companies—the East India Company, for example—and later helped to ease the way for the industrial revolution.

Early immigrants to this country, of course, knew of the corporation (some colonies were actually corporations), but in colonial America corporations were not plentiful. According to Lawrence Friedman, not counting towns and churches, only seven corporations were formed prior to the American Revolution (1985a, 189). Why? In the first place, people were concerned with survival and had little time for entering into complex formal business arrangements. Most business enterprises were carried out by one person, by members of a family, or by small partnerships. More important, perhaps, there was a distrust of activities whose goals were primarily mercenary—especially in the Northern Colonies.

As people got more settled and were ready to invest in larger enterprises (and wanted the protection of being in a corporation), they found that it was difficult to form a corporation. To start a corporation, one had to apply to the state legislature for a special charter. Each article of incorporation or charter was voted on separately by the legislative body in the state in which the group wanted to incorporate. This was a bulky and time consuming procedure and often not worth the effort. Eventually, however, between 1850 and 1900, most states abolished the requirement of special charters and instead instituted something called "general articles of incorporation," creating a system that was more like what we have today—where forms get filled out and fees get paid, and then a corporation is born.[2]

Prior to the Civil War some U.S. courts viewed corporations with distrust; these potentially powerful actors lacked both soul and conscience (Hall 1989, 109-110). One sort of control over corporations was effected through use of the doctrine of *ultra vires*. This doctrine was invoked to restrain corporations from acting "beyond the scope" of the powers granted them by their charters. As legal historian Kermit Hall noted, "this doctrine contributed an element of uncertainty to business dealings, because it meant that a person who entered into a contract with a corporation did so at some risk. If the contract was declared [by the courts] *ultra vires*, it could not be enforced and damages could not be collected" (1989, 110).

Ultimately, however, the law helped corporations more than it hindered them. In 1819 the U.S. Supreme Court, under the leadership of Chief Justice John Marshall, took the first step toward granting business corporations the mantle of Personhood. In *Dartmouth College v. Woodward*, the Court held that corporate charters were contracts protected by the contract clause (Article 1, §10) of the U.S. Constitution. As a result, the Court said, a contract between a corporation and another legal actor must be respected as much as any legal contract between two mortal persons (4 Wheaton 518 [1819]). [3]

---

2. By the late nineteenth century, corporations in the United States were encouraged not only by the ease of incorporation and the rule of limited liability but also by the fact that incorporation was done under the jurisdiction of states rather than of the federal government. This arrangement helped because the states wanted corporations to come into their jurisdiction and do business (and, of course, pay taxes). States competed to attract corporations, and many found it to their advantage in this competition to pass laws of incorporation that were especially helpful to corporate leadership. What was most attractive to those who actually ran the corporations was being legally as free as possible to do as they wished without having to be accountable to the stockholders and investors.

The state of Delaware probably could be declared the overall winner in this corporation derby—it passed laws allowing corporations to take actions approved only by a majority of the stock holders rather than by unanimous votes and to hold annual corporate meetings in places not easily accessible to the stockholders. The result was that the corporate officers were able to enter new forms of enterprise and achieve spectacular growth and profits (not to mention, spectacular losses) much more readily than they could under more restrictive rules.

3. A discussion of how one "decodes" case citations follows the list of "Cases Cited" at the back of the book in "A Brief Guide to Case Citations."

A new phase began in 1868, when the Fourteenth Amendment to the U.S. Constitution was ratified and became part of the law of the land. Eighteen years later, in 1886, the status of the corporation as a juristic Person was enhanced—perhaps beyond any corporate officer's dreams. This was when the Supreme Court decided the case of *Santa Clara County v. Southern Pacific Railroad Company* (118 U.S. 394 [1886]). In that case the question was, Did the Fourteenth Amendment's equal protection clause bar the state of California from taxing corporate property differently than property that was owned by individuals? The Court's answer? Yes. In the process of answering this question, the Court ruled that corporations were no longer legal Persons for limited purposes only, but fell under the definition of Personhood embraced by the crucial Fourteenth Amendment provision that, "No State shall deprive any person of life, liberty, or property, without due process of law; nor deny to any person within its jurisdiction the equal protection of the laws."

What did this decision mean? It meant that corporations could not only enter into contracts and court cases but could now exercise legal rights as Persons.[4] This interpretation of the Fourteenth Amendment was perhaps the greatest boon to corporations that had ever been discovered or invented, and corporations made great use of it. In fact, during the fifty years that followed the Court's ruling in *Santa Clara*, no one made more use of the Fourteenth Amendment than corporations. In cases in which the Court applied the Fourteenth Amendment between 1886 and 1936, "Less than one-half of one percent invoked it in protection of the Negro race, and more than 50% asked that its benefits be extended to corporations" (*Connecticut General Life Insurance Company v. Johnson*, 303 U.S. 77 [1938]. Hugo Black, *dis.*).

In passing, it might be noted that although the idea of corporations as Persons is a relatively recent one (Coleman 1974, Chapter 1), attributing Personhood to nonhumans is not a uniquely modern phenomenon. According to law professor Christopher Stone, "If one traces culture back far enough, there must certainly have been times when things (for example, totems) were regarded as having an

---

4. Corporations are not citizens and therefore cannot vote, but they are entitled to most other rights accorded Persons by the law--including rights to due process and free speech. Some commentators have suggested that giving such rights to corporations is not fair because corporations do not carry the same duties that human persons do. The typical example is that corporations cannot be drafted (of course, neither can women in the United States).

independent moral and legal existence. Even in twentieth-century India we have a case in which an interfamily dispute regarding custody of the family idol was reversed with orders that, on retrial, counsel be appointed for the idol" (1987, 21-22).

Human Persons

For the most part, the concept of Personhood is offered here as something of an ideal or pure type (Weber 1978, 20-21). Unlike the true ideal type, however, "Person" is not simply an analytic construct or heuristic. Although there may be no entity that exactly matches, say, the ideal typical bureaucracy, in each society there are at least some individuals with full legal standing (Persons). Likewise, there are individuals or entities in each society with no legal standing (Nonpersons). However, though pure examples of each type exist in each society, when I write of "Persons" and "Nonpersons," it is with the understanding that the attributes of Personhood can (and in many cases, do) exist along a continuum and that, depending upon the civil society under study, there may or may not be what lawyers call a bright line between them.

In some societies, however (and in times past, perhaps in all societies), the line between Person and Nonperson is not only bright, but shining. Ancient Roman law, for example, distinguished between citizen *(civis)* and mere inhabitant *(incola)*, and further, between those who lived under the control of others *(alieni juris)* and those with the legal ability to manage their own affairs *(sui juris)*. In Roman law, then, it was very clear who was and who was not a full party to the civil contract. Several hundred years later, English legal historians Pollock and Maitland (1898) offered a list of individuals who were not Persons in the eyes of old English law. The list included infants, lunatics, idiots, Jews, monks, married women, and other suspect characters. Many examples, of course, can be drawn from the American experience. The Constitution as it was originally interpreted and executed for the most part excluded women and African and Native Americans from the list of "We the People."

It must not be forgotten that any notion that all (adult) people in a society have a claim to Personhood is a fairly recent one. Historically, in most societies large portions of the population had no legal standing or—at best—were clearly second-class citizens. One nineteenth-century commentator explained the traditional view this way:

In all human society, and under every form of government, we find two general divisions of persons; the one holding an *immediate,* the other a *mediate* relation to the community in which they live. It is competent to persons of the former description to dispose of themselves and their affairs as they please, with no other limitation than that which is laid on them by the laws of the community to which they belong. . . .

But, besides these persons, there have always been, under every form of government, from the most stringent despotism to the purest democracy, a large number of persons who stand only in a *mediate* relation to society, or to its governing power; or who, in other words, are related to it through the medium of others. In every civilized country all persons, who have not attained their majority, are of this description; to a certain extent, also, all married women, without regard to age, are of this description; and in many ages and countries, the relations of master and servant have been such, that servants have been all their life long persons of the same description. . . . The relation of this whole description of persons to the society in which, or to the government under which, they live, is such that they are incapable of direct communication with it, and enjoy its benefits, and receive its protection only through the medium of others. This distinction of persons into those who act in their own right, and those who act only in the right of another, is fundamental; and having obtained under all governments, must be confessed to be found in Nature, and a necessary element of social order. (Seabury 1861, 65-67)

In the United States in the eighteenth and nineteenth centuries, even so-called free or emancipated blacks were essentially legal Nonpersons in most states, a fact that illuminates one difference between a merely emancipated individual and an enfranchised one. In 1796, St. George Tucker, one of Virginia's most eminent jurists, outlined some of the legal "incapacities and disabilities" borne by emancipated blacks: "No negroe or mulattoe can be a witness in any prosecution, or civil suit in which a white person is a party. . . . Emancipated negroes may be sold to pay the debts of their former master contracted before their emancipation." In addition, although the U.S. Constitution (Article 4, §2) requires that each state respect the freedoms of *citizens* from other states, the laws of Virginia prohibited "the migration of free negroes or mulattoes" into its territory and stipulated that "those who do migrate hither may be sent back to the place from whence they came" (Tucker 1796, quoted in Kurland and Lerner 1987, 1: 561).

The free black-as-Nonperson was not simply a southern phenomenon. In September 1865, Governor Oliver P. Morton of Indiana described the disabilities of African Americans in his state this way:

"We not only exclude them from voting, we exclude them from testifying in courts of justice. We exclude them from our public schools, and we make it unlawful and criminal for them to come into the state. No negro who has come into Indiana since 1850 can make a valid contract; he can not acquire title to a piece of land, because the law makes the deed void" (Voegeli 1967, 179). As Voegeli found in his study of the midwestern states, Indiana's position, although extreme, was not unique: "The severity of the discriminatory legislation varied, but every state imposed legal disabilities upon its black residents" (1967, 2).

In U.S. society (and presumably, in most societies), the status of Nonperson has typically been an ascribed one, but it may also be achieved. For example, in many societies, people convicted of a serious crime may lose—generally, in addition to their freedom—their standing as Persons in the eyes of the law. The extreme case is something called "civil death" *(civiliter mortuus)*, which, as *Black's Law Dictionary* explains it, "means that all rights and privileges . . . including the right to contract and to sue and be sued are forfeited." It may well be that in some societies civil death ultimately means death in the physical sense. In Bali, according to Geertz, there is a saying that "to leave the community of agreement is to lie down and die." Geertz characterized being forced to exit from the community as the "next best thing" to capital punishment (1983, 177). In his study of archaic Western law, Harold Berman also illustrated the potentially dire consequences of one form of civil death when he noted that the status appropriately known as "outlawry"—the equivalent to being put out of civil society or civil death—involved the "forfeiture of all goods and liability to be killed by anyone with impunity" (1983, 61). As Pollock and Maitland noted with respect to the outlaw, "It is the right and duty of every man to pursue [the outlaw], to ravage his land, to burn his house, to hunt him down like a wild beast and slay him; for a wild beast he is; not merely is he a 'friendless man,' he is a wolf. . . . *Caput gerat lupinum*—in these words the courts decreed outlawry" (1898, 2: 449).

Civil death is not always literally fatal, and notwithstanding the imagery of the outlaw as beast, it is not my intention to argue that Nonpersons will always be regarded as literally nonhuman. In Blackstone's time, monks were considered to have achieved the status of Nonpersons in the eyes of the law as they were, in effect, "dead to the world." In England, well into the nineteenth century, marriage for women involved a similar fate for, upon marriage, "the very being or legal existence of the woman is suspended" (Blackstone [1769] 1979, 4: 430). In the New World, the tendency among settlers was to follow the

English tradition with respect to women; although her legal disabilities varied somewhat from colony to colony, the married woman was considered, expressed in Law French,[5] to be under cover of her husband's person *(coverture)*—as a result, she had no legal identity of her own. Legal historian William E. Nelson, drawing upon a number of early cases, showed that in Massachusetts, until the mid-nineteenth century, the married woman

> was incapable of entering into contracts, of managing or disposing of her own property, or of suing and being sued. "Upon strict principles of law, the *feme-covert* . . . [was] not a member . . . [and had] no *political* relation to the *state*. . . ." Married women were even deemed incapable of committing crimes, at least when they were in the presence of their husbands, since a wife was presumed to be under her husband's command, and "if he commanded it, she was bound to obey him by a law paramount to all other laws—the law of God." (Nelson 1975, 103)[6]

---

5. Law French was one of the last remnants of the influence of the Norman Conquest in England. Until about 1400, French was the language of choice among England's educated upper class; Law French as a highly technical language of art retained its influence on the law well into modern times.

6. Nelson noted that this incapacity to perform criminal acts did not necessarily extend to all types of cases—especially when it came to "crimes forbidden by the law of nature, which are *mala in se* [evil in and of themselves], and some where the wife may be presumed the principal agent" (1975, 228*n*178). Legal historian Kermit Hall's accounting of this adds two important points: First, in some cases where the layperson would be tempted to label the woman as the principal agent of the offense, such an assessment would be in error, for the law would assume "that she had done so under her husband's coercion." This was true even in instances in which the crime was obviously against the husband's interests. Second, the fact that married women were disabled from committing crimes did not necessarily mean that their legal transgressions went unpunished—their husbands might be punished instead. In some cases this led to what some might view (today) as bizarre consequences, as when a man was whipped for his wife's adultery (1989, 35).
The principle of vicarious liability has proved to be an enduring one. Although it is more typical in tort/civil liability cases (for example, it is fairly common for employers to be held vicariously liable for the negligent acts of their employees or for parents to be held liable for the wrongs of their children) the possibility of vicarious criminal liability still exists. For example, in many jurisdictions, people can be held vicariously liable for a "murder" committed by their pit bulls.

Some might be troubled by lumping such disparate types of individuals into a single group under the heading of Nonpersons—even as an exercise in ideal-typical analysis. What is to be gained by considering married women, slaves, children, outlaws, monks, convicts, and lunatics as members of a single category? Surely, their respective life chances and conditions were varied enough to rob this categorization of all analytic value? On this very point, in their study *Gender Justice*, David Kirp, Mark Yudof, and Marlene Strong Franks criticized (with justification) some antebellum southerners' attempts to justify the treatment of slaves by lumping together women and African Americans. Here they discuss a passage from George Fitzhugh's *Sociology for the South* (1854):

> "Two-thirds of mankind, the women and the children are everywhere the subjects of family government" wrote George Fitzhugh, in his impassioned antebellum defense of slavery. "In all countries where slavery exists, the slaves are also the subjects of this kind of government." That slaves were treated just as women and children, Fitzhugh argued, made slavery somehow more acceptable. "God has . . . provided a better check, to temper and direct the power of the family and the master than any human government has devised."

> Yet, despite this attempt to liken the treatment of blacks to that of women and children . . . historically the analogy seems little more than a rationale for oppression. . . . However misguided their actions might seem to the contemporary observer, men sought to dignify women by elevating and protecting them; whites, by contrast, insisted upon the subservience of blacks. (1986, 43-44)

Kirp, Yudof, and Franks suggested that lumping African slaves, women, and children into the same group could not justify the treatment of slaves, and it is difficult to quarrel with that. Although this lumping certainly could not justify the treatment of African Americans, however, it can and does shed light on the legal system's treatment of women and children, for the system's treatment of women and children had a great deal in common with its treatment of slaves.

What is to be gained by this lumping of people into the category of Nonperson, then, is a better understanding of how legal standing (the ability to invoke the law in one's defense and to enforce one's claims) affects life in society. There is no gainsaying that—in most cases—the actual life conditions of Nonpersons varied depending upon the Nonpersons' relations to the Persons. Although to ensure their cooperation, a man might cajole his children with sweets and his wife with jewels but beat his slaves with whips, at base neither the children, the wife, nor the slaves had legal recourse should the father/master elect to abuse them.[7]

John Stuart Mill took this notion a step further and argued that slaves tended to be better off than wives! "I am far from pretending that wives are in general no better treated than slaves; but no slave is a slave to the same lengths, and in so full a sense of the word, as a wife is. . . . [Her husband] can claim from her and enforce the lowest degradation of a human being, that of being made the instrument of an animal function contrary to her inclination." This, said Mill, is the "worst description of slavery" (1869, 463). The similarity between slaves' and married women's positions was not something that was only noted by a few. Ursula Vogel, for example, noted: "That the legal condition of women in modern society was virtually indistinguishable from the institution of slavery was a common phrase in the political vocabulary of nineteenth-century feminism" (1988, 139). As Mary Boykin Chestnut, herself a slave mistress, observed in the nineteenth century, "There is no slave, after all, like a wife" (Chestnut 1980, 49).

I will have more to say in the next chapter on the implications of Nonpersonhood, but for now it is important to note that most fundamentally what these disparate types of Nonpersons (women, children, slaves) had in common as a result of their exclusion from the civil domain was their inability to do specific legal acts (e.g., to make contracts, hold public office, obtain occupational licenses, etc.) or to make claims on the transformation of resources that law provides. They were, in other words, legally disabled from participating in the civil domain of their society and from gaining access to law's power.

InterPersonal Relationships

For those who are parties to the civil contract, that is, for those who are legal Persons, the law treats different types of interPersonal relationships differently. More specifically, relative to the civil contract interPersonal relationships will fall into one of two categories.

First, there are relationships that are purely communal or extralegal. These involve role configurations to which the civil contract attaches no special rights and duties and, indeed, to which it

---

7. I can hardly let this moment pass without noting that, in my judgment, it is incredibly naive to believe that women's place in society (and lack of place in the civil domain) was a result of men's desire to "elevate" and "protect" them and that men did not "insist upon subservience" from women.

pays no attention (such as friendship). Even when they exist between legal Persons, such relations are altogether communal and therefore subject only to social (and not legal) norms and sanctions.

Second, there are relationships that are recognized by the law and therefore regarded as civil. One subset of civil relations includes those relationships that receive positive or enabling civil recognition; these are relationships in which participants may invoke the sovereign power to protect their rights (e.g., marriage, business partnerships, and employer-employee relations). In some cases the law will even protect the integrity of the civil relationship itself from the interference of outsiders. For example, until fairly recently in the United States it was possible for a Person to sue someone who seduced or "alienated" the Person's spouse's affection (in U.S. law this "tort" or civil wrong was called "alienation of affection"; in English common law it was called "enticement"). Similar rules, at various times, have protected employer-employee relations.

A second subset of civil relations includes what can be called "prohibited" relations. Entering into these sorts of relationships makes Persons vulnerable to punitive responses from civil society. Examples of prohibited relations in our society include polygamous marriages, relations between businesses that violate antitrust statutes, master-slave and prostitute-client relationships.

Persons in relationships that lack positive civil recognition (that is, relationships that are communal or prohibited) cannot call upon the power of the sovereign either to protect their rights in the relationship or to insure the integrity of the relationship itself. That this is no trivial matter might be seen by comparing heterosexual and homosexual marriages. In most contemporary jurisdictions, gay and lesbian partnerships have no civil existence as couples. It is true that, at this writing, in at least one-half of the United States, people in same-sex relationships are not subject to legal sanctions, and so their relations are not prohibited. But, as things are presently constituted, gay and lesbian relationships remain purely communal. As couples these partners have no legally enforceable rights or privileges—no rights of inheritance or to privileged communication, and even no rights to visit one another in the hospital beyond those of any nonrelated individuals. In many jurisdictions, the situation is (or has been) likewise precarious for heterosexual couples who—for whatever reasons—have failed to marry formally. In some states, heterosexuals who "cohabit" are at least technically in violation of the law and hence vulnerable to sanction. In U.S. society, polygamy (or plural marriage) creates similar problems for participants. The difference, of course, is that because polygamy is everywhere in this country forbidden by law, those involved not only have an unprotected relationship but are also vulnerable to a punitive response from the civil domain.[8]

Figure 2.1 illustrates one possible constellation of Persons and Nonpersons and civil and communal relationships in a relatively simple society. Circle A includes all the people and all the social or interpersonal relationships that actually exist within a society. Circle B, which includes only Persons and civil relationships, represents the civil domain. Finally, the relationship between the civil domain and society is illustrated in Circle C. As Circle C illustrates, only some people and some relationships are included in the civil domain. Because many people and relations are excluded from the civil domain, it is quite a bit smaller than the communal domain.

In this chapter I have laid out some of the effects of the civil contract on relationships between Persons. But what of Nonpersons? As I discuss in the next chapter, although Nonpersons are not parties to the civil contract, they are subject to it, and this fact has a number of important implications for how Nonpersons live out their lives.

---

8. States that criminalize heterosexual cohabitation are Arizona, Florida, Idaho, Illinois, Michigan, Mississippi, North Carolina, North Dakota, and West Virginia (Duff and Truitt 1991). Generally, these laws are not enforced, but they do exist and so cohabiters are vulnerable. In states where cohabitation is not criminalized, the legal disabilities of cohabitants are being remedied to an extent in those jurisdictions that allow for "domestic partnership" contracts.

Admittedly, while polygamy is prohibited by the law, the degree to which polygamists are likely to be sanctioned depends upon where they reside. In some places in the Western part of the United States, for example, polygamy appears to be quite widespread. Nonetheless, polygamists do run a constant risk of exposure and sanction as one deputy sheriff in Utah found. He lost his job because he practiced polygamy. In appealing his firing, Deputy Sheriff Potter claimed that since so many people openly practiced polygamy, the law had fallen into desuetude (i.e., had been abandoned by the government) and that therefore he should not be punished. Potter's appeal did not succeed. The court ruled that the law forbidding polygamy was so fundamental in the United States, that it could not be abandoned (*Potter v. Murray City,* 760 F.2d 1065 [1985]).

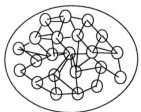 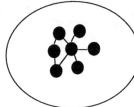 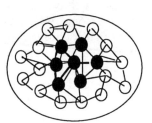

A. All people and all relationships that actually exist in the society.

B. Persons and relationships that comprise the civil domain.

C. The civil domain in society.

FIGURE 2.1. Relations between the civil and the communal domain in a simple society. Note: The figure is misleading in that it might suggest that relations between Persons are necessarily civil ones. This is not the case. In this country, for example, a friendship between two persons is not a civil relation in that friendship, per se, involves no special *legal* rights and duties. In other words, in the eyes of the law, friends owe each other only that which they owe to nonfriends. Morally, of course, friendship creates many obligations.

3

The Civil Domain
and Nonpersons

Ye shall have one manner of law, as well for the stranger, as for one of your own country.

— *Leviticus 24:22*

Although Personhood and Nonpersonhood exist at opposite ends of a continuum, when it comes to Nonpersons there is no shortage of examples illustrating the extreme case: The Jews of Nazi Germany; the *hinin* and *eta* of Japan;[1] those of African descent in the antebellum American South; Japanese Americans during World War II; and of course slaves in any society in any era.

Typically, in such cases Persons will view Nonpersons as (at best) greatly inferior or (at worst) literally not human. What W. E. B. DuBois wrote with respect to African Americans in the United States illustrates one possibility: "The second thought streaming from . . . the older South [is] the sincere and passionate belief that somewhere between men and cattle, God created a *tertium quid*, and called it a Negro—a clownish, simple creature, at times even lovable within its limitations, but straitly foreordained to walk within the Veil" (quoted in Stone 1974, 9*n*25).

---

1. The hinin and eta ("heavily polluted") were a people who were believed to have less than full human status. In the nineteenth century, when these caste distinctions were "officially" abolished in Japan, the eta and the hinin were grouped together into a new "status" group known as *burakumin* ("people of the hamlets").

Many even disputed that Africans and members of other nonwhite races were set above the beasts in the natural order of things. Here's one example of such reasoning from a late nineteenth-century "scholar":

> Thus, scientific research demonstrates that man (the pure-blooded white), whom God designed, equipped, and clothed with authority to subdue the earth, never descends to savagery. On the other hand, the Negro, when uncontrolled by the White, becomes "a mere wanderer in the woods," and like any other animal, subsists upon the spontaneous products of the earth, and proceeds of the chase. This indicates that the natural relation between the White and the Negro is that of master and servant. . . .
>
> [The] mass of scriptural and scientific evidence clearly indicates that the pure-blooded White is the creature whom God designed should perform the mental labor necessary to subdue the earth; and that the Negro is the creature whom God designed to perform the manual labor. The Negro, in common with the rest of the animals, made his appearance upon the earth prior to the creation of man. With the Negro and the animals of draught, burthen and food, it was possible for man to develop all the resources of the earth and not personally till the ground. (Carroll [1900] 1991, 101-102)

Historians continue to debate whether slaves were actually regarded by early U.S. law as mere chattel—like cattle and other nonhuman forms of life—or as true human beings (see Tushnet 1975). Some argue that the essential humanity of slaves was indeed acknowledged and cite as proof the fact that slaves were held responsible for their crimes. As a judge said in one case, "The law views [slaves] as capable of committing crimes. This can only be upon the principle, that they are men and rational beings" (*State v. Jones*, 1 Miss. [Walk.] 83 [1820], quoted in Tushnet 1975, 119). Although I do not wish to enter into this debate, I can point out that historically whether a being (human or otherwise) is held responsible for its crimes has not always proved a good way to test its humanity. In the Middle Ages, for example, animals and other nonhuman entities were sometimes tried in courts of law for manslaughter (Pollock and Maitland 1898, 2:472).[2]

---

2. *Deodand* is from Latin, *Deo dandum*, a thing to be given to God. Originally, wild animals were tried in ecclesiastical (church) courts while domesticated animals were tried in secular courts.

At first I was greatly puzzled by the idea of Deodand, but now I wonder whether what seems to be a historical novelty of animals being treated as people in court has blinded us to the historical norm of most people/Nonpersons being treated as beasts.

The principle of *Deodand* allowed the courts to forfeit the life of nonhuman chattel—including oxen, trees, and wagons—responsible for the death of humans.

Theories about the inferior nature of Nonpersons are important in sustaining the Nonperson's status and tend to be incorporated into formulas or cognitive conventions used to legitimate and to reinforce the exclusion of Nonpersons from the civil domain. Chief Justice Roger Taney drew upon this sort of legitimating theory to justify his unhelpful response to Dred Scott when the former slave petitioned for his freedom:

> The words "people of the United States" and "citizens" are synonymous terms, and mean the same thing. . . . They are what we familiarly call the "sovereign people," and every citizen is one of this people, and a constituent member of this sovereignty. The question before us is, whether the class of persons described in the plea in abatement compose a portion of this people, and are constituent members of this sovereignty? We think they are not, and that they are not included, and were not intended to be included, under the word "citizens" in the Constitution, and can therefore claim none of the rights and privileges which that instrument provides for and secures to citizens of the United States. On the contrary, they were at that time considered as a subordinate and inferior class of beings, who had been subjugated by the dominant race, and, whether emancipated or not, yet remained subject to their authority, and had no rights or privileges but such as those who held the power and the Government might choose to grant them. (*Scott v. Sandford*, 60 U.S. [19 How.] 393 [1856])[3]

In a more pithy statement of a similar socially constructed reality, "A handbook published by the [Japanese] Ministry of Justice in 1880 referred to . . . *hinin* as 'the lowliest of all people, almost like

---

3. Dred Scott, a slave, was taken by his owner (Dr. Emerson of the U.S. Army) to Illinois, where slavery was prohibited by statute. Later, he was taken to Louisiana (to an area where the Missouri Compromise prohibited slavery). Eventually, Scott was brought back to Missouri, where he brought suit to recover his freedom. Just before his suit commenced, Scott was sold to John F. A. Sanford of New York. As it turned out, Sanford had very little to do with the case. By the time the Supreme Court heard the case, Sanford had been consigned to a mental hospital (some scholars have asserted that he had been driven mad by the whole controversy). A typographical error at the Supreme Court is responsible for the misspelling of Sanford's name in the title of the case.

animals'" (Hane 1982, 146). It is perhaps no coincidence that such statements are reminiscent of the ways in which people tend to depersonalize (even de*humanize*) their wartime enemies.

Nineteenth-century U.S. apologists often rationalized the patent injustice of segregation and other forms of discrimination against African Americans by invoking the idea that the different social and legal treatment of African Americans and whites was "natural" owing to their "obvious" physical differences (e.g., Carroll [1900] 1991; Seabury, 1861). The fact that such theories were applied even to individuals who were "mostly white" genetically (e.g., those who had one grandparent of African descent and three of European descent),[4] of course, casts doubt on the validity of such reasoning. (James F. Davis, in his recent book *Who Is Black? One Nation's Definition,* pointed out that the United States was unique in following what was known in the South as the "one-drop rule"—"meaning that a single drop of 'black blood' makes a person black" [Davis 1991, 5]).

The situation of outcaste peoples in Japan is even more telling, for it suggests that polygenistic theories will be invoked and hold sway even where racial differences are objectively illusory. As recently as 1965, for example, a government survey in Japan revealed that 70 percent of the people polled believed that members of such outcaste groups as the hinin "were of a race and lineage different from [and inferior to] the Japanese" (Hane 1982, 140). No objective scientific evidence can be found to support such a theory.

Whatever the reason for their exclusion, the unfortunate individuals who inhabit society but lack membership in the civil domain endure an uncertain existence. In many respects, the Nonperson's position relative to the civil contract mirrors that of beasts or people living in territories occupied by foreign powers. Excluded from the civil domain, the Nonperson is dependent upon the capricious benevolence of Persons who hold sovereign power. The Nonperson's existence is essentially lawless. Although they are *subject* to law, Nonpersons typically have no right, or only limited rights, to invoke it. In their part of the society, outside the civil domain, the rule is "might makes right." (Actually, with respect to Person/Nonperson relationships, this characterization is exactly correct only if we

---

4. By way of example, it can be noted that Homer Plessy, who in the late nineteenth century challenged the right of railroads to require segregated seating, was—as the U.S. Supreme Court made a point of mentioning—"seven eighths Caucasian and one eighth African blood [and] that the mixture of colored blood was not discernible in him." Nonetheless, Plessy was relegated to the Nonwhite section of the train (*Plessy v. Ferguson,* 163 U.S. 537 [1896]).

acknowledge that the Person has, simply by virtue of being a Person, the *might* of the law on his or her side. In this sense, the sovereign power, when used by Persons against Nonpersons, is perhaps better construed as martial force than legal action.)

The idea that Nonpersons exist in an "occupied territory" is apt; the occupying forces of Persons may ignore not only the humanity of the Nonpersons, but also their individuality. While not all societies place a premium on the idea of individuality, or even recognize it, most modern societies do. And in modern society one benefit of Personhood is the right to be treated as an individual. Nonpersons often are not treated as individuals. In many cases, their individuality is denied to the extent that they are not even allowed to have surnames of their own. This was true, for example, of slaves in the antebellum South (Hast 1969) and, of course, of married American women who—for years—lost their birth names when they married. In a decision that was later cited as an important precedent in a number of cases, a judge suggested that the woman's loss of name was an age-old phenomenon: "For several centuries, by the common law among all English-speaking people, a woman, upon her marriage, takes her husband's surname. That becomes her legal name, and she ceases to be known by her maiden name" (*Chapman v. Phoenix National Bank*, 85 N.Y. 437 [1881]).[5]

The implications of losing one's name did not escape early feminists. As Elizabeth Cady Stanton pointed out in a letter to Rebecca Eyster in 1847:

> There is a great deal in a name. It often signifies much, and may involve a great principle. Ask our colored brethren if there is nothing in a name. Why are slaves nameless unless they take that of their master? Simply because they have no independent existence. . . . The custom of calling women Mrs John This and Mrs Tom That, and colored men Sambo and Zip Coon, is founded on the principle that white men are lords of all. (Quoted in Stannard 1977, 3-4)[6]

Forbidding Nonpersons names of their own is not exclusively a U.S. or even Western phenomenon. The hinin and eta of Japan were not allowed surnames either (Hane 1982); indeed, Orlando Patterson, in his historical and cross-cultural study of slavery, observed that the

---

5. In fact, as I explain in the next chapter, the judge in this case misread history.

6. A more recent examination of the relationship between women and slavery can be found in Chevillard and Leconte, 1986.

prohibition may be well-nigh universal for slaves: "In every slave society one of the first acts of the master has been to change the name of his slave. One must reject any simplistic explanation that this was simply a result of the master's need to find a name that was more familiar, for we find the same tendency to change names when slaves come from the identical society or language group as their masters" (1982, 54).

Elizabeth Cady Stanton anticipated the observation since made by many social scientists: Taking away a person's name is an effective de-individuation technique. As Erving Goffman put it, de-naming is "a great curtailment of self" (1961, 18). Orlando Patterson explained it thus, "A man's name is, of course, more than simply a way of calling him. It is a verbal signal of his whole identity, his being-in-the-world as a distinct person" (1982, 54). This "de-naming" took its toll. Even today, among African Americans, the expression to "call out of one's name" means "to insult" (Gwaltney 1980, xv).

In modern Western culture, a variation of the use and misuse of names to depersonalize is to call another by his or her first name when such intimacy has not been earned. Cheryl Townsend Gilkes wrote of how some African Americans in the late nineteenth century effectively preserved their individuality in the face of such overfamiliarity by refusing to tell whites their first names or use their first names "in any public settings that could be interracial." This practice, said Gilkes, "was (and still is) intended to prevent white racists" from using first names "as a strategy to depersonalize and to devalue black people" (Gilkes 1985, 683). Some African Americans named their children in ways that would conspicuously frustrate whites' attempts to devalue them: "Miss," "Sir," and even "King."[7]

Once someone ceases to be an individual in his or her own right, or is judged to be a Nonperson, how is that unfortunate being treated? Georg Simmel supplied part of the answer when he noted "that peculiarly ideal unity in which men lump them together when they simply speak of 'the women.'" He observed that the "contrast between the sexes fully has the character of a *party* contrast," and highlighted his observation by quoting this German ditty:

---

7. My thanks to Anna Riley and Magalene Taylor for pointing this out to me.

Man bears his shame alone,	*Der Mann trägt seine cshmach*
	allein,
But let a woman fall,	*Doch Kommt ein Weib zu Falle,*
The blame rests on them all.	*So schilt man auf sie alle."*

(Simmel 1955, 95)

The implication is this: Because Persons tend to lump Nonpersons together, if a Nonperson disobeys the law, his or her entire group may be made to suffer.

Harold Berman's work on the development of Western law provides an interesting example of this practice. He noted that the students who flocked to Italy from all over Europe in the late eleventh century to study law were in "a precarious legal situation." The law of Italy treated foreigners from a particular country as interchangeable. For example, "Any alien might be liable for the debts of his fellow countrymen. A Bolognese merchant with a claim against a London merchant could extract damages from any of the English Law students at hand" (1983, 124).[8]

When the government of a country takes umbrage at some wrong done to it by members of another country, any sanction that results is generally referred to as "reprisal." Thus, in response to terrorist activities in the 1980s, the U.S. government ordered the bombing of Libya as reprisal. Similarly, in the early 1990s, when it was believed that former President George Bush had been the target of an assassination attempt by some Iraqis, the U.S. government ordered a bombing of government buildings in Iraq as reprisal. The point was not to punish the terrorists or assassins themselves but to effect reprisals on the country that (we supposed) produced and harbored the terrorists. Very often, Persons' responses to Nonpersons manifests a similar dynamic. Thus, when Persons hold Nonpersons vicariously liable for the wrongs of others of their group, their actions are perhaps more accurately labeled "reprisals" than "punishment." Applying or threatening to apply (group) reprisals rather than (individual) punishment not only denies the individuality of the wrongdoer but pushes the wrongdoer back under the extralegal social control of his or her group. In essence, this practice may enlist the support of the Nonperson's social group in maintaining social control.

---

8. Max Weber (1978, 46) touched on this notion in his discussion of basic sociological terms. He noted that, under some circumstances, "certain kinds of actions of *each* participant may be imputed to *all* others." In such cases, he said, we speak of "mutually responsible members."

The nature of this dynamic, or at least its flavor, was illustrated dramatically in Vrba and Bestic's book *I Cannot Forgive*. In the following excerpt, the authors demonstrate how the threat of reprisal can encourage group members to ward off reprisal by sanctioning rulebreakers themselves. The scene is Auschwitz, 1942; the prisoners are preparing for an inspection by Heinrich Himmler.

> In the tenth row outside our Block, the Block Senior found Yankel Meisel without his full quota of tunic buttons.
>
> It took some seconds for the enormity of the crime to sink in. Then he felled him with a blow. . . . I saw the Block Senior, with two of his helpers, hauling Yankel inside the barrack block.
>
> Out of sight, they acted like men who have been shamed and betrayed will act. They beat and kicked the life out of him. They pummelled him swiftly, frantically, trying to blot him out, to sponge him from the scene and from their minds; and Yankel, who had forgotten to sew his buttons on, had not even the good grace to die quickly and quietly.
>
> He screamed. It was a strong, querulous scream, ragged in the hot, still air. Then it turned suddenly to the thin, plaintive wail of abandoned bagpipes, but it did not fade so fast. It went on and on and on, flooding the vacuum of silence, snatching at tightly-reined minds and twisting them with panic, rising even above the ugly thump of erratic blows. At that moment, I think, we all hated Yankel Meisel, the little old Jew who was spoiling everything, who was causing trouble for all with his long, lone, futile protest. (1964, 12)

The prisoners' response to Yankel Meisel is startling, but predictable given the power of reprisals to force Nonpersons to police their own. Examples of reprisal can be found much closer to home and in far more familiar settings than Nazi Germany; indeed, the technique seems well-nigh universal when it comes to Persons and Nonpersons' relationships. For example, punishing the group for the misdeeds of a single individual is an accepted technique for exerting social control over children. Thus, the teacher who requires an entire classroom to forgo recess owing to the misdeeds of a single student who was chewing gum, or the parent who threatens to require expiation of some sort from all the children unless the miscreant confesses his or her guilt, ignores principles of due process that, when it comes to Persons, are basic and even sacred.

Consider, for example, what would happen if the supervisor of a work group (of adults) made the following announcement: "Someone wrote obscene words on the bathroom wall. Because of this, we will deduct $15 from each worker's paycheck to pay the cost of repainting the bathroom." Or, "Someone has been stealing supplies and each of you will be charged a share in order to reimburse the company." It is not difficult to imagine how outraged the adult workers (the guilty as well as the innocent) would be—it is unacceptable to punish a group of Persons for the misdeeds of an individual, and it is likewise unacceptable to punish a guilty Person unless one has proof.[9] Still, this sort of treatment is a time-honored way of "teaching" children right from wrong. This speaks to the fact, I think, that children—in important respects—are not regarded fully as Persons.

Even when it targets only individual offenders, punishment against Nonpersons seems to have a special quality—in many cases, compared to punishment meted out to Persons, it is more intense and often more dramatic in terms of the suffering that it entails. Why might that be so?

In "Two Laws of Penal Evolution" Durkheim argued that as society "progresses," punishments inevitably become more humane. He noted, for example, that the notion of capital punishment has changed over time.

> In a very large number of ancient societies, death, pure and simple, did not constitute the supreme punishment; it was augmented, for those crimes held to be the most heinous, by supplementary penalties, which had the effect of making it more hideous. Thus, the Egyptians, aside from hanging and beheading, employed burning at the stake, torture by ashes, and crucifixion. In punishment by fire, the executioner began by making several incisions in the hands of the guilty party with sharp-ended cane stakes, and only then was the latter made to lie on a fire of thorns and burned alive. Torture by ashes consisted of suffocating the condemned man under a heap of embers.
>
> . . . The people of Asia appear to have pushed cruelty further. "Among the Assyrians, guilty parties were thrown to ferocious beasts or into a flaming furnace; they were roasted in a brass basin over a low fire; their eyes were put out. Strangulation and decapitation were rejected as insufficient measures! Among the various peoples of Syria,

---

9. This rule is strongly felt in the United States. In the jails of Cook County, Illinois, for example, I spoke to many frustrated burglars who felt the system had abused them by convicting them of burglaries they had not committed (even though they had committed several other burglaries that the authorities didn't get them on).

criminals were stoned, pierced with arrows, hanged, crucified, their ribs and entrails burned with torches, they were quartered, thrown from cliffs, . . . crushed under the feet of animals, etc." ([1901] 1978, 158)

Of course, social enthusiasm for augmenting the death penalty is neither an exclusively Eastern or ancient phenomenon. Consider the following account from Michel Foucault's *Discipline and Punish* as he writes about the death warrant of Damiens who was convicted of attempting to take the life of King Louis XV:

On 2 March 1757 Damiens the regicide was condemned "to make the *amende honorable* before the main door of the Church of Paris," where he was to be "taken and conveyed in a cart, wearing nothing but a shirt, holding a torch of burning wax weighing two pounds"; then, "in the said cart, to the Place de Grève, where, on a scaffold that will be erected there, the flesh will be torn from his breasts, arms, thighs and calves with red-hot pincers, his right hand, holding the knife with which he committed the said parricide, burnt with sulphur, and, on those places where the flesh will be torn away, poured molten lead, boiling oil, burning resin, wax and sulphur melted together and then his body drawn and quartered by four horses and his limbs and body consumed by fire, reduced to ashes and his ashes thrown to the winds." (1979, 3)

Things have changed. These days, people in many societies have condemned even the simple, unadulterated death penalty as a barbaric practice. In the United States, the last bastion of capital punishment in the West, many people have taken pride in our invention of modes of "humane" killing and in the fact that there are constitutional prohibitions against administering the death penalty in ways that are "cruel and unusual."

Why have these changes occurred? Why the increasing stress on *humane* punishment? Durkheim suggested that two factors have played a role in this development. In the first place, in premodern society, acts designated as crimes were mostly those that offended transcendent sentiments (e.g., blasphemy, treason, etc.). Crime, therefore, was responded to with fierce and intense punishment because it outraged the gods, and outraged gods might be tempted to effect group reprisals on the humans (whose status, relative to the gods, was that of Nonpersons). In modern society, in contrast, the influence of the gods is no longer so strongly felt (or feared); it is the interests of individuals that society wishes to protect. Yet, in the second place, what tempers outrage (and punishment) in response to acts that offend individuals is that, at the same time society has come to respect (and even revere) the interests of individuals, it has come to recognize the humanity of the criminal offender. Therefore, as Durkheim put it, punishment (in part) becomes more humane because "there is no longer the same distance between the offender and the offended; they are more nearly on an equal footing" ([1901] 1978, 175).

Durkheim's account is persuasive, but I would add that in some societies, the distance between Person and Nonperson may be nearly as great as it ever was between Person and god. Durkheim's assertion that "the attack of a man against a man could not incite the same indignation as the attack of a man against a god" is hardly an accurate description of the situation in which a Nonperson attacks a Person. Instead, acts by Nonpersons that result in injury to Persons are often responded to as if they contain as least an element—if not a ripe case— of lèse-majesté (or high treason); and, given the domination of Persons over Nonpersons, lèse-majesté is a fitting description of any Nonperson's violation of the laws of a civil domain. The Nonperson's status in society helps to explain why societies often mandate harsher penalties against Nonpersons than they do against Persons for the same proscribed behaviors.

An interesting example of this can be found in what Blackstone described as the "elderly" English law ([1769] 1979, 1:421). The English law of domestic relations focused not on husband and wife but on baron and feme, or *Lord* and woman. This difference in men's and women's legal status had some interesting consequences when it came to specific criminal acts: For example, women who killed their husbands were punished more harshly than men who killed their wives.

> Traditionally the slaying of wife by husband was simple murder, while the slaying of husband by wife was "petit Treason." This feature of English law [had the] clear intent of vicious punishment for the [husband] murderer (such as death by burning). . . . [T]he old tradition of treating baronicide as treason reveals many of the basic English assumptions about a wife's political identity. It could not be simpler: her husband was her king. (Kerber 1986, 119-120)

Another example is from the United States. One thing that distinguished early American criminal law from its British counterpart was the fact that most jurisdictions abolished capital punishment for the crime of theft (McIntyre 1987, 14). Slaves who committed theft were exempted from such leniency. In fact, nearly any offense of law placed the slave in jeopardy of death (Stroud 1856).

Nonpersons also may be in jeopardy of being punished for what we now call "status offenses"—or legal wrongs that can only be committed by members of certain categories of people. The behaviors that constitute status offenses are not, in and of themselves, proscribed (for Persons, that is); these behaviors are only wrong when done by Nonpersons. For example, the following statute regarding children's behavior was still on the books in South Dakota until 1968. It lists the behaviors (status offenses) that would result in a child being judged "delinquent:"

> Any child who, while under the age of 18 years . . . who is incorrigible, or intractable by parents, guardian or custodian; who knowingly associates with thieves, vicious, or immoral persons; who, without cause and without the consent . . . absents itself from its home or place of abode; who is growing up in idleness . . . who wanders about the streets in the nighttime without being on any lawful business or lawful occupation, or habitually wanders about any railroad yards or tracks, or jumps or attempts to jump onto any moving train, . . . who writes or uses vile, obscene, vulgar, or indecent language, or smokes cigarettes or uses tobacco in any form; who drinks intoxicating liquors on any street, in any public place, or about any school house, or at any place other than its own home; or who is guilty of indecent, immoral, or lascivious conduct. (Quoted in Empey and Stafford 1991, 59-60)

It was often argued that the intent of these statutes was to protect the well-being of the child. As Judge Julian Mack, one of the first juvenile court judges in the United States, put it: "not so much to punish as to reform, not to degrade but to uplift, not to crush but to develop, not to make him a criminal but a worthy citizen" (Empey and Stafford, 59-60). But such statutes clearly had the effect of keeping the children-Nonpersons "in their place." An inspection of laws that were established to regulate the behaviors of slaves demonstrates this point more clearly. The following sorts of provisions were typical of "Slave Codes" in the antebellum South:

> If a slave shall presume to come upon the plantation of any person, without leave in writing from his master, employer, &c., not being sent on lawful business, *the owner* of the *plantation* may inflict ten lashes for every such offense. (Stroud 1856, 161; emphasis in original)

> *For being guilty of rambling, riding or going abroad in the night, or riding horses in the daytime without leave*, a slave may be whipped, cropped, or branded on the cheek with the letter R, or otherwise punished, *not extending to life* or so as to render him unfit for labour. (Stroud 1856, 167; emphasis in original) [10]

---

10. Historically, the status offenses for which women were in jeopardy in U.S. society were similar to those that applied to children in that special emphasis was placed on "morals." For women, the most obvious status offense

Even "free blacks" were liable for status offenses. Anticipating Chief Justice Taney's assertion in the *Dred Scott* decision that African Americans, "whether emancipated or not," remain subject to the authority of whites, the laws of Louisiana, for example, contained the following provision: "Free people of colour ought never to insult or strike white people, nor presume to conceive themselves equal to the whites; but, on the contrary, they ought to yield to them on every occasion, and never speak or answer them but with respect, under the penalty of imprisonment according to the nature of the offense" (1 *Martin's Dig.* 640, quoted in Stroud 1856, 157).

The hinin and eta and other Nonpersons in Japanese society were subjected to similar restrictions:

> All sorts of restrictive measures were imposed to abuse the *eta-hinin.* They were restricted in where they could live, quality of housing, mobility in and out of their hamlets, clothing, hairdo, and even footwear. One *burakumin,* reflecting on the plight of his ancestors, remarked, "[They] were not treated as human beings. They were not allowed to wear any footwear but had to go about barefoot. They could use only straw ropes as belts, and only straws to tie their hair. They were forbidden to leave their hamlet from sunset to sunrise. . . . When it was necessary to see others [i.e., Persons], for some business reason, they had to get on their hands and knees before they could speak." (Hane 1982, 142)

Nonpersons, then, are different from Persons in a number of important respects. Legally, they may not be regarded as individuals and hence may be subject to reprisal for the wrongful acts of other Nonpersons. Their lack of individuality may be indicated by a prohibition against having legal surnames. Finally, even when they are treated as individuals, their behavior is subject to stricter legal scrutiny and their legal infractions are likely to be punished more harshly.

---

was that of prostitution, which—in several jurisdictions—could only be committed by women. In *United States v. Bitty* (208 U.S. 393 [1908]), the U. S. Supreme Court held that prostitution "refers to women who for hire or without hire offer their bodies to indiscriminate intercourse with men." In some cases, as in colonial Massachusetts, sexual misbehavior was an offense for both men and women, but it was a more serious offense for women. "Colonial authorities also considered copulation between a married man and a single woman as an act of fornication. Such an offense by a married woman was adultery [a more serious offense]. The sexual code, reflecting the early existence of a double standard in America, was rarely very harsh on males" (Flaherty 1978, 55).

What is perhaps most telling of their legal status (or lack thereof), is the fact that Nonpersons, by definition, cannot commit "civil wrongs" (torts, breaches of contract, etc.), for these imply that the wrongdoer has failed in his or her duty. Duties go hand in hand with rights and Nonpersons are denied both. Contracts between Nonpersons and between Persons or Nonpersons are generally void and unenforceable as the Nonperson has no right to contract. Thus, Nonpersons are usually not allowed to enter into legal (i.e., enforceable) marriage contracts or to make wills. It was long the case (and in many jurisdictions still is) that children could not be held responsible for their contracts and so, contracts between children or between children and adults were unenforceable. To the extent that duties must be accompanied by rights, the Nonperson is exempted.

Between parties to the civil contract (that is, between Persons), there are limits to how far one can go to effect a remedy of a wrong (i.e., invoke "self-help") in a relationship even if it is a noncivil one. Acts toward fellow Persons must be *infra vires*—or within the powers allotted to citizens.[11] Within some civil domains (as will be shown in the next chapter in a discussion of archaic German society), staying within the scope of legally acceptable behavior allows one tremendous latitude. But in other societies (e.g., the United States today), interPersonal behavior is very much constrained by the law.

Frequently, Persons have much more latitude with respect to how they behave toward Nonpersons than they do with respect to how they behave toward Persons. The restraint Persons must show in behavior toward Nonpersons depends on the benevolence of the sovereign, or of the Persons holding sovereign power. Generally speaking, however, good treatment is a result of charity, not entitlement. In *Uncle Tom's Cabin*, Harriet Beecher Stowe summed it up this way: "There is, actually, nothing to protect the slave's life, but the *character* of the master" (1965, 444).

It may seem as if the law "protects" Nonpersons. And it often does, just not in the same way or for the same reasons that it protects Persons. For example, many of the southern states passed laws ostensibly to protect slaves:

> Any owner or employer of a slave or slaves, who shall cruelly treat such slave or slaves, by unnecessary or excessive whipping, by withholding proper food and sustenance, by requiring greater labour from such

---

11. Hence, the legal principle *sic utere tuo ut alienum non laedas*—use your own so as not to injure another. This principle does not necessarily apply, of course, to relations between Persons and Nonpersons.

slave or slaves than he or she or they are able to perform, or by not affording proper clothing whereby the health of such slave or slaves may be injured and impaired, or cause or permit the same to be done, every such owner or employer shall be guilty of a misdemeanour, and on conviction shall be punished by fine or imprisonment in the common jail of the county, or both, at the discretion of the court. (Act of 1833 [Georgia], 2 *Cobb's Dig.* 827, quoted in Stroud 1856, 41)

Such laws had very little meaning because no slave could testify against a white person. More important, perhaps, was the fact that, when given in response to misdeed or offense, no punishment was considered unnecessary or excessive: "Thus, the master was virtually free to inflict mortal wounds and, whether justifiable or not, these acts would practically be beyond the purview of the law" (Higginbotham 1978, 188). The crucial difference between laws protecting Persons and those protecting Nonpersons is the implication that the *Nonperson does not have a legally cognizable independent interest in preserving his or her own life.* Thus, in the South, "Restricting the power of the masters, even to the point that slaves could be taken from them for mistreatment, had no liberating implications for those who were unfree. Once again, the fact that the master's power was less than absolute did not imply that the slave's subordination was less than total. The Kentucky laws, like most of its kind, provided only that expropriated slaves be sold to other, presumably more humane masters" (Oakes 1990, 158).

Because they exist more to protect the sensibilities of Persons than to protect Nonpersons from injury, laws that protect Nonpersons are more accurately compared to laws written to protect dumb beasts than to laws created to protect Persons. For example, the Georgia statute purported to protect slaves cited above has much in common with one of the earliest anti-cruelty (to animals) statutes passed in this country: "If any person shall override, overdrive, overload, torture, torment, unjustifiably injure, deprive of necessary sustenance, food or drink; or cruelly beat or needlessly mutilate . . . any living creature, every such offender shall, for every offense, be guilty of a misdemeanor" (Mississippi *Rev. Code*, §98.41.1, quoted in Favre and Loring 1983, 123-124)

Even when, in their beneficence, the authors of the civil contract specify that Persons cannot unjustly injure Nonpersons, the punishment given Persons who breach this provision is apt to be proportionately less than what might be meted to Persons who hurt Persons and will certainly be less than that given Nonpersons who hurt Persons. This difference is reflected in a song that, according to Stetson Kennedy (1959, 166), was sung by African Americans in the South in the 1950s:

When a white man kills a Negro,
They hardly carries it to court.
When a Negro kills a white man,
They hang him like a goat.

Making a similar point, Hane recounted the tale of the judicial response to the murder of an eta youth in Japan: "In 1859, when an *eta* youth tried to enter a Shinto shrine in Asakusa in Edo (Tokyo), he was beaten to death by the residents of that district. When the chief of the *eta* community appealed to the magistrate to punish the culprits, the magistrate is said to have responded, 'The life of an *eta* is worth about one-seventh the life of a townsman. Unless seven *eta* have been killed, we cannot punish a single townsman'" (Hane 1982, 142).

Nonpersons in Modern Society

Is the distinction between Person and Nonperson still relevant in modern society? At a fairly superficial level, it does not seem to be. It is more difficult to identify examples of Nonpersons in modern society than in societies either historically or geographically distant from our own. But, it is unlikely that Nonpersons do not exist in modern society. It may be just that, generally, we Persons find it difficult to see Nonpersons in our midst.

What is the source of this difficulty? I think it is that most Persons do not see Nonpersons as beings who are owed legal abilities. A Nonperson is not simply a being who lacks legal abilities. The list of examples of Nonpersons upon which I have relied here has included nineteenth-century married women, slaves of African descent in the antebellum South, Jews in Nazi Germany, and the hinin and eta in Japan, but it has not included dolphins, cats, dogs, horses or trees. Yet at various times and in various places, married women and slaves have had as little claim to the status of Persons as cats and dogs. The implication is that a Nonperson is not only an individual or being who lacks legal abilities but, an individual or being who *ought to have* these abilities. For most Persons, Nonpersons either should never have had rights in the first place (as in the present day case of infants or trees, or in days gone by, of married women and African Americans), or deserved to have their rights withdrawn through their own fault (as in the case of convicted felons). Hence, Thomas Jefferson and his colleagues could write sincerely, "We the People of the United States," in full knowledge that more than half of the humans were excluded from the civil domain (e.g., women, Native Americans, and African Americans).

Consider the "animal liberation" movement. To most Persons in U.S. society the idea of giving legal rights to animals is manifestly absurd; it just doesn't make sense. Thus, although animals are clearly not Persons, most of us would not think of them as Nonpersons either. But, there are some with broader vision. Animal rights advocate Peter Singer has maintained that even though the idea of "animal liberation" sounds "more like a parody of other liberation movements than a serious objective," it is not. In his judgment, "All animals are created equal." Indeed, Singer pointed out,

> The idea of "The Rights of Animals" actually was once used to parody the case of women's rights. When Mary Wollstonecraft, a forerunner of today's feminists, published her *Vindication of the Rights of Women* in 1792, her views were widely regarded as absurd, and before long an anonymous publication appeared entitled *A Vindication of the Rights of Brutes*. The author of this satirical work (now known to have been Thomas Taylor, a distinguished Cambridge philosopher) tried to refute Mary Wollstonecraft's arguments by showing that they could be carried one stage further. If the argument for equality was sound when applied to women, why should it not be applied to dogs, cats, and horses? The reasoning seemed to hold for these "brutes" too; yet to hold that brutes had rights was manifestly absurd; therefore the reasoning by which this conclusion had been reached must be unsound, and if unsound when applied to brutes, it must also be unsound when applied to women, since the very same arguments had been used in each case. (Singer 1975, 1)

Nearly 200 years later, Singer played off Taylor's argument by asking: If such reasoning is not unsound with respect to women, how can it be unsound with respect to brutes?

The fact that Nonpersons are difficult to see does not mean they are not to be found in modern society. Children are the most obvious Nonpersons in this society—in that they have the greatest number of legal disabilities. And then there are others who fall into categories of individuals who, if not Nonpersons in the most extreme sense, are nonetheless handicapped by significant legal disabilities: homosexuals (who in some jurisdictions are disabled from retaining custody of their children, joining the military in times of peace, or holding jobs requiring government security clearances [Rivera 1985]); convicts; the mentally incompetent; and illegal aliens. New categories of Nonpersons are emerging. The legal rights to privacy, to insurance and to health care of Persons living with AIDS are precarious at the present time (Mohr 1988). The homeless are essentially disabled from many legal rights: Without an address it is difficult if not impossible to register to vote or to receive social security checks or other forms of public assistance. More than ever, in recent times poverty, per se, has become legally disabling: For example, many people are too poor to avail themselves of the legal protections afforded by bankruptcy laws (Sullivan, Warren and Westbrook 1989). Although it has long been the case that poor people have less access to legal counsel than wealthy persons when accused of crimes (McIntyre 1987), today in many urban jurisdictions poor people may be denied access to sovereign protection even when *victimized* by crimes. When police are afraid or otherwise unwilling to venture into inner-city neighborhoods the neighborhoods' residents are exiled from the civil domain and forced back into a Hobbesian state where might makes right. During the time I spent doing research in the courts of Cook County, Illinois, I was frequently reminded of the great "distance" of many Chicago neighborhoods from the civil domain. Depending upon the neighborhood, in the event an African American killed his (African American) spouse, the act might be called a "South Side divorce" by police officers; in one neighborhood just south of the University of Chicago's campus, city police would jokingly deem a black-on-black homicide a "63rd Street misdemeanor."

The poor, the homeless, and people living with AIDS may not be Nonpersons to the degree that women and slaves were in the early nineteenth century, of course. They nonetheless must live with significant legal disabilities, as well as the social consequences of those disabilities.

Finally, technological "advances" are fuzzing the line between Person and Nonperson. For example, at what point does an embryo or fetus become a child and thus gain the benefits that accrue to those destined to become Persons?

Less obvious, perhaps, but potentially just as pressing, is the question of those who are dying. Death can no longer be regarded as an "event" (if it ever could have been); it is now clearly a process (Gervais 1986, 3). A dead human is not a Person, but at what point in the dying process does one become a Nonperson and lose, for example, one's rights to self-determination? A "fully competent" Person can refuse medical treatment; this is not true in all cases of those who are terminally ill. (Of course, the laws of our civil domain do require that we abide by a dead Person's will, but only if the will was authored by a fully competent Person.)

Thus, although historical and cross-cultural evidence seems to provide "cleaner" examples, Nonpersons (or at least individuals with significant legal disabilities) are with us still.

A Caveat

The distinction between Person and Nonperson leaves unanswered, and indeed, unaddressed, some important questions about dealing with legal disabilities that are de facto rather than de jure. Thus, although an individual may have a legal—*de jure*—right to invoke the law, that individual might be situated in such a way that in fact he or she cannot do so. The ability to invoke the law often requires more than technical standing—it frequently requires having access to nonlegal resources as well. Having the technical legal power to institute a suit to redress a wrong does not guarantee access to the courts when lawyers, and even filing fees, are beyond one's financial resources. Likewise, having the legal power to vote does not guarantee access to the ballot box when it is guarded by a phalanx of Klansmen. Technical legal rights are often only one of the resources that need to be mobilized to gain the benefits of Personhood. However, they are a necessary first step, and the fact that in many cases technical legal ability is a necessary but not sufficient resource does not mean that technical legal rights must be regarded as trivial resources. (And the fact that many of those in power have ignored the reality that having technical legal ability is not enough to gain access to law's resources may explain the enthusiasm of sociologists and legal scholars for documenting instances of de facto legal disabilities.)

Having technical legal advantages is important. By way of example, as I will explore further in Chapter 7, consider how family dynamics can change when married women have as much right as men to choose their domicile (where they will live) or to control their own money and sign contracts. Even when such rights are not explicitly invoked, knowledge that wives have a legal right to their own income must have an impact on the nature of family decisionmaking. The same is true when the right to vote is extended to minorities. Although making the civil domain more inclusive has not accomplished all that one might hope it would, it has had an impact on the nature of politics and political discourse.

Moreover, bringing specific social relations out of the communal domain and into the civil one has had a tremendous impact on social life. Some of the implications of such changes are considered in following chapters, but—as a preview—imagine how family dynamics change once people have a legal right to divorce. Imagine too how the dynamics of the workplace change once workers have a legal right to unionize. Finally, consider how the dynamics of the classroom change once professors can be held legally accountable for sexual or racial harassment. Even when husbands and wives, workers, and students do not invoke their rights to divorce, unionize, or sue, the nature of the social interaction in each situation will be affected by the *potential* that Persons will mobilize law's resources on their own behalf.

Law: Conflict or Consensus

Distinguishing between Persons and Nonpersons allows one to make use of both of the ascendant views of law in social science. One view (often called the "functionalist" view) sees law primarily as an "integrative mechanism": "The function of law is the orderly resolution of conflicts. . . . Someone claims that his interests have been violated by someone else. The court's task is to render a decision that will prevent the conflict—and all potential conflicts like it—from disrupting productive cooperation" (Bredemeier 1962, 74). From this perspective, law and legal mechanisms primarily serve an integrative function.

The other view is that law, far from being an integrative, consensus-based entity, is the "tool of the dominant class [that] ends by maintaining the dominance of that class. Law serves the powerful over the weak; it promotes the war of the powerful against the powerless. Moreover, law is used by the state (and its elitist government) to promote and protect itself. . . . [Law is] nothing other than official oppression" (Quinney 1972, 42).

Each view of the law accurately reflects part of the reality—but only a part. The functionalist (or, more properly, the "consensus") view reflects the way law works between Persons within the civil domain; while the "conflict" view depicts the way the law acts between Persons and Nonpersons.

This is not to suggest that all Persons stand equal before the law within the civil domain. As I noted at the beginning of this chapter, the distinction between Person and Nonperson properly belongs on a continuum. It is likely that in most civil domains varying levels of Personhood exist. Thus, it would be more accurate to say that consensus theories of law reflect how law works between Persons at equal, or approximately equal, points on the Person-Nonperson continuum. Yet, as I discuss in the next chapter, owing to the idea of "right makes might" and (especially) to a legal system's needs to be perceived as legitimate, at times consensus-based theories prove more powerful than expected in explaining how law works between Persons, even between Persons with significantly different degrees of legal power and abilities.

4

The Civil Domain
in Society

How the law works as a contract between Persons, and how it affects Person-Nonperson relations is just part of the story of the law in society. In this chapter I will look more broadly at the relationship between the two domains of society—the civil domain (into which the law may intrude) and the communal domain (which is, at base, "lawless"—though certainly not "normless"). The goal is to show that an understanding of the relationship between the civil domain and the larger society constitutes an important link in understanding the relationship between law and society.

Where the size of the civil domain is large relative to a society's population (as it is in the United States and in most other Western democracies), by definition a great deal of life as it is played out between individuals is affected by the transformation of resources that the law provides. Simply put, most relations are civil ones. Indeed, as Robert Gordon has observed, today "it is just about impossible to describe any set of 'basic' social practices without describing the legal relations among the people involved." These legal relations, he suggested,

> don't simply condition how the people relate to each other but to an important extent define the constitutive terms of the relationship. . . . For instance, among the first words one might use to identify the various people in an office would likely be words connoting legal status: "That's the owner over there." "She's a partner; he's a senior associate; that means an associate with tenure." "That's a contractor who's come in to do repairs." "That's a temp they sent over from Manpower." (Gordon 1984, 103)

As more and more relations come to be included in the civil domain, more and more relations become such that Persons may call upon the power of law to remedy breaches of expectations. Thus, even the size of the civil domain with respect to the rest of society is telling. We might begin simply by asking, How large is the civil domain relative to that society?

The civil domain may be minuscule relative to society or nearly coterminous. At one extreme, Weber (1978) reported that, relative to the size of archaic Germanic society itself, the civil domain was very small. Most members of society were excluded from civil society (the exception being male heads of households or kinship groups), and most relationships were extralegal. Within households or kinship groups, disputes were arbitrated by elders who were, within that context, a "law unto themselves." Weber wrote, "It is true that the punitive powers of the master of a household became to some extent restricted by the intervention of the elders of his own kinship group or the religious or military authorities in charge of certain intra-group relations, but by and large the master remained a law unto himself within his sphere and he was bound by legal rules only in very special cases" (Weber 1978, 651). Truly, in those days, a man's home was not only his castle, but his kingdom.

Because most social relations, including relations between members of households or kinship groups, existed in the communal domain and outside the civil domain, law played a very limited role in society. As Weber noted, most disputes were settled extralegally: "Among kinship members . . . there could be neither vengeance nor litigation but only arbitration by the group elders; against those who resisted, only the sanction of boycott or social ostracism could be applied. Legal procedure and law in the sense of claims guaranteed by judicial decision and coercive power attached thereto existed only between those different kinship groups and their members who belonged to the same political community" (Weber 1978, 677).

Even between those kinship groups belonging to the same political community, civil expectations were minimal. The provisions of the earliest civil contracts were concerned primarily with conduct that endangered the entire community and not, for example, with offenses to individuals:

A primitive form of criminal law did develop outside the boundaries of the household, particularly in situations in which the conduct of an individual endangered all members of his neighborhood, kinship or political association. Such situations could be brought about by two types of misconduct: religious blasphemy or military disobedience.

> The whole group was endangered when a magical norm, e.g., a taboo, was infringed and, in consequence, the wrath of magical forces, spirits or deities, threatened to descend with evil consequences not merely upon the blasphemer (or criminal) himself but upon the whole community which suffered him to exist within their midst.... The second source for such punishment was political or, originally, military. Anyone endangering by treachery or cowardice the security of the collective fighting forces or, after disciplined combat had come into being, by disobedience, had to reckon with the punitive reactions of the war lord or the army. (Weber 1978, 651; see also, Diamond 1971, 62)

It was this minimal intrusion of law, or the civil contract, into society and social relationships that Durkheim was perhaps referring to when he said, "The most ancient [legal] codes are veritable international treaties, concluded by sovereign groups in order to insure peace; they are therefore only concerned with those acts which involve relations of one group to another and which in consequence could threaten peace" ([1904] 1983, 155).

What of other sorts of disputes or breaches of expectations? More specifically, what of disputes arising from breaches of social expectations about the propriety of, say, homicide, theft, or assault between members of different households? Even a cursory knowledge of human nature makes us certain that such acts must have occurred and must not have gone unnoticed; knowledge of history, however, makes us almost as certain that these disputes and injuries were dealt with extralegally; that is, according to social norms and not according to law.

These practices were based, in part, on customary distinctions between public wrongs (i.e., wrongs against the interests of the sovereign group) and private wrongs (wrongs against the interests of an individual). This distinction is a long-standing one, and as Blackstone noted, it "seems principally to consist in this: that private wrongs or civil injuries, are an infringement or privation of the civil [i.e., legal] rights which belong to individuals, considered merely as individuals; public wrongs, or crimes or misdemesnors, are a breach and violation of the public rights and duties, due to the whole community in its social aggregate capacity" ([1769] 1979, 4:5).

In the United States today, almost all possible *legal* wrongs are still defined as public or private wrongs (or, in some cases, both). The crucial difference between these types of legal wrongs is not the nature of the act committed but rather whose interests are seen as having been offended or injured. Public wrongs or crimes are acts that are seen as offending the interests of the sovereign entity. In other words, crimes are acts that breach duties owed to the sovereign or sovereign group.[1]

Broadly speaking, U.S. law recognizes two principal types of private wrongs. Breach of contract and tort.[2] Breach of contract refers to a failure to perform a specific duty (owed to specific individuals) that one has taken on by signing a contract.[3]

A tort, like a breach of contract, involves conduct that violates a duty owed individuals, hence, both torts and breaches of contract are "private wrongs." But a tort is different from a breach of contract in that it involves a breach of a general duty. This sort of duty is imposed by law and generally owed to all other members of the society or of a particular group.

The distinctions between crime, tort, and breach of contract can be somewhat confusing and so more explanation is warranted. First, what is the difference between crime and tort? Here is one way to think of it: In our society, one has a legal duty to respect other people's property and (as a corollary) a right to expect other people to respect one's property. Because these expectations are derived from law, or the civil contract, it follows that, should someone breach this expectation, there is recourse to a sovereign-supplied remedy. That is, the victim can take the offending party to court. But failing to respect another's property could be a crime or a tort (or both) and the type of remedy as well as the

---

1. Technically, as Blackstone implied, public wrongs violate public law—or laws that pertain to the relations between the sovereign entity and the individuals who live within the sovereign's domain. Thus, if the sovereign denied an individual's right to some constitutionally guaranteed benefit, this offense would also qualify as a public wrong. Private wrongs, in contrast, are those acts that violate private law—or the laws that regulate relations between individuals.

2. In exact translation, the Norman word "tort," like the Latin word "delict," simply refers to a "wrong." However, it is used here in the more specialized sense that it has come to have in law, viz., a noncriminal but justiciable or legal wrong not arising from breach of a legal contract.

3. Breach of contract can also be thought of in terms of the more abstract designation that is sometimes used, and that is "breach of duty." This category of wrongs refers more broadly to wrongs committed when special duties, generally ones assumed voluntarily by an actor, are breached. For example, along with breach of contract, the breach of duty category includes breach of trust—a wrong that can only be committed by a trustee or someone with specific fiduciary responsibility.

procedure followed in pursuit of remedy will depend on whose interests are seen as having been offended: In the U.S. legal system, for example, stealing a car is an act deemed to offend the interests of the sovereign as well as the interests of the car owner. For this reason, it is both a crime (theft) and a tort (conversion). In contrast, accidentally bumping into someone's car and denting its fender is not deemed a crime. The sovereign is typically interested in getting involved only when there has been an *intentional* offense to its interests; therefore, such an act is merely an offense to the car owner or a tort (negligent harm to property).

Generally speaking, respecting the property of other Persons is a general duty that all members of society have—there is no escaping it because it is imposed on everyone by the civil contract (though sometimes only implicitly). In contrast, breach of contract refers to a failure to perform a duty that one has voluntarily accepted and thus involves a breach of a duty that one has imposed upon oneself. For example, there is no general duty to share one's property with others. But, if in return for a "consideration" (money or some other form of payment), one agrees to lend or give some piece of property to another, then reneges on the deal, one offends the interests of that other individual and thereby commits a wrong.[4]

Because public (e.g., criminal) wrongs are acts judged to be against the interests of the civil domain or sovereign, the state has a direct

---

4. In the United States (and in England) the difference between tort and breach of contract was once much more significant than it is today. Until the mid-twentieth century, a "formalist" theory of contract prevailed. Simply put, a formalist theory of contract holds that everything in the contract is contractual. Such a theory, especially when coupled with a rigid adherence to the "technicalities" of contract law, creates a very narrow view of contractual liability. Under this view, if the parties do not put a specific provision into their contract, then no matter how unfair the result, the contract is binding even to the smallest of fine print.

In light of his view that not everything in the contract is contractual (1933, 211), Durkheim, of course, would have held such a theory of contracts to be untenable as, indeed, it has proved to be. As noted in Chapter 1, no society gives complete freedom to contract. In the United States, the formalist approach has been modified and such concepts as "quasi [or implied] contracts," "unjust enrichment" and "unconscionability" (all of which allow for taking into account the noncontractual elements of duty in contract law) were invented to make contract law more fair. For this reason, according to some legal scholars, the distinction between tort and breach of contract is disappearing. See, for example, Gilmore 1974, *The Death of Contract*.

interest in the affair and typically will be the party that instigates legal action (especially if the sovereign employs police and prosecutors).[5] To find remedy for a private wrong, however, the offended individual must instigate action (bring suit in court).

Private wrongs are not, however, "all wrongs that are not criminal wrongs," for not all noncriminal wrongs are remediable through law. What members of a modern society generally refer to as "private wrongs," are really "private" only in the sense that the sovereign's interest is only *indirect* and so it is the individual who must bring suit— or instigate legal action—to win legal remedy. The sovereign does have an indirect interest in torts and breaches of contract, and it is only because of that indirect interest that the offended individual *can* bring suit and call upon the power of the sovereign entity to enforce a judgment.

The concepts of public and private wrongs do not exhaust the list of wrongs. There are wrongs that are extralegal that the law ignores. I refer to these wrongs as "truly private" wrongs because they involve instances of harm or dispute in which the sovereign has *no interest* and will not intervene—even if asked. Truly private wrongs are thus extralegal and belong in the communal domain, as illustrated in Figure 4.1.

Civil Domain   Communal Domain

The *civil domain* contains all wrongs   The *communal domain* contains all
that are remediable through legal   wrongs that are NOT remediable
action   through legal action

FIGURE 4.1 Primary domain locations of public wrongs, "private" wrongs, and "truly private" wrongs. In many cases, acts that violate legal norms violate social norms as well.

---

5. In the U.S. legal system, when both individual interests and sovereign interests are offended, the sovereign has precedence in seeking remedy. For example, as noted above, theft is a tort as well as a crime, but the state's (criminal) case against the alleged thief takes precedence over the (tort) claims of the person who has actually lost property as a result of the theft.

Some specific examples of truly private wrongs can help to make this point more clear:

1. Mary and Bob are going steady. Bob discovers that Mary is cheating on him with Peter, Bob's best friend. Bob feels wronged.

2. Mary and Bob are married. They each have jobs, and each regularly contributes funds to a joint savings account in hopes of one day purchasing their dream home. One day, Mary withdraws $100,000 from the savings account, flies to Reno, and loses the entire amount playing Blackjack. Bob feels wronged.

In each case, Bob has every reason to feel wronged, but in *neither* case (in the U.S. legal system, at least) does he have any recourse to a sovereign-supplied remedy. In each of these instances, Mary has breached social/normative expectations about acceptable behavior. However, she has in neither case breached the civil contract; she has not broken the law. What Mary has done is to commit wrongs that are *truly* private. Of course, she has harmed Bob, but the harm (even when both severe and tangible, as it is in the second example) is not a legally relevant or justiciable one.

The fact that under the U.S. civil contract Mary's first injury to Bob is not a justiciable one may be explained by invoking the legal maxim *De minimus non curat lex*—the law does not concern itself with trifles. (The sociologist would caution, of course, that what is a trifle in some societies could be a heinous offense in others.) The fact that Mary's second injury to Bob is not justiciable suggests the following caveat to that maxim—"nor does the law concern itself with all nontrifles." What is considered justiciable can change—even thirty years ago wife-beating was generally only a truly private wrong in the United States. Although a husband who blackened the eyes of his wife may have violated social norms, his violent acts were not breaches of legal (civil) expectations. Hence, the battered wife had no *legal* recourse.[6] The private wrongs with which the law is concerned are those that

---

6. Of course, in the United States wife-beating has never been totally unrestrained by the law. Many jurisdictions had so-called "rules of thumb" (i.e., it's okay to beat your wife as long as you did it with a stick that was thinner than your thumb) or "stitch rules" (beating your wife was legal as long as the resulting injuries didn't require more than a particular number of stitches).

constitute infringements of *civil* (or legal) rights; that is, private wrongs are breaches of civil expectations as opposed to purely social/normative expectations.[7]

In their discussions of premodern societies, most commentators have missed this important point and treated the idea of private wrong (or civil injury) as if it meant any significant wrong, or any nontrifling injury against an individual that was not criminal. In other words, many writers seem to have assumed that any significant injury that was not reacted to as a criminal offense must have been, by definition, a civil (i.e., legal) one. For example, A. S. Diamond defined crime as "conduct which is an offense to all" and civil wrongs as "conduct which is an offense only to individuals" (1971, 167). The implication is that every wrong belongs in one *legal* category or the other—civil or criminal.

I suggest that this "operationalization" of wrong is incomplete. In archaic societies especially, the majority of wrongs against an individual's interests, even significant wrongs, were *truly* private. They were, in other words, extralegal. Being extra legal meant that the damage could be remedied only through "self-help," which, in archaic society, often meant recourse to blood feud (or "might makes right"). It is important to note that however much self-help is guided and restrained by social norms (as it usually is), it must be distinguished from remedies that are accorded by law; as I illustrate below, the dynamics of legal action and self-help are different in important respects.

What is confusing is that there survives from the early days evidence that—at first pass—seems to imply that there were legal remedies for truly private or extralegal wrongs. For example, one of the oldest surviving European codes is the law of the Salic Franks (*Lex Salica*) issued by King Clovis around 496 A.D.[8] This code "starts by listing monetary sanctions to be paid by a defendant to a plaintiff for failure to respond to the plaintiff's summons to appear in the local court. It also lists monetary sanctions to be paid by wrong-doers to injured parties for various kinds of offenses, including homicides, assaults, thefts" (Berman 1983, 53). Conceiving of these "offenses" as

---

7. The relationship between civil (or legal) and social expectations is discussed at length in the next two chapters.

8. The Salicans were the Frankish people of Germany who settled in Gaul—a division of the ancient Roman Empire (including what is now mainly France and Belgium).

civil, and of the prescribed monetary "sanctions" as legal, however, is misleading. Although such cases might be heard before a public assembly *(moot)* and decisions rendered, that process could be more accurately labeled nonbinding arbitration or mediation than lawsuit. Unlike tort actions of today (where one ignores a summons to court at one's peril), participation was optional for both defendant and plaintiff, and "even if they consented to appear, they might not remain throughout" (Berman 1983, 56).

More important, judgments rendered under such circumstances were not authoritative, and a finding for one of the litigants in no way guaranteed the outcome.

> Where . . . the trial took place before an assembly of the whole community, with all members participating in the making of the judgment . . . it might be expected that as a consequence of such cooperation in the rendering of the judgment none of its members would obstruct its enforcement, provided it had not been publicly challenged in the assembly. Nevertheless, the victorious litigant could not depend upon anything more than mere passivity on the part of those outside of his own kinship group. It was entirely incumbent upon him, by way of self-help, to enforce the judgment with the assistance of his kin-folk unless, of course, the unsuccessful party obeyed the judgment. (Weber 1978, 648)

There is a striking similarity between these proceedings and the situation now typically seen in the "World Court." A century ago, Frederick Pollock noted this parallel between international and primitive "law":

> [Law's] jurisdiction began, it seems with being merely voluntary, derived not from the authority of the state but from the consent of the parties. People might come to court for a decision if they agreed to do so . . . but the court could not compel their obedience any more than a tribunal of arbitration appointed at this day under a treaty between sovereign states can compel the rulers of those states to fulfill its award. (Quoted in Maitland and Montague 1915, 11-12)

Just as Bob has no legal case or recourse against the erstwhile Mary in the examples given above, in archaic German society if Wulfslan assaulted Gandolf, the latter had no legal recourse. Again, a wrong was committed, but it was an extralegal one. Recall that law involves a particular transformation of resources. Gandolf might well have taken his case to the moot and "won," but the victory was an empty one if Wulfslan could not be sufficiently intimidated by public opinion. In such a case, Gandolf's win was—at best—a symbolic one.

"Symbolic victories" are not, of course, totally without value and indeed can be quite compelling. Public opinion and shaming, for example, can be very effective social sanctions. Although such victories may result in social (informal) pressure being brought to bear on the loser, however, they do not change the winner's resources in the same way that a legal victory would. As I discuss below (in Chapter 5), in a pluralistic society especially, informal social control may be of very little use. Symbolic victories are not legal victories.

Other illustrations may be drawn from the anthropological literature. A. S. Diamond's account of the "judicial" process in a gathering and hunting society, for instance, reveals it to be similarly *extra*legal: "The chief announces what the council or the community agrees and a family who desires to do so may disregard his wishes and take independent action. In regard to disputes and disorder arising from alleged wrongs, the Chief's function and efforts are to preserve or restore peace: he may offer advice or moral suasion but not a judgment" (1971, 185). Essentially, the difference between the mechanisms used to settle extralegal or truly private wrongs and those used to settle legal wrongs (whether private or public) is akin to what Gulliver (1969a; 1969b) identified as the difference between dispute settlement by *negotiation* and dispute settlement by *adjudication*. Negotiation seeks to make a settlement that is a "mutually acceptable, tolerable resolution of the matter in dispute, based on the assessed or demonstrated *strengths of the parties*" (1969a, 17; emphasis added). In other words, insofar as the civil contract perspective is concerned, pure negotiation is not a legal process because there is no transformation of resources; a negotiated settlement is one in which *might makes right*.

Adjudication is different: Adjudicated settlements are "in some way coercive in that the adjudicator . . . has not only both the right and obligation to reach and enunciate a decision but also power to enforce it" (1969a, 17). Adjudication, then, is a legal process because there is a transformation of resources.

To the extent that the distinction between adjudication and negotiation implies there is no room for negotiation in the legal process it is misleading. In fact, most legal cases are settled through what appears to be negotiation. In the criminal justice process this is typically known as "plea bargaining"; in civil suits we generally refer to cases being "settled out of court."

But this sort of negotiation is not really true negotiation (as defined above) because it is played out against a background of potential adjudication. So, for example, when a plaintiff's attorney "negotiates" a deal with a defendant's attorney, the negotiation is not worked in terms of the resources at the command of each party but rather in terms of how much the evidence accrued by each side is expected to be worth should they have to go to trial and have the case adjudicated. In a civil case, the winner is not necessarily decided by who has the most money or political pull, but by who has the facts on their side (again, right makes might) (McIntyre 1987, 148-150). In other words, this sort of negotiation is influenced by the transformation of resources that the law provides. (I think of the difference between pure negotiation and negotiation conducted with adjudication in the background this way: When I was a child my older brother and I would often "negotiate" who got control of the television set. When such negotiations took place in the absence of my parents, my older (and *much* larger) brother would always win. When my parents were home, he would only win a portion of the time.)

Durkheim's View
of Legal Evolution Rehabilitated

Durkheim, in *The Division of Labor* (1933), argued that criminal (repressive) law dominated over civil (restitutive) law in early society. Yet beginning with Faris's (1934) review of the first English translation of Durkheim's book, it has been fashionable to assert that Durkheim was wrong about this; indeed the view that Durkheim erred on this point has become the majority one among sociologists and other social scientists. A. S. Diamond, for example, argued that criminal law arose not only later than tort, but *from* tort (1971, 68). In this view, Diamond was following a precedent set by Sir Henry Maine in *Ancient Law*. "The penal law of ancient communities is not the law of Crimes," he wrote, "it is the law of Wrongs or, to use the English technical word, of Torts. The person proceeds against the wrong-doer by ordinary civil action, and recovers compensation in the shape of money damages if he succeeds" ([1861] 1986 307-308).

The idea that the earliest legal systems were dominated by concerns about private or civil wrongs (specifically, torts) is deeply entrenched. As L. S. Sheleff summed up contemporary assessments of Durkheim's work on this matter: "Durkheim was probably right in his theoretical premise that the law is the visible outer symbol of the nature of a society. He was almost certainly wrong in his empirical assessment of the direction of the law from repressive to restitutive" (quoted in Reiner 1984, 196).

This position, despite its popularity, needs reassessment. On the one hand, Durkheim may have erred when he implied that individuals in early societies had no interests that could be injured apart from their share in "society's" interests. On the other hand, it was nevertheless true that the law in early societies took little notice of injuries to personal interests, and Durkheim was almost certainly correct when he claimed that the *law* of those earliest societies was dominated by repressive and not restitutive law.

Confusion on this point has led to misleading accounts of the relationship between law and society. It is a significant mistake to equate the condition of the tortfeasor who is judged liable for making restitution in modern society with that of a wrongdoer found "guilty" and liable for making "composition" in archaic society—in the latter case, there was no sovereign enforcement of judgment and hence no real transformation of resources of the injured party. *Composition* was money or goods (*wergild*) given to an injured person by the guilty party in lieu of blood feud or other forms of revenge-seeking behavior.

These early codes did not provide *legal* remedy; they simply provided a normatively or socially accepted "market value" for certain *truly private* or extralegal wrongs.[9] The "laws" of King Æthelbert (600 A.D.), for example, consisted simply of ninety statements of equivalency. Here are three of them as listed by Colby (1915, 195-196):

> If an ear be struck off, let "bot" [amends] be made with xii. shillings.
> If the other ear hear not, let "bot" be made with xxv. shillings.
> If an ear be mutilated, let "bot" be made with vi. shillings.

By way of example, assume it is the year 602 A.D. Wulfslan's teenage son has taken a jar of oil from Gandolf's dwelling. Gandolf has been wronged and must respond (else all the other hoodlums in the neighborhood will believe that they can play fast and loose with Gandolf's stuff). One possible response is for Gandolf to injure Wulfslan to the same (or greater) degree. Gandolf doesn't really relish this prospect, however, because such a move could escalate into more conflict than Gandolf wants. So instead, Gandolf consults the "law" and finds the following: "If any one take property from a dwelling, let him pay a three-fold 'bot'" (Colby, 1915 195). Gandolf proposes to Wulfslan that the wrong be "composed"—that is, that he be paid three times the

---

9. German sociologist Georg Simmel made a somewhat similar point in his discussion of the origins of wergild in *The Philosophy of Money* (1978, 356-366); his discussion focused on wergild in terms of "fines."

value of the stolen jar of oil. Now Wulfslan must choose: If he pays, then Gandolf will not feel obliged to take other action for he will have received his due. If he refuses to pay, Gandolf will feel obliged to take action. However, no sovereign entity will step in to force Wulfslan to pay the bot.

"Composing" a blood feud, then, involved making a payoff that pacified the injured party. Composition is similar to civil action in that the intent (ostensibly, at least) is not to punish but to restore the status quo; it is unlike civil action in that it only works for those who can enforce it.

As long as the sovereign group will not enforce the "judgment," composition can hardly be thought of as judicial, though certainly it may be "normative"—but that's extralegal. For "law enforcement" to exist does not require a designated police force (*cf.* Schwartz and Miller 1964, but see also, Baxi 1974), or even, contrary to Weber's view, a "staff," but it does require some action (force or threat of force) on the part of the collectivity. As long as such disputes can be resolved only through "self-help" (e.g., blood feud or threat of blood feud), they remain extralegal. Setting monetary amounts for the composition of the blood feud merely helped to forestall bloodshed by providing an alternative currency for remedy, a way to resolve disputes that did not involve bloodshed. Where satisfaction of "honor" was perhaps as important as the actual remedy, the wronged party did not lose face by allowing a feud to be "composed"—for he got what society and his neighbors saw as his due. Therefore, accepting composition in lieu of bloodshed did not involve a loss of face, or constitute an invitation for abuse from others. As Harold Berman said, "The substitution of fixed rates of payment gave dignity to a settlement short of violence" (1983, 56). Thus, composition satisfied honor. Composition was not law; it was (to paraphrase Redfield) merely the blood feud shortened (Redfield 1964, 12).[10]

---

10. Durkheim's discussion of the vendetta and its relation to punishment adds to the confusion on this issue. "The vendetta," he wrote, "is evidently a punishment which society recognizes as legitimate, but which it leaves to particular persons to inflict." But, he said, "it is far from true that private vengeance is the prototype of punishment; it is, on the contrary, only an imperfect punishment" (1933, 94). The distinction between punishment and vendetta, and hence between legal and extralegal process, was made a bit more clear (though not much) when Durkheim distinguished in a later work between "vengeance" (i.e., personal retaliation) and "punishment" (group response to criminal act): "Vengeance, is not a punishment; it is modern warfare that it resembles. It was not able to transform itself into punishment

The Civil Domain: The Modern Contrast

Contemporary American society represents a point of extreme contrast to archaic German society. In the latter case, civil ties were few and thus the law hardly intruded at all into society. Most of archaic society involved, in fact, "lawless" communal relationships, and consequently, most disputes were settled extralegally. Extralegal solutions might involve anything from shaming to blood feud, but however extreme, they took place in the communal domain, where there was, as Beccaria said in his discussion of dueling, "the anarchy of the laws" ([1764] 1963, 73).

It is difficult, in contrast, to conjure up images of relationships in modern U.S. society that are *not* civil ones; where once it may have been commonplace to hear people mutter "there ought to be a law," more than likely now there is a law. Where historically people in certain sorts of relations (e.g., husband and wife, parent and child, minister and parishioner, teacher and student, little league coach and player) could not invoke the law to remedy breaches of expectations, this is no longer true. In other words, the size of the civil domain, relative to society, has increased dramatically.

What determines the size of the civil domain? Durkheim argued in *The Division of Labor in Society* (1933) that as society grows larger and more complex, individuals within society become much more interdependent at the same time as they become more autonomous. With this development, society's ability to tolerate both "wrongs" and remedies involving "self-help" may decrease. Intuitively, given the degree to which law is about relationships, it does seem that an increase in the variety and interpenetration of social relationships necessitates an increase in law. Still, this observation has only to do with the amount of law in the absolute sense. To the extent that more social relationships imply more "society," as the number of relationships and laws to govern these relationships increases, the size of the civil domain relative to society, in theory, could remain the same. At the very least, an increase in social complexity (on the face of it) seems to provide no reason for the absolute size of the communal domain to become smaller.

Let's say that in a particular society (at Time One) there are 100 distinct social relationships (e.g., father-son, father-daughter,

---

since everywhere it tends to give rise to composition, that is, to damages" ([1904] 1983, 154).

husband-wife, mother-son, mother-daughter, master-servant, lord-peasant, and so on). Of these relations, thirty are civil. That is, thirty percent of all social relationships involve specific legal advantages and disadvantages; in thirty percent of all social relationships breaches of expectations may be resolved legally.

Time passes and life becomes more complex. At Time Two there are 175 distinct social relationships. (Thus, instead of just father-son relationships there are father-oldest son and father-second son relationships, etc.)

One would expect that more law would be needed in this more complex society, but there would be no reason to expect that the proportion of civil relations would have to increase relative to the number of relations. Thus, one would expect that the size of the civil domain would increase, but that it would remain about the same relative to the size of the overall society. Hence, about thirty percent of all social relations would be civil ones.

The amount of social complexity in any society will, at least in part, determine the absolute size of the civil domain. But in and of itself the number of relationships does not determine the ratio of civil relations to social ones, or of the size of the civil domain relative to the size of society. And yet, in the United States the relative size of the civil domain has increased tremendously. A number of relations that were until very recently considered to be outside the civil domain (say, between little league player and coach) are now civil (and hence, in such relations, breaches of expectations are subject to litigation).

It has often been remarked that the size of the civil domain in this country is noticeably larger relative to society as a whole than in other societies with about the same degree of social complexity. Compared to the United States, the proportion of Japanese society that is included in the civil domain is smaller. So, while social complexity seems to be involved, it does not account for all the variance.

But the comparison between Japan and the United States suggests another explanation of what is, or is not, excluded from the civil domain. The following hypothesis seems plausible: To the degree that Persons in the civil domain share values and expectations about appropriate behavior, interPersonal relations will be excluded from the civil domain. In other words, where values are mostly shared among parties to the contract, most interPersonal relationships will be communal ones governed by social norms, not law. Like the marriage contract between two people in love, the provisions of the civil contract will tend to affirm or to reiterate group values and articulate collective goals in relatively vague ways rather than spell out expectations in detail.

This hypothesis does not, however, necessarily imply a peaceful society or one in which conflict is lacking. The consensus in such a society may simply be based on a normative acceptance of the "law of the jungle." One can imagine a society (such as archaic Germany, or perhaps one ruled by nineteenth century-type American corporate officers) in which there is a great deal of competition for resources, yet very little rule of law.

This relates to a distinction that Vilhelm Aubert made between two types of conflict. One type of conflict, he said, involves a "conflict of interests"—this sort of conflict generally "stems from a situation of scarcity. Both want the 'same thing,' but there is not enough of it available for each to have what he wants" (1989, 96). The second type of conflict is, I think, more fundamental, and involves "dissensus" or disagreement over "facts and/or values" (95). Aubert suggested that the different types of conflict are amenable to different types of resolution: "conflicts of interest may often lend themselves to settlement by negotiation within a dyadic arrangement. Dissensus may be harder to settle by negotiation and will often demand some kind of triadic structure for settlement" (95).

To put Aubert's insight into the language I've been using in this book, conflicts of interest between Persons lend themselves to resolution in the communal domain through negotiation. Dissensus too may arise and be resolved within the communal domain, but will more likely cause people to resort to civil domain structures (e.g., the courts) for authoritative resolution. (There is always a possibility, of course, that when conflicts arising from dissensus cannot be resolved peacefully in the civil domain, they might be thrown back into the communal [i.e., "lawless"] domain, as happens in civil wars.)

The focus here is on values shared by those who are party to the contract, or Persons—and that group is not necessarily the same as the sum of people who reside in a country. The amount of specificity and precision in the civil contract varies not with how *heterogeneous society itself is* but with how *heterogeneous the civil domain is.*

Modern Japan is often held up as an example of a society in which people are loath to litigate:

> The belief that the Japanese are an exceptionally nonlitigious people is remarkably pervasive. Commentators, both within and without Japan, are almost unanimous in attributing to the Japanese an unusual and deeply rooted cultural preference for informal, mediated settlement of private disputes and a corollary aversion to the formal

mechanisms of judicial adjudication. . . . As explained by Kawashima Takeyoshi, one of Japan's leading legal sociologists and most articulate exponents of this belief, the endurance of a traditional concern for preserving cooperative personal relationships makes unwanted any definitive delineation of rights and duties through litigation. (Haley 1978, 359-360; see also Yoshiyuki 1976)

Professor Kawashima's position reflects a great deal of scholarly and popular "wisdom" about the nature of Japanese society and the role played by law in that society. It is an empirical fact that in Japan, despite its seeming complexity, there are comparatively few lawyers and laws, and low levels of litigation. Japanese society confounds any Durkheimian conception of the relationship between social complexity and the evolution of law.

The paucity of lawyers, laws, and litigation suggests that the civil domain is small in Japan. The question is, Why is this so? One's first guess would be that Japan's civil domain is small because of widespread societal homogeneity. But is this true? Interestingly, some evidence suggests Japan's civil domain is actually homogeneous because its membership is limited; in other words, those Persons who are party to the civil contract purposefully exclude most types of relationships and most people from full membership, denying them full access to sovereign power.

Thus, Robert L. Nelson (citing Galanter 1983) noted that: "some of the societies held up as ideals of nonlitigiousness, most notably Japan, manifested low levels of litigation and few lawyers not because of a cultural predisposition against formalized conflict but as a result of conscious decisions by political elites to limit the institutional resources given to formal dispute resolution structures" (Nelson 1988, 678). Similarly, John O. Haley noted that, in Japan, "governmentally imposed restrictions limit total entry into the legal profession— private attorneys, government lawyers and judges—to less than 500 persons a year. As a result Japan has fewer lawyers and judges per capita today than it did in the mid-1920s. . . . This is not, I must emphasize, the result of any lack of demand" (1982, 273).

By these lights, those who take the small number of lawyers in Japan as an indication of low demand for lawyers' services (e.g., Kawashima 1973) are probably wrong. Although a multitude of factors no doubt shapes the civil domain in any particular society, in Japan the fact that so few resources are dedicated to litigation is as much owing to people's disability to litigate as it is to their disinclination (see also Kidder and Hostetler, 1990). In other words, it may be that to say that

Japanese people tend not to litigate may be like saying that women and African Americans in nineteenth-century America were not litigious. Empirically, the assessment is correct, but it begs the question.

If the Japanese have been perceived as loath to litigate, many writers have asserted exactly the opposite about U.S. citizens. In fact, it has often been suggested that litigiousness is a cultural value (or, as some put it, "a national disease") in the United States. The national reputation for being lawsuit-happy actually predates the American Revolution. As one early visitor to these shores saw it:

> A litigious spirit is very apparent in this country. The assizes [court sessions] are held twice in the year in the city of Annapolis and the number of causes brought forward is really incredible. Though few of the gentlemen who practice have been regularly called to the bar, there are several who are confessedly eminent in their profession; and those who are possessed of superior abilities have full employment for the exertion of their talents. (William Eddis, *Letters from America*, 1770, excerpted in Kurland and Lerner 1987, 1:516)

What is interesting is that the first European settlers in America were anything but litigious. As I have noted elsewhere (McIntyre 1987, 15-16), colonial lawyers, even those "regularly called to the bar," were rarely encouraged and sometimes forbidden to practice their craft at all. *The Massachusetts Bay Body of Liberties* (1641) forbade pleading for hire; Thomas Merton, who has been called the first Massachusetts lawyer, was jailed and later expelled for "scandalous behavior." The writers of *The Fundamental Constitutions of the Carolinas* (1669) declared to all attorneys that it was a "base and vile thing to plead for money or reward" (Friedman 1985b, 81). One of the settlers in William Penn's settlement enthusiastically proclaimed the community's rejection of both doctors and lawyers and remarked his relief at the fact that his settlement had no need for either the "pestiferous drugs of the one or the tiresome loquacity of the other" (Beck 1930, 97).

The colonies that banned lawyers had civil domains populated by Persons united by a strong consensus about values and expectations. As these civil domains became more heterogeneous, resort to courts of law became more frequent. There may be something to the notion that litigation is valued in and of itself in the United States, but it is clear that the nation's heterogeneity, and especially its Persons' access to the courts, are important factors. (This topic will be taken up again in Chapter 7).

Changes in the Size of the Civil Domain

What causes the civil contract to become more or less inclusive of people and/or relationships?[11] This issue is particularly striking when it comes to "Persons," since any change in the number and categories of people included in the contract seems apt to be quite revolutionary. In other words, it is one thing to bring a new type of relationship into civil society but quite another to bring in a new category of individuals.

For example, why is it that the civil contract in the United States has moved (at least in the technical sense) from according the status of Person only to white adult males to granting Personhood to women, African Americans, Native Americans, and—to a lesser extent—minors?

In theory, at least, it seems reasonable to presume that Personhood may be gained by excluded individuals (Nonpersons) in one of two ways. First, and perhaps most obviously, Personhood may be gained by war or what amounts to war. The social movements literature and especially writers coming from the resource mobilization school of thought argue persuasively that groups often demand, take, and win standing over and against the resistance of those who have it (see, for example, McAdam, McCarthy and Zald 1988).

If it is not realized as a result of war, Personhood must come as a result of "treaty." In other words, it must be because those who are already party to the civil contract admit Nonpersons to the status of Persons. Law Professor Christopher Stone has suggested that giving legal status to a new category of individuals often has very little to do with an altruistically inspired recognition of value of those individuals as Persons or of their inherent rights. Instead, he said, the motive is typically to protect the rights of those who already have legal status (1987, 43). Historians have argued, for example, that in this country the Married Women's Property Acts—which in the early 1850s began to extend to married women in the United States the right to own property—was engendered by their fathers' desires to protect

---

11. It does not do to think that the civil contract can change only in the direction of becoming more inclusive. The colonial treatment of Africans was an example of the contract becoming more *exclusive*. At first, in some colonies, Africans were not treated much differently from white indentured servants (Hast 1969). Then the contract only treated free Christian Africans as Persons; then—when it was forbidden to baptize Africans—all Africans were excluded from franchisement.

family estates from improvident sons-in-law (Sachs and Wilson 1979, 77).

It seems that Personhood is most often extended by treaty under threat of war. After the American Revolution, when decisions were being made about the conditions of Personhood, there was a great deal of discussion about restricting the right to vote to those with significant property or financial resources. This was a touchy question because many colonial leaders agreed with Thomas Paine, who in his *Dissertation on the First Principles of Government* (1775) argued, without a great deal of success, that "it is possible to exclude men from the right of voting, but it is impossible to exclude them from the right of rebelling against that exclusion; and when all other rights are taken away the right of rebelling is made perfect" (Kurland and Lerner 1987, 1:219-220). In a similar fashion, some believe that African Americans, women and other minorities were able to make civil rights gains during the 1960s and 1970s because the "majority" (i.e., "Persons") feared open rebellion.[12]

Civil recognition of newcomers generally is not total—typically there are lingering legal disabilities.[13] But in the long run, once any

---

12. It is unlikely that women were perceived as a threat. What, then, are the origins of their legal gains during this period? Some of it, at least, may have been accidental. As Jeanne Gregory has explained, "In the United States, the employment rights of women and racial minorities are embodied in the same law, although the legislators had not originally intended it to be so. Ironically, the amendment to include 'sex' along with 'race' in Title VII of the Civil Rights Act of 1964 was introduced by a Southern Congressman [Howard Smith] who regularly voted against civil rights measures and who wished to discredit the Bill. Although discussion on the amendment was punctuated with hysterical laughter, Congress accepted it and the Bill became law" (1987, 31). In a footnote, Gregory stressed that legal recognition of Personhood is a necessary but not sufficient resource for actually gaining the benefits of Personhood: "Once the law was passed feminists then had to campaign to insure that the provisions in respect of women were taken seriously" (46n).

13. Of course, an extension of rights to Nonpersons may be a temporary maneuver intended to pacify Nonpersons while allowing Persons time to regroup and bolster their resources to exterminate the threat. Historically, this approach was used by the U.S. government, for example, when dealing with Native Americans; it is also what happened to workers in Czechoslovakia in 1969. More recently, some have argued that a similar regrouping and subsequent rescinding of civil rights for women and minorities occurred in this country during the Reagan-Bush administrations (Chambers 1990).

recognition or standing is achieved—once a group of Nonpersons gets a toehold in civil society—there is the *possibility* that they can litigate for a stronger position (i.e., "give them an inch and they'll take a mile").

One thing seems fairly certain: granting the status of "Person" to new categories of individuals is bound to make the civil contract (law) more complex, more precise, more detailed, and less a simple affirmation or reiteration of shared values. If the fact that these individuals were not previously accorded recognition as Persons means anything, it is that they were perceived to be "different" from Persons in some important and significant way. Certainly this is true of former Nonpersons in our society—African Americans, Native Americans, and women. Being perceived as different has important consequences.

For example, as noted in Chapter 3, in U.S. society the important difference between Person and Nonperson was often alleged to be one involving the Nonperson's "reasoning" abilities; there was a perception (on the part of the white males who authored the Constitution) that these civil disabilities were fair owing to the alleged inability of these Nonpersons' to make appropriate decisions—either owing to their "situation" or to their innate characteristics; the white male Persons believed that the members of these groups lacked "a will of their own":

> All members of the state are qualified to make the election, unless they have not sufficient discretion, or are so situated as to have no wills of their own. Persons not twenty one years old are deemed of the former class, from their want of years and experience. . . . Women what age soever they are of, are also considered as not having a sufficient acquired discretion; not from deficiency in their mental powers, but from the natural tenderness and delicacy of their minds, their retired mode of life, and various domestic duties. . . . Slaves are of the latter class and have no wills. (*The Essex Result 1778*, quoted in Kurland and Lerner 1987, 1:396-397)

In societies where one's ability to "reason" is not so highly prized, other kinds of perceived differences are used to support and justify exclusion. A century ago, those who were parties to the civil contract in Japan legitimated exclusion of individuals who were members of the outcaste group hinin (or "non-human") on the basis that they were "polluted." In 1907, government officials in one prefecture made their view explicit:

> The people of this race [the hinin] in this prefecture are devout believers of Buddhism, and thus they should be sincere and virtuous

. . . but instead they are ruthless and cruel. Not only do they steal and kill cats and dogs, but they also steal other property. . . . This race of people stands outside of society and knows nothing of morality. By and large they are lazy and addicted to gambling. Because of their perverse nature, they have a strong inclination to unite for unjust purposes. They join in groups of threes and fives, vandalize the homes of good people, and steal [anything that they can get their hands on]. (Hane 1982, 146)

Granting new groups of individuals legal abilities and standing brings into the civil domain people who are (or have been) judged to be different in important ways. Granting Personhood to former Nonpersons means an increase in the perceived differences among Persons *within* civil society; it also means that dominant groups have given up at least some of their power to use force legitimately against the former Nonpersons. Notwithstanding the perceived nature of the differences between new and old Persons, once civil recognition is granted, the civil contract will have to be adjusted to deal with these differences in some way.

When new Persons are brought into a civil domain, it is likely that two things will occur. First, there must almost certainly be a decrease in reliance upon informal (that is, extralegal) mechanisms of social control among Persons who are party to the civil contract (because informal mechanisms of social control gossip and disapproval do not exist, or are not as effective, *across* communal groups). Second, as a result of the impotency of informal (communal) control, there likely will be an increased reliance upon more concrete law and legal standards to guide, evaluate, and control behavior. One example can be drawn from the experience of female U.S. soldiers who fought in the Gulf War in the early 1990s. In Saudi Arabia, before the war, police (i.e., "the law") rarely had to get involved in enforcing the custom that women not wear shorts in public. The American women, however, wore shorts in public and had "no shame" about doing so. As a result, the legal apparatus was invoked to enforce the custom. In the aftermath, similar legal coercion was used to put uppity Saudi women (e.g., those who wished to obtain drivers' licenses)—who had presumed to follow the American women's example—back into their place.

One likely outcome of bringing more Persons into the civil domain is that more types of relationships, heretofore communal, will become "civil," or legally relevant. In Chapter 1 I argued that the degree of specificity in a legal contract is negatively related to the amount of trust existing between the contracting parties. Here the argument is basically the same. All in all, there is a positive relationship between the specificity of the civil contract and the heterogeneity of the civil domain.

Why this is so can be explained by the fact that trust is based on a perception of commonality. When the members of one group perceive the members of another group as being "different," this usually means they feel that group cannot be trusted, especially if they consider the differences to be important ones. A lack of trust betrays the belief that the means of informal social control are impotent; that, for example, the weight of informal group opinion is not enough to ensure that someone will "do the right thing" (McIntyre 1989). In such situations, resort to law is the logical outcome because, when it is not purely affirmative, law is a contrivance that can be used to establish and, if needed, force compliance with common standards of minimally expected behavior.

Thus, when a body of law (i.e., a civil contract) is highly specific, it usually exists in conjunction with a civil domain that has (or has had) a heterogeneous population. A clear illustration of this is the difference between English common law and French or German civil codes. Common law, or a variation of it, exists in most English-speaking countries—England, Wales, Ireland, United States, Canada, Australia, Scotland, South Africa, and Rhodesia. These countries have based their legal systems, at least in part, on the English system which allows law to develop over time through decisions made by judges in particular cases.[14] Common law, then, tends to emerge haphazardly from the usages and customs of the people and is apt to be vague and imprecise. Civil codes, on the other hand, are unquestionably enacted and tend to be precise and specific. Common law tends to exist where the civil domain (though not necessarily society) is relatively homogeneous; civil codes, as in the case of France and Germany, may be enacted to help unite balkanized states and territories; to unite, in other words, several different civil domains.

Similarly, historians studying U.S. law have shown that early colonial codes were often drafted as a result of the civil domain becoming more inclusive of those who were formerly Nonpersons. Legal historian Lawrence Friedman noted, for example, that in Massachusetts, after "early political struggles weakened the power of

---

14. This is not to say that statutory laws (even "codes") do not play a role in common law systems. They certainly do. In the United States most criminal law, for example, is statutory law. Case law, in contrast, tends to have no place in systems based on civil codes.

the oligarchy . . . the colony embarked on an extraordinary course of drafting codes" (1985b, 69).

Two other important examples from U. S. history come to mind; in each case, groups of Nonpersons had made progress in gaining legal standing (that is, progress in mitigating their disabilities). In other words, in each case new categories of Persons were working their way into the civil domain. One response from the Persons already in the civil domain was to create new (and more complex) laws intended to cement superior advantages for those who had been Persons longest, to regulate the behavior of new Persons and to regulate interPersonal relations.

The first case involves African Americans after the Civil War. It is notable that *laws* requiring segregation (viz., "Jim Crow laws") were not created until well after African Americans had been granted the nominal status of Personhood as a result of post-Civil War constitutional amendments:

> The caste system as it had existed [in slavery] was maintained not by law but by a body of customs that was more or less self-enforcing. One evidence of the change in race relations, as a result of emancipation, was the efforts of the southern communities to enforce by statute racial distinctions and discriminations which it was difficult or impossible to maintain by custom and tradition.
>
> Most of the racial conflicts and controversies in the southern states during Reconstruction and after seem to have had their origin in the caste system, and in the efforts to maintain it by law and force when it was no longer sustained by the inertia of tradition and the force of public opinion. (Park 1950, 185; quoted in Ringer 1983, 234)

Many historians have agreed that "the segregation statutes that appeared in the late 1880s and 1890s did not replace a scheme of social integration, but rather one in which blacks were excluded by customary understanding" (Hall 1989, 147; see also, Vann Woodward 1966, 65). But Charles Lofgren, for one, has added persuasively that "the most direct trigger for the initial wave of Jim Crow legislation was increasing black unwillingness to defer to whites. A new generation, raised outside the confines of slavery and the web of antebellum restrictions on free blacks, was coming of age. Negro newspapers perceived growing black assertiveness in the face of indignities inflicted by whites; and among the white population, stories of 'uppity' Negroes increased during the late 1880s" (1987, 25). (Moreover, as I will discuss in Chapter 7, it was not until well after the Civil War

Reconstruction Era that antimiscegenation laws, which prohibited interracial marriage, became commonplace.)

The other historical example of how incorporating "uppity" new Persons can lead to new legislation that takes over where custom fails involved women. Until about 1850, married women in the United States were disabled from earning money, making contracts, and buying and selling property. After sustained effort, women gained some headway through passage of the Married Women's Property Acts, which gave them the right to own and manage their own property. However, while the Married Women's Property Acts provided limited relief, such cases as *Chapman* served as reminders of what the woman's place in society was. (The reader will recall from Chapter 3 that in the case of *Chapman v. Phoenix National Bank*, 85 N.Y. 437 [1881], the judge ruled that women had no right to continue using their birth names after marriage. Although this case was frequently cited in subsequent cases, recent scholarship has proved that the judge in *Chapman* was in error. As Justice Heffernan noted in 1975, the notion that common law requires the woman to take her husband's name "is merely the ipse dixit of the author of that opinion. . . . Sixty years before Chapman, an English case, *The King v. The Inhabitants of St. Faith's Newton* (1823)...held that a woman is not required to bear the surname of her husband.")[15]

Predictably, after the women's civil rights gains of the 1960s and 1970s, in the 1980s there occurred another "backlash"—a series of "reprisals" well documented by Susan Faludi in her book *Backlash: The*

---

15. *Ipse dixit* is legalese/Latin for "unsupported assertion." It would be surprising that, independent of some political or personal agenda, any judge would find that *Chapman* provided a compelling precedent. As Justice Heffernan pointed out, the circumstances were "bizarre" and the case provided a good example of a "hard case making bad law": "Verina Chapman, a married school teacher living in South Carolina, held a few shares of stock in a New York bank, which she had purchased under her maiden surname, Moore. In an excess of patriotic zeal during the Civil War, she was charged falsely with being a rebel, a confederate officer, a judge, and a member of the Congress of the Confederacy. Under the Confiscation Act of 1862, an action was brought to confiscate her bank shares. The action was brought in her maiden name of Verina Moore, and notice was posted under that name. There was no answer to the libel, and confiscation was effected by default. [In 1881] the New York court held that the default could be set aside because of insufficient notice, i.e., no person such as Verina Moore existed after marriage, only Verina Chapman. It therefore held there was no jurisdiction over the defendant. The case stands as an example of legal fabrication designed to effect a good result" [*Kruzel v. Podell*, 67 Wis. 138, 226 N.W. 2d 458 (1975)].

Undeclared War Against American Women (1991). For one example of this backlash Faludi turned to so-called fetal protection policies:

> Starting in the late '70s and accelerating in the '80s, at least fifteen of the nation's largest corporations, from DuPont to Dow to General Motors, began drafting "fetal protection policies" that limited or barred women from traditionally "male" higher-paying jobs that involved exposure to chemicals or radiation—exposure that the companies said might cause birth defects. By mid-decade, hundreds of thousands of employment opportunities had been closed to women in this way. (Faludi 1991, 437)

Were these policies simply a result of corporate concern for the next generation? Why then was there so little concern for the effects of chemicals and radiation on sperm? Faludi, among others, has found the employee-concern theory to be unpersuasive.

> Fetal protection policies actually had more in common with the backward "protective labor policies" that had proliferated at the turn of the century, policies that restricted the hours, pay, and type of work women could do. . . .

> In the 1980s, neither corporate America nor the U.S. government made reproductive safety a real priority. In fact, the corporate desire to guard female fertility vanished mysteriously for women who worked outside the high-paid circle of the "male" workplace. (Faludi 1991, 437)

The American (and European) public has once again been reminded of another possible effect of incorporating former Nonpersons into the civil domain. This is the reemergence of "hate crimes," or "crimes which manifest prejudice based on race, religion, sexual orientation, or ethnicity" (Hate Crimes Statistics Act HR 3193 [1988]). The essence of a hate crime is that the victim is targeted because of his or her membership in some category of individuals. Perpetrators of hate crimes deny the individuality of the victim insofar as they treat him or her as a representative of that category. Arguably, what is so hateful about a hate crime is that it is an attempt by some individual or group to treat a Person as a Nonperson. In effect, a hate crime is an illegitimate reprisal, an attempt to put groups of individuals back into the category of Nonpersons. In hate crimes, groups of individuals who have made progress in overcoming legal disabilities are made the target of violence (e.g., the lynching of African Americans after the Civil War).[16]

The relationship between the civil and communal domains and society as a whole, in important respects, is fairly straightforward. On the one hand, the more homogeneous the group of Persons who make up the civil domain, the smaller the civil domain will be relative to society as a whole. On the other hand, as the civil domain becomes more inclusive of disparate types of Persons, more interPersonal relations are brought out of the communal domain and into the civil. Looking at the relationship between the social norms of the communal domains and the laws of the civil domain within society makes the dynamics of the relationship between the two domains more clear; this, then, is the focus of the next chapter.

---

16. Even when it does not approach the level of a violent hate crime, responses by Persons to gains made by former Nonpersons often seem way out of proportion to the actual gains made. A few women break into a previously male-dominated factory line, and suddenly signs appear: "Shoot a woman, save a job" (save a job for whom?) (Faludi 1991, 443). Education does not seem to make Persons necessarily more accepting of former Nonpersons. It's embarrassing to admit, but even highly educated sociologists have been known to succumb. One is apt to hear Anglo male professors, for example, bemoan the fact that a white male Ph.D. can't get a job because (to quote a colleague of mine) "all the jobs go to women and minorities." Still, I look around my campus and I don't see any signs that white males are being overwhelmed.

5

Social and Legal Expectations

I have proposed that sociologists ought to view law as a contract between Persons that articulates expectations about minimally acceptable behaviors in certain kinds of relationships. I have argued that the law as contract is an apt analogy because, in essence, law, like contracts, involves a transformation of resources such that when expectations are breached, the injured Person may call upon the sovereign power to effect a remedy.

Along the way I examined two analytically separate domains of society, the civil and the communal, and suggested that the more homogeneous the group of persons who make up the civil domain, the more interPersonal relations will stay in the communal domain of society, out of law's reach.

One important component of the law-as-civil contract metaphor remains thus far underexplicated: If law has to do with *expectations about minimally acceptable behaviors,* what are the sources of these expectations? How do legal expectations (i.e., laws) differ from social ones (i.e., norms)? What is the relationship between law and norms? To answer these questions, in this chapter and in the one to follow the focus of the discussion switches from Persons and relationships to ideas and expectations.

Durkheim's Legacy: Law and Solidarity

For Durkheim, the pressing question was this: What holds society together? Or, What is the basis of social solidarity? Durkheim distinguished between "mechanical solidarity" and "organic solidarity." Mechanical solidarity predominates in societies with the simplest division of labor, societies in which people are alike and share common ideas and values. In simple ("mechanical") societies people tend to be engaged in the same sorts of labor—gathering and hunting, or agriculture, for example. This commonality of labor gives rise and is tied to common interests and goals (i.e., "the collective conscience"). Thus, in such a society, no one profits from a bad crop or hunting year.

Organic solidarity is a product of more complex divisions of labor. Here the collective conscience is more limited and individuality and individual interests are more developed. In such societies, solidarity is based not on commonality of interests but on diversity. As the labor of people in society comes to be more diverse and more specialized, people come to be more interdependent. Labor is specialized and interests diverge. Thus, sheep owners and wool spinners profit when cotton farmers are wiped out by the boll weevil. At the same time, owing to their specialized labor, people come to be more dependent on one another. The farmer needs the manufacturer who in turn relies upon teamsters and grocers. Solidarity in such societies is based on people's interdependence. In short, mechanical solidarity exists to the degree that people are alike and have values in common; organic solidarity exists to the degree that people *need* the products of one another's labor.

For Durkheim, the problem with studying social solidarity is that it is "a completely moral phenomenon which, taken by itself, does not lend itself to exact observation nor indeed to measurement." To unravel the enigma of social solidarity, Durkheim said, "we must substitute for this internal fact which escapes us an external index which symbolizes it and study the former in light of the latter. This visible symbol is the law" (1933, 64).

For Durkheim, the law symbolizes and objectively *indexes* the bases of social solidarity; it mirrors and organizes crucial but invisible social things. Concomitantly, as society changes, so too will law. In societies based on mechanical solidarity law is mostly repressive or penal and expresses strongly felt beliefs held in common. Repressive law punishes those who violate the tenets of the collective conscience. In societies based on organic solidarity, restitutive law holds sway; it seeks not to punish but to keep relations going and to regulate business, property rights, and the like. When there is a breach of legal expectations, restitutive law does not seek to punish but to restore things to their normal state. Thus, according to Durkheim, as society advanced from mechanical solidarity, based on likeness, to organic solidarity, based on dissimilarity and interdependency, law progressed from mostly repressive to mostly restitutive (1933).[1]

It was for such reasons that Durkheim was convinced that a study of law would greatly augment sociology's ability to understand the nature of social life. Yet, ironically, it is from this same logic that one can derive justifications for why sociologists need *not* study the law. If law is important only as an index of reality, it ceases to be important (or becomes less important) for sociologists to the degree that other indices are discovered and/or other ways of measuring social reality are invented.

There can be little doubt that law still has value as an index of solidarity—at least insofar as law reflects the foundations of solidarity among Persons. Moreover, law can be used to index the civil domain's relationship to the wider society (for example, Who is a Person? How is a Nonperson to be treated?). Yet, a more interesting and pressing question is this: Does law merit attention from sociologists only because of its value as an index? Answering that question requires a closer look at the relationship between social and legal norms.

From the Durkheimian perspective the relationship between social and legal norms is straightforward: Law emerges from social norms. Durkheim was not alone in his view. The idea that law implements custom and social expectations and norms, and that it is not the other way around, is firmly embedded in both folk and scholarly wisdom. The commonsensical notion that "you can't legislate [new] morality" could be heard in William Graham Sumner's argument that "legislation can't make mores" (1906, 77) (or, law-ways cannot change folkways). Similarly, the French philosopher Voltaire warned, "Let law never be contradictory to custom: for if the custom be good, the law is worthless" (James and Stebbings 1987, 38). Jurist Oliver Wendell Holmes put it this way: "The first requirement of a sound body of law is that it should correspond with the actual demands of the community, whether right or wrong" (1963, 36).[2]

---

1. Durkheim described a more sophisticated vision of law's development in his "Two Laws of Penal Evolution" ([1901] 1978), first published some eight years after publication of *The Division of Labor*. I have stressed Durkheim's earlier work here because it is my impression that *The Division of Labor* has been more widely read by sociologists. Notwithstanding the fact that many social scientists disagree with the chronology of law's development that Durkheim gives in that book (see Chapter 4 in this work), *The Division of Labor* has had a tremendous impact on how sociologists think about the law.

2. To be sure, many sociologists would offer much more sophisticated analyses of the relationship between law and norms than are expressed in

Given the view of law and society offered in *The Division of Labor*, Durkheim would have applauded such sentiments. And, although he was obliged to admit that it "often happens that custom is not in accord with law," he discounted the importance of any such discordance. In Durkheim's view, opposition between law and social norms is either short-lived (as a sort of cultural lag between social and legal changes) or "crops up only in quite exceptional circumstances. . . . It arises only in rare and pathological cases which cannot endure without danger." Normally, he said, *"Custom is not opposed to law, but is, on the contrary, its basis"* (1933, 65; emphasis added).

In my view, however, the relationship between law and social norms is not so easily stated. First, the civil contract perspective alerts us to the fact that where law does reflect social norms, it indexes the norms of *Persons* inhabiting the civil domain. Thus, law may reflect the norms of only a subset of society. Second, to the extent that the civil domain is heterogeneous, the relationship between law and social norms may not be a direct one. These concepts are the focus of this chapter. In chapter 6, I will examine the possibility that, in at least some cases, the law may be of greatest consequence to sociologists not because it reflects existing social norms and expectations but because of the role it plays in constructing *new* social norms and expectations.)

The Civil Contract and Legal Expectations

Explicit in the concept of the civil contract is the idea that expectations about appropriate behavior play an important role in both the content and processes of law. If a breach of legal (i.e., civil) expectations occurs, the law may be invoked.

This is not to say, of course, that law operates only in the breach. Although both the law's contents and its operations are most obvious in the breach, the law's role is usually unobservable. Like a legal contract, law acts as a point of evaluative reference for people about who should be doing what, etc., as well as a warning about what may be the consequences of a breach, even when it is not being overtly invoked. Thus, as Malcolm Feeley noted, "The law is most often set in motion by people who apply it to themselves and to each other without

---

these quotations. However, it is my guess that *most* sociologists (if only because they really haven't stopped to consider the nature of law since they took sociology 101) would be satisfied with the assertion that law generally is little more than a codification of important social norms.

benefit of explicit mobilization of legal institutions" (1976, 515). Much of the time the expectations that are enshrined in law stay in the background. Yet law's presence is felt by people as they go about their daily lives. As a matter of course, I pay my rent on time each month and I file my income tax each year on April 15. Every four years I go to the Department of Motor Vehicles to renew my driver's license, and I always carry proof of insurance when I drive. At work, I take care not to be seen as exploitative or harassing of my students, and when I shop I always pay for items I take out of the store.

Hence, my routine takes into account the fact that many of my relations are civil ones; I consciously orient to certain people in my environment knowing that my acts have legal as well as moral implications. Some might object that having to worry about the legal ramifications of, for example, one's relationships with one's students is a burden—that it robs the professor-student relationship of some of its richness. But sometimes the existence of the restraints and resources of the civil domain are what allows people to enter into relationships that otherwise they might not. For example, female graduate students might be more willing to work with male professors knowing that they have legal recourse should anything untoward happen. Likewise, signing a prenuptial agreement that protects their children's inheritance in the event they die before their spouse may allow senior citizens to feel more free to marry without worrying about greedy in-laws. In short, the protections afforded by the law can give people a sense that it's safe to enter into certain types of relationships even where there is no personal basis for trust.

Indeed, as one legal scholar observed, the existence of law in the background of relationships can facilitate a process in which "civil" relationships take on "communal" overtones:

> It should be noted that there are many transactions . . . that are not solely or explicitly constituted by rights and contracts. Transactions in the local store, for example, may be governed by implicit friendship and goodwill as much as by self-interest and legal obligations. Someone may ask, "why can't all economic transactions be like that?" . . . It is important to stress that, even if they were, there would *still* be a role for [law] to play. My grocer can deal with me in an informal, friendly way, sometimes giving me credit when I need it, or ordering some trivial item that I want, and so on, only if he has confidence that in the last resort he would be able to recover the money I owe him if I abused his friendship. . . . He may hope (just like the partners to a normal marriage) that he never has to invoke these formal guarantees, but that is quite compatible with the proposition that his

assurance of their existence is one of the reasons he is able to act as informally as he does. (Waldon 1988, 642)

Laws, Social Norms, and Morals

For Durkheim, legal or civil expectations about how people ought to behave stem from social custom and norms. Law, for Durkheim, is ultimately derived from the community's sense of morality (which, in many cases, may have been religious in origin). More specifically, Durkheim saw law as essentially a codification of a society's most important norms. Durkheim's idea of the derivative nature of law is most obvious in his analysis of criminal or repressive law, for crime is, by definition, any act that "offends strong and defined states of the collective conscience" (1933, 80). If crime is that which offends the collective conscience, criminal law reflects expectations that derive from the collective conscience.

But, unlike many modern sociologists, Durkheim did not ignore noncriminal law. Indeed, what he called "restitutive law"—or law that arranges relations between individuals and can be invoked in order to reinstate the status quo after a legal breach—was of particular concern to Durkheim as he sought to understand the dynamics of modern society. Restitutive laws, he said, emerged not from the center of the common conscience, but from "very ex-centric regions"—individual interests (1933, 113). Hence, restitutive laws "do not totally derive from the collective conscience, or are only feeble states of it" (112).

This does not mean, however, that restitutive law has no social component, nor does it mean that even in modern society the sovereign's role can be reduced "to that of a conciliator of private interests." "Nothing," said Durkheim, "is more incorrect than considering society as sort of a third-party arbitrator" (1933, 113). Even law that appears to be private (that is, law that arranges relations between individuals) is ultimately concerned with social relationships and reflects social values. To illustrate this principle, Durkheim used the example of the legal contract and reminded his readers that the sovereign only enforces contracts that are in keeping with social values: "It is true that obligations properly contractual can be entered into and abrogated solely through the efforts of those desiring them. But it must not be forgotten that if the contract has the power to bind, it is society which gives this power to it. . . . [Society] lends this obligatory force only to contracts which have in themselves a social value" (1933, 114).

Of course, questions remain: What constitutes "social value"? According to whose calculus is value determined? In other words, if law does reflect social values, morality, and customs, the sociologist must still ask: Whose values? Whose morality? Whose customs?

At one level, the answer is easy. As social conflict theorists have persuasively demonstrated, the law reflects the interests of those with the ability to be heard (or make themselves heard). In terms of the civil contract perspective, the law is likely to reflect the interests and values of Persons over Nonpersons. In the nineteenth century, for example, the law reflected the values, morality and customs of white Persons—not African-American or Native-American Nonpersons. Further, among Persons, law is more likely to reflect the interests and values of those with the fewest legal disabilities. (However, one must not simply assume that a perfect correspondence exists between the content of law and the interests of Persons with the fewest legal disabilities. Why this is so is a topic that is explored in Chapter 6.)

Within any particular civil domain that is not perfectly homogeneous, a legal system must confront conflicting definitions of social value. This problem is exacerbated to the degree that the Persons who inhabit the civil domain do not adhere to common moral values. Norms and customs are products of interaction among subsets of society (groups within the communal domain, or normative collectivities or communities). For this reason, norms are used by sociologists (as well as laypersons) to define the boundaries of communal groups (see Meier 1987). Yet, as explained below, it is important to remember that norms, by definition, imply consensus, and consensus is frequently a relatively small-scale phenomenon.

Norms, in the sense of "oughts" (as opposed to "regularities") may be thought of as a group's articulation or specification of its moral values (Smelser 1963). When the civil domain is made up of a homogeneous group of Persons, the laws that do exist will likely correspond closely to social norms and expectations of that group. For example, in many instances, the earliest American colonists simply wrote down their norms—in an "affirmative" way—and called them law. Generally speaking, however, it is logical to suppose that the less homogeneous the civil domain, the less direct the correspondence between laws and social norms. So, as sociologist Robert F. Meier said, "It has been usual to view law as norms (e.g., Black 1976), but laws are normative only to the extent that they reflect evaluative agreement among citizens to whom they apply. That is, laws are rules, but they may not be norms" (Meier 1981, 15).

Law has often been referred to as some sort of "ethical minimum." As Georg Zellinek asserted: "The law does not aim at the realization of an ethical ideal. . . . The law is simply a guardian at its outer limits, so that the principle is upheld and not contradicted. Morals give the idea the fullest reality and its positive aspect; the law, on the other hand, acts on it only negatively and at its outermost periphery" (Zellinek 1878, 42; quoted in Aubert 1989, 84).

Depending upon the nature of the civil domain, the distance between law as an ethical minimum and morals as an ethical maximum will vary. In heterogeneous civil domains (or in civil domains that consist of Persons from disparate normative collectivities), the distance between laws and social norms (the latter operationalizing ethics and values) will be greater than in homogeneous civil domains. If law is defined as a civil contract about minimally acceptable behaviors, it stands to reason that in heterogeneous civil domains, laws will *require* less of Persons than norms do. Those who make laws will seek out the common denominator between groups; that common denominator will be lower or higher depending upon the disparateness of civil society.

This observation brings to mind Durkheim's oft-quoted remark that, within a "society of saints" (which, one supposes, must be a very homogeneous group), even the most "venial" of faults will be responded to as major crimes (1938, 68-69). In other words, in a society of saints, law as an "ethical minimum" will be very close to the "ethical maximum" of morality.

These days, most civil domains are hardly so homogeneous, and hence one would expect law to be at some distance from morals. For example, in a heterogeneous civil domain, law may prohibit murder. But in one particular communal group (i.e., normative collectivity) norms may require the wealthy to feed starving people, while in another communal group it is perfectly acceptable to shun charity ("God helps those who help themselves"). A law may forbid interracial marriage, but a particular communal group norm may prohibit interclass marriage as well; the law may forbid adultery, but a particular communal group's norms may even regulate flirting behavior. Norms, then, can be said to demand *a higher standard of behavior* (and thus, offer less freedom of action without fear of sanction) than laws. In fact, relative to law, the behavior required by norms may well be supererogatory.

The reason for this gap between norms and law, as I illustrate in Figures 5.1 and 5.2, is essentially one of logistics: Even if members of all normative collectivities within a society can agree on basic moral values (e.g., "everyone is equal before the law," "there is a right to life," or whatever), the inevitable translation of these moral standards into behavioral prescriptions or norms will differ for different groups. Given relative equality of Persons (i.e., people with the same legal abilities and legal disabilities), the law of the civil domain will articulate a standard that reflects the common denominator of all normative collectivities or communities of Persons who inhabit the communal domain.

For example, say that the norms of all groups within a particular civil domain specify that "everyone is equal." Such norms typically mean "roughly" equal because "exactly equal" would be an impossibility. Diversity is likely to occur because there will be intergroup differences in how equal "roughly equal" must be. Similarly, say that the norms of all groups within a particular civil domain proscribe discrimination between job candidates on the basis of "irrelevant" characteristics. The question then becomes, What sorts of characteristics are job-relevant? Relevancy will no doubt be judged differently by different people. (In one town, gender may be a relevant job characteristic for school teachers, but not in another town).

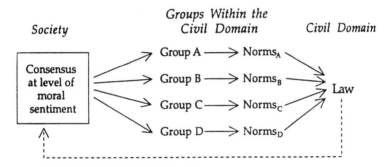

FIGURE 5.1 Relationships between morals, norms, and law. The dotted line illustrates the feedback loop that exists between law and morality. This line represents the "constitutive" effects of law.

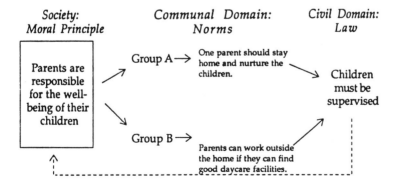

FIGURE 5.2 Example of the relationship between morals, norms, and law.

Differences in social "operationalizing" of moral values occurs with less grand issues as well. One of my more observant colleagues (who wishes to be unnamed here) questioned my assertion that norms are relatively small-scale phenomena by asserting that—across all communal groups in the United States—"nose-picking in public" is non-normative behavior. Granted that, the question then becomes, What constitutes "public"? In some communal groups or normative collectives, nonpublic or private in this context may mean strictly solitary behavior; other groups may allow that nose-picking "in front of spouse" or even "in front of co-workers" is permissible (not norm-violating) behavior.

The "Operationalization" Process

Just as norms are articulations of people's values in the communal domain, law is the articulation of Persons' values or moral principles in the civil domain. And within the civil domain, the constitutive principles of law will be subjected to an "operationalization" process that is similar to the process in which norms emerge from moral values. For example, in order that the principle "equality before the law" be realized, it first must be translated into legal procedures. As with the legal contracts discussed in Chapter 1, the civil contract will spell out these legal procedures with more or less precision depending upon the amount of trust that exists among Persons in the civil domain. The amount of trust, in turn, has to do with the degree of homogeneity present. When trust is high (when people have confidence that they share important values and are all acting in good faith to realize those values), such homilies as "Everyone is entitled to a fair trial" will suffice as ways of operationalizing the principle of equality before the law.

Here trust means an acceptance that others will act within the realm of "fair play." The sorts of behaviors that constitute fair play, of course, will vary from group to group; the rules may vary from Marquis of Queensbury rules to no holds barred. In other words, the meaning of fair play may range from having to follow a number of specific rules (no hitting below the belt, no hitting when your opponent is down, etc.) to "anything goes." This sort of trust may arise from personal experience, but as I have noted elsewhere,

> people may also choose to bestow trust because a potential agent has been "certified" or credentialled by others who the principal trusts. Thus, when a bishop consecrates a priest, this act of consecration

alone may be enough to cause believers to bestow trust on the priest. In this sense, a bishop is a gatekeeper of what might be called a "moral community," or community of believers. Likewise, at one time, it may have been that admission to the bar was the equivalent of consecration for young lawyers. This sort of derived trust is not only bestowed on professionals; other moral communities exist: It is said, for example, that members of certain fraternal organizations (e.g., Rotary, Masonic Temple) will loan money to a "brother" in difficulty even when that brother is a stranger from out of town. (McIntyre 1989, 134*n*)

Where trust is present, the civil contract (i.e., the law) will be vague. For example, such concepts as "fairness," "equality," "due process," and even "contract" and "commerce" will be defined according to commonsense understanding. Once a perception arises that trust is being abused, however, there may be a movement (on the part of those who feel betrayed, or who speak for those who have been betrayed) to make the law more specific. Where trust is lacking, either because it never existed or because it has been abused too frequently, it is likely that the civil contract will become more detailed.

Prior to the so-called Due Process Revolution in the United States (that is, prior to the 1960s), for example, the guarantees offered criminal suspects and defendants were quite vague, if not Delphic, in character (Kurland 1970, xvi). Everyone had a right to a "fair trial," but what did that mean in practical terms? It meant, for one thing, that the court would appoint an attorney to represent an indigent individual if the judge thought he or she "needed one"—but not as a matter of course. Similarly, a defendant's right to be presumed innocent until proved guilty was expected to be watched over by both police and courts.

If someone who had been convicted believed that he or she had not been given a fair trial, the case might be heard by an appellate court. Following a standard set by the U. S. Supreme Court, the appellate court judges would invoke equally vague standards to judge whether the conviction had been won fairly. They would ask, for example, whether the action of the state violated those "fundamental principles of liberty and justice which lie at the base of all our civil and political institutions?" (*Palko v. Connecticut*, 302 U.S. 319 [1937]).

What principles were considered "fundamental?" That would vary depending on the nature of the case. Sometimes, for example, fundamental principles required having an attorney to represent poor defendants; in other cases the failure to appoint defense lawyers did not constitute a breach of any fundamental principles (*Betts v. Brady*, 316 U.S. 255 [1942]). Sometimes, being tried twice for the same offense was a fundamental breach of fairness; in other cases, it wasn't (*Palko v. Connecticut,* 302 U.S. 319 [1937]).

All other things being equal, allowing courts latitude to operate within the "spirit" of the law without being tied to the letter of the law was seen as desirable. Up through the middle of the twentieth century, the U.S. Supreme Court wanted to leave the states a measure of discretion to respond to their own particular needs (*Wolf v. Colorado,* 338 U.S. 25 [1949]). The Court justified the extension of such discretion to states by saying that police, prosecutors, and judges could be *trusted* to do the right thing.

Howeverm by the 1960s, events had eroded the Supreme Court's trust in those in charge of the various states' criminal justice systems. By then it had become very clear that, when it came to certain categories of defendants (minorities, indigents, etc.), the ideas of some states about "fairness" left much to be desired—that what had been promised to all "Persons" was not being delivered to all Persons. In consequence, the Court perceived that the legitimacy of the entire criminal justice system was threatened. As the Court ruled in *Mapp v. Ohio,* "Nothing can destroy a government more quickly than its failure to observe its own laws" (367 U.S. 643 [1961]). So, during the late 1960s and early 1970s, the Supreme Court abandoned vague admonitions "to be fair" and instituted precisely detailed procedures: no felony trials without legal counsel; no use of evidence gained from searches without warrants; no questioning of suspects without Miranda warnings, and so on. In each case, the Court made it obvious that these new "procedures" were being instituted owing to the Court's perception that at least in some cases, police, prosecutors, and judges had abused the trust placed in them (see, for example, *Mapp v. Ohio,* 367 U.S. 643 [1961]; *Gideon v. Wainwright,* 372 U.S. 335 [1963]; *Miranda v. Arizona,* 384 U.S. 436 [1966]; *In re Gault,* 387 U.S. 1 [1967]).[3]

Parenthetically, the movement from trust in the good faith of judges and other members of the criminal justice system to reliance on procedures is illustrative of how, even for those Persons who lack significant resources, *right can make might.* For this one important reason, we ought not to assume a perfect correspondence between the

---

3. The Supreme Court's movement from "trust" to "proceduralism" is discussed in more detail in McIntyre 1987 (Chapter 1). A similar movement from trust to proceduralism is documented in Richard K. Scotch's book on the growth of federal disability policy, *From Goodwill to Civil Rights* (1984). Some implications of the difference between confidence based on trust in the goodwill of others and confidence based on reliance on procedures in another sociolegal context are discussed in McIntyre 1989.

content of law and the interests of those with the strongest voice and fewest disabilities. Law not only reflects society's power structure but can be used to alter it. This is a topic that will be explored in the next chapter.

Looking Ahead:
The Role of Ideas in Law and Society

Sociologists have long attended to questions about the deterrent effects of law; about (in other words) the value of force or threat of force in controlling behavior. Less attention has been paid to another, more subtle—but nonetheless important—aspect of law. As Harvard law professor Mary Ann Glendon recently pointed out, "We are accustomed to viewing law as importantly shaped by beliefs and behavior, but we frequently overlook the reflexive and continuous nature of the interaction among laws, ideas, feelings and conduct. Often mesmerized by the coercive power of law, we tend to minimize its persuasive and constitutive effects" (1989, 10).

The role of law in ordering ideas is of particular interest, for ideas are important in ordering social relations. As Peter Winch argued, one's social relations with others "are permeated" with one's ideas about reality. "Indeed," he wrote "'permeated' is hardly a strong enough word: social relations are expressions of ideas about reality" (1963, 23).

In this sense, for example, I would argue that, even in the absence of law, the structure of marital relations reflects ideas about the "real nature" of men and women. In societies in which men are believed to be superior to women, the structure of marital relations reflects this belief. Consider this nineteenth-century assessment of what was the "natural" configuration of men's and women's roles in marriage and family:

> Nature indicates the man as the proper party to propose and originate marriage. By endowing him also with the greater strength of body and mind (for though particular women may, and, doubtless, do excel particular men in both these respects, yet a comparison of the sexes on the whole leaves no reasonable doubt that the superiority belongs to the man), she [Nature] unequivocally points him out as the head of the woman; and in so doing, she plainly designates the father as superior to the mother, in the rule and government of the family. (Seabury 1861, 73)

Relations between children and parents similarly reflect society's view of children vis à vis adults. In each case, as these ideas change, so too does the relationship.

This is not to argue that ideas are necessarily controlling. As Weber pointed out, "Not ideas, but material and ideal interests, directly govern men's conduct." Yet Weber added an important caution: "Very frequently the 'world images' that have been created by 'ideas' have, like switchmen, determined the tracks along which action has been pushed by the dynamic of interest" (1946, 280). As I will show in the next chapter, insofar as law has ideas embedded in it, it can be constitutive of relationships and how people act within those relationships.

6

The Constitutive
Effects of Law

A decade ago, Clifford Geertz suggested that social scientists move beyond the functionalist view of law to a "hermeneutic" one; such a view, he said, sees that "law is not a bounded set of norms . . . , but part of a distinctive manner of imagining the real." Law, Geertz stressed, is "meaning" as well as "machinery"; law is "a species of social imagination." It is "constructive of social realities rather than merely reflective of them" (1983, 173, 232).

The idea that law provides categories through which we come to understand day-to-day reality has been emphasized in the works of a number of the so-called Critical Legal Scholars. According to Robert Gordon, with respect to modern society,

> Many critical writers would, I think, claim not only that law figures as a factor in the power relationships of individuals and social classes but also that it is omnipresent in the very marrow of society—that law making and law-interpreting institutions have been among the primary sources of the pictures of order and disorder, virtue and vice, reasonableness and craziness, Realism and visionary naiveté and some of the most commonplace aspects of social reality that ordinary people carry around with them and use in ordering their lives. To put this another way, the power exerted by a legal regime consists less in the force that it can bring to bear against violators of its rules than in its capacity to persuade people that the world described in its images and categories is the only attainable world in which a sane person would want to live. "Either this world," legal actions are always implicitly asserting, "some slightly amended version of this world, or the Deluge." (Gordon 1984, 109)

Others have stressed that this categorization process is not altogether benign. Carol Smart (1989), for example, pointed out that law not only constructs but destroys. Law is a kind of knowing, she said, that disqualifies and overpowers other forms of knowing; legal rhetoric forces the richness of life into narrow legal categories and thereby robs them of their essential meaning. And, because these are essentially males' categories, the resulting distortions have the greatest impact on cases involving women.

By way of example, Smart cited the experiences of a rape victim in court. Smart noted that when a rape victim must recount her experiences in keeping with the laws of evidence, she loses parts of the story that are meaningful to her: "The legal form through which women's accounts of rape are strained constitutes a very precise disqualification of women and women's sexuality. This 'precision' is imparted by the legal method that is deployed during the rape trial" (1989, 26). More specifically, the binary logic—or the insistence on such opposites as truth/untruth, guilt/innocence, consent/nonconsent—is completely inappropriate to the "ambiguity of rape" (33). As Smart explained, "This is not to say that women themselves do not know whether they want a sexual encounter or not, but the 'telling' of a story of rape or abuse inevitably reveals ambiguities. Hence a woman may agree to a certain amount of intimacy, but not to sexual intercourse. In the legal model, however, consent to the former is consent to full intercourse" (33-34).

It has not been the usual thing for social scientists to view law as constructive or destructive, however, and indeed, even many legal scholars without a social science background have resisted seeing law as an autonomous force. Professor Lawrence M. Friedman, for example ignores (or tries to ignore) the possibility that law might have a constitutive impact in society and clings to the neoDurkheimian view that, as Friedman put it, law is "relative [to] and molded by economy and society." In the Introduction to his *History of American Law*, Friedman said that his perspective on law "takes nothing as historical accident, nothing as autonomous." Law, he says, is only a "mirror of society" (1985, 12).[1]

---

1. *A History of American Law* was first published in 1973. A decade later, Friedman seemed more willing to concede law's constitutive aspects, a point of view more in keeping with the perspective stressed in the present chapter. Thus, in 1984, Friedman seemed to abandon the law-as-mirror viewpoint: Law, he said in this later work, is "a toolbox of practical instruments ... heavily freighted with norms and ethical values. In every complex society there are conflicting and contending values and norms. The legal system names winners

Professor Kermit L. Hall's recent work on the development of American law is actually entitled *The Magic Mirror*. Hall explained his choice of title by citing Oliver Wendell Holmes, who once referred to law as "a magic mirror, [wherein] we see reflected, not only our own lives, but the lives of all men that have been!" (quoted in Hall 1989, 17).

For legal scholars the view of law as mirror has its roots in the revolt of many early twentieth-century legal thinkers against the traditions of "legal formalism." According to legal formalists, law was a closed system in which legal decision making could always be explained as the straightforward application of a legal rule to the case. Hence, to understand the law, one need only look to the law. Extralegal factors (economic and social) had no place in legal analysis.

A group of law professors, now collectively remembered as "Legal Realists,"[2] condemned the formalist approach to law by saying that it was grounded in an unbelievably naive conception of the world. Realists argued that a realistic study of the law—one that looked at the influence of social and economic factors on legal development—was required (Purcell 1973, 82).[3]

As an anodyne to the legal formalists' view of law as a closed and totally autonomous system, the law-as-mirror perspective has value. But, as Professor Mark Tushnet wrote in his careful review of Friedman's historical opus *A History of American Law*, this point of view leads one to ignore "the possibility that the legal order may become an active influence, to some degree, on the social and economic order" (Tushnet 1977, 83). Such an oversight would be an unfortunate error.

---

and losers among these norms. It plucks some values out of the mass and gives them official status. The others it ignores; or, even worse, it may blacken their names and proscribe them" (1984, 665).

2. Among the most prominent of the Legal Realists were such scholars as Jerome Frank, Karl N. Llewellyn, Thurman Arnold, Herman Oliphant, William O. Douglas, and Underhill Moore.

3. Realists demanded an empirical approach to the study of law. As Robert M. Hutchins, then dean of the Yale Law School put it, "We believe that the way to escape from the morass into which law administration has fallen lies through study. This study should be directed to discovering the working in practice of our present rules." Hutchins was most emphatic about the need for empirical research: "We regard facts as the prerequisite of reform" (Quoted in Schlegel 1979, 468).

An important caveat: It is difficult to talk about law as constitutive without seeming to invest it with a life of its own; a life independent of those who use it. It is not my intention to promote a view of "the law" as some mystical entity; in my mind, law per se is not an "engine of action" (Coleman 1988, S96). Rather, law is a resource (and constraint) that must be invoked and directed by people.

Still, to argue that law is constitutive is not only to maintain that the law provides categories that "filter" or organize events but to argue also that it can be used to change ideas. Consequently, such an argument suggests that law can be used to affect people's behavior in significant ways. In addition, to argue that law is constitutive is to fly in the face of a great deal of popular scholarly opinion. Most people can cite examples of failed attempts to use law as a means of social engineering. Prohibition, of course, is the example that first comes to mind, but one could generate a lengthy list that includes both mundane and magnificent illustrations of society's failure to achieve reform through law. Society, it seems, is not as pliable as many legal (and social) thinkers once hoped (Pound 1930).

In their paper "The Legal Threat as an Instrument of Social Change," Zimring and Hawkins (1971) astutely observed that law is not always impotent as an agent of social chanutive is to fly in the face of a great deal of popular ge but that it tends to be singularly ineffective when charged with changing behavior that has acquired "a moral significance." On the face of it, this seems a reasonable argument. Consider, for example, what would follow a change in the law that regulates income tax payments. Say that from now on, the law dictates that taxes are due on May 15 instead of April 15. Although this change in the law would likely engender some confusion for a year or so, one doubts that it would occasion much conscious disobedience: The date one pays income taxes has very little moral significance (in U.S. society). The public's response would be much different, however, if a law was passed that attempted to restrict the freedom to marry or to have children, for these sorts of behaviors do have tremendous moral significance in U.S. society.

Must we conclude from this that law is not really constitutive of anything that is very important? No. Understanding the constitutive effect of law requires looking past its prescriptions and proscriptions to see as well the moral, legal, and social contexts in which these are embedded. Social and legal scholars may then see that the failure to achieve important reform through law has at times resulted not just from law's impotency, but at least in part from policy-makers' lack of understanding of how law works in society.

How Law Creates a World

There are two obvious ways in which law can become constitutive of new social expectations rather than simply functioning as a mirror of existing social norms: First, *law may be the source of new social expectations for novel situations.* Second, *law may be the source of new expectations for existing relations.*

Law as Constitutive of Expectations in Novel Situations: The Law of Negotiable Instruments

The most obvious case in which law is constitutive involves situations in which Persons find themselves in (or about to enter into) a relationship they value and then discover there are no shared social norms—that is, no consensus about appropriate behavior. As a result, these Persons experience uncertainty about how they ought to behave and about how they ought to expect others to behave. Such uncertainty may exist even when everyone wishes to act within the bounds of propriety. When the rules of behavior have not been set and Persons are precluded from generating a "communal" or normative consensus, then lawgivers may be asked to create laws to guide expectations. Once they are created, it is likely that such laws will acquire normative connotations insofar as they come to make up the expectations of the Persons who rely upon them. (And, to the extent that these laws give rise to normative expectations, they in effect create "community.")

This was the sort of situation that existed at the end of the nineteenth century among U.S. business leaders who believed that their activities were being constrained by a lack of uniformity across jurisdictions when it came to regulations regarding commercial paper and other types of "negotiable instruments." Some of the problems were really fundamental ones. For example, if Abel owes Baker $150, and he has signed an IOU to that effect, can Baker "assign" this debt to Cook? Especially crucial were questions about privity of contract:[4] If Baker gives the note to Cook and Abel decides not to pay, does Cook have a right to sue Abel? In some states, the courts said yes, in others, they said no. The situation was confusing: "A report of the American Bar

---

4. Technically, privity of contract has to do with relations between contracting parties. Generally, it allows each party to the contract to sue other parties to the contract but generally disables a third party from suing on the contract. Thus, questions of privity typically arise when the issue is who can sue whom.

Association, in 1891, complained that there were 'fifty different languages' of law. The businessman had a right to ask why 'the meaning and effect of a promissory note' should not be 'as certain and definite' in all states 'as the meaning of words in an American dictionary.' 'Variance, dissonance, contradiction' causes 'perplexity, uncertainty and damage'" (Friedman 1985b, 539-540).

Congress's response to the business community's perplexity was to draft a Negotiable Instruments Law. Although Lawrence Friedman argued from his law-as-mirror perspective that this law was merely a "restatement" of rules that were, for the most part, "already accepted, either as businessmen's norms or as established courtroom doctrine" (Friedman 1985b, 340), I would argue that the law certainly did not restate a consensus but helped to create one by picking out specific rules in use and making these into law.

Law as Constitutive of New Expectations in Existing Social Relations: The Emergence of a "Right to Privacy"

Much less frequent, perhaps, but certainly more dramatic, are instances in which legal principles are used to create new expectations about long-established social relations. Consider, for example, social norms and expectations about "privacy." Contemporary expectations about privacy did not emerge from social norms but from the works of modern legal thinkers who chose to go against existing social norms.

The concept of privacy itself is an ancient one and can be traced back to Roman times at least (Duby 1988). Privacy was invoked as a legal concept as early as medieval times. Although it has been argued that "the concept remained constant over the ages" (Duby 1988, 6), there is reason to challenge this statement. Relative to the contemporary view, the traditional idea of privacy was a truncated one; it limited privacy to certain spheres of life (one's home and one's business) into which government did not intrude.[5]

---

5. In the United States, such expectations were enshrined in the Fourth Amendment to the Constitution which affirmed, inter alia, "the right of the people to be secure in their persons, houses, papers, and effects, against unreasonable searches and seizures." The first overt articulation of this right came in the case of *Boyd v. United States* in which the Supreme Court asserted that people were entitled to protection against all government invasions of "the sanctity of a man's home and the privacies of life" (116 U.S. 616 [1886]). Interestingly, however, until the 1960s, in many places the legal expectation that the government would not intrude, derived from the Fourth Amendment, only really applied against the federal government. The Fourth Amendment

One doubts, however, that colonial leaders could have conceived of a society in which people thought that they *ought* to have privacy in the face of neighbors' curiosity (however much people might have wished to have such privacy). Although certainly the walls of one's house or workshop afforded some de facto privacy (Shils [1966] 1970), people expected their privacy to be invaded; indeed, the expectation was that people had a moral duty to invade the privacy of others and to scrutinize their behavior. As historians have noted of Puritan communities, for example, "Neighbors were expected to watch each other so that the sins of a few would not jeopardize the standing of the entire community in God's eyes" (Pleck 1987, 18). The church elders had ultimate responsibility for supervising people's conduct, and they were assisted "by the members of the congregation, who exercise mutual inspection, or 'holy watching,' over one another's lives, and reported delinquencies that came to their attention. . . . John Cotton had preached to the Winthrop group as they left England, 'goe forth, every man that goeth, with a publicke spirit, looking not on your owne things onely, but also on the things of others'" (Haskins 1960, 91).

Even after it ceased to be a strict religious duty, many continued to take seriously the obligation to keep holy watch. Nancy Cott's study of eighteenth-century divorce records found that what most of us would consider to be the most private areas of life were routinely intruded upon by "neighbors, lodgers, and kin." In one case, for example, Mary Angel and Abigail Galloway of Boston, out for a walk, looked through an open window and saw their neighbor Adam Air "in the Act of Copulation" with Pamela Brichford. Testimony about what happened next conveys a sense of their zeal for "overseership":

> On Seeing this We went into the House, & stood behind them as they lay on the Floor, and after observing them some time, the said Abigail Galloway spoke, & asked him if he was not Ashamed to act so when he had a Wife at home, he got up & answered, one Woman was as good to him as another he then put up his nakedness before our faces, & went away, and she on his getting off her, jumped up & ran away into another part of the House. (Cott 1976, 22)

---

right to privacy against the intrusion of *state* government officials was affirmed by the Supreme Court in 1949, when it ruled that privacy against unreasonable governmental intrusion was required by the Fourteenth Amendment right to due process (*Wolf v. Colorado*, 338 U.S. 25). Nationwide, no teeth were put into the ruling until 1961 (*Mapp v. Ohio*, 367 U.S. 643).

The mid-to-late nineteenth century has been identified by historians as a time when, owing principally to changes wrought by the Industrial Revolution, there occurred a separation of the public and private spheres of life. Still, private in this sense did not mean *protected* from nongovernmental intrusion. Private continued to mean only *separate* from public. Stephanie Coontz summed up the evidence: although privacy was an ideal, a goal of middle-class existence, "there were important limits on the privacy of the middle-class family. Male business and female kin networks cut across the couple relationship, while the family often felt it had to live its life on display, proving to neighbors, peers, and social superiors its 'respectability' and conformity to middle-class standards" (Coontz 1988, 306). The situation was similar for working-class families who did not even make a pretence of seeking privacy as an ideal: "Conditions of life in the industrial working class strongly militated against" privacy (Coontz 1988, 306).

The first inkling of change came in 1880 when Judge Thomas McIntyre Cooley wrote, in his *Treatise on the Law of Torts*, that individuals had the right "to be let alone" (Cooley, 1880, 27).[6] Ten years later, law partners Samuel D. Warren and Louis D. Brandeis cited Cooley's point to lend authority to their *Harvard Law Review* article entitled "The Right to Privacy" (1890):[7]

---

6. Sociologists, perhaps, would be impressed to learn that, in addition to many fine legal articles and decisions, Judge Thomas McIntyre Cooley fathered early social psychologist Charles Horton Cooley.

7. Although most legal historians trace the discovery of the right to privacy back through the Warren and Brandeis article and then to Cooley (e.g., Keeton et al. 1984, 849), it does not seem fair that Cooley should share much of the credit. Judge Cooley did indeed use the now famous expression "the right . . . to be let alone," but it was only to justify laws that provided remedy to victims of assault, hardly a revolutionary contribution: "The right to one's person may be said to be a right of complete immunity: to be let alone. The corresponding duty is, not to inflict any injury, and not, within such proximity as might render it successful, to attempt the infliction of an injury. In this particular the duty goes beyond what is required in most cases; for usually an unexecuted purpose or an unsuccessful attempt is not noticed. But the attempt to commit a battery involves many elements of injury not always present in breaches of duty; it involves usually an insult, a putting in fear, a sudden call upon the energies for prompt and effectual resistance. There is very likely a shock to the nerves, and the peace and quiet of the individual is disturbed for a period of greater or less duration. There is consequently abundant reason in support of the rule of law which makes assault a legal wrong, even though no battery takes place. Indeed, in this case the law goes still further and makes the attempted blow a criminal offense also" (Cooley, 1880, 29).

The press is overstepping in every direction the obvious bounds of propriety and of decency. Gossip is no longer the resource of the idle and of the vicious, but has become a trade, which is pursued with industry as well as effrontery. To satisfy a prurient taste the details of sexual relations are spread broadcast in the columns of the daily papers. To occupy the indolent, column upon column is filled with idle gossip, which can only be procured by intrusion upon the domestic circle. The intensity and complexity of life, attendant upon advancing civilization, has rendered necessary some retreat from the world, and man, under the refining influence of culture, has become more sensitive to publicity, so that solitude and privacy have become more essential to the individual; but modern enterprise and invention have, through invasions upon his privacy, subjected him to mental pain and distress, far greater than could be inflicted by mere bodily injury (Warren and Brandeis 1890; quoted in Prosser 1960, 383*n*)

The conception of privacy offered by Warren and Brandeis had a tremendous impact on both social and legal expectations; within a couple of decades, judges in many jurisdictions had accepted the Warren and Brandeis thesis as authoritative, and it continues to be used as a resource for litigants who remedy for "harms" to their sensibilities. No doubt that at least some people had long wished to be free of spying neighbors and other intrusions into their personal lives, and the Warren and Brandeis article, and its acceptance by judges, provided one way to win that remedy.

Parenthetically, although the greatest "advances" in law often have been born out of the tribulations of the petty and mean, the right to privacy has a much more aristocratic heritage:[8]

In the year 1890 Mrs. Samuel D. Warren, a young matron of Boston . . . held at her home a series of social entertainments on an elaborate scale. She was the daughter of Senator Bayard of Delaware, and her husband was a wealthy young paper manufacturer who only the year before had given up the practice of law to devote himself to an inherited business. Socially Mrs. Warren was among the élite; and the newspapers of Boston, and in particular the *Saturday Evening*

---

8. Of course, the greatest advances in law usually occur when the courts or legislators take steps to assist the petty and mean (often Nonpersons or those with significant legal disabilities). Persons are accorded rights against the government as a matter of course (almost by definition). What Mr. Warren wanted, in contrast, was something different: he wanted protection against the intrusions of the communal domain.

Gazette, which specialized in "blue blood" items, covered her parties in highly personal and embarrassing detail. It was the era of "yellow journalism," when the press had begun to resort to excesses in the way of prying that have become more or less commonplace today; and Boston was perhaps, of all of the cities in the country, the one in which a lady and a gentleman kept their names and their personal affairs out of the papers. The matter came to a head when the newspapers had a field day on the occasion of the wedding of a daughter, and Mr. Warren became annoyed. It was an annoyance for which the press, the advertisers and the entertainment industry of America were to pay dearly over the next seventy years.

Mr. Warren turned to his recent law partner, Louis D. Brandeis, who was destined not to be unknown to history. The result was a noted article, The Right to Privacy, in the Harvard Law Review, upon which the two men collaborated. It has come to be regarded as the outstanding example of the influence of legal periodicals upon American law. (Prosser, 1960, 383-384)[9]

As they have evolved over the past hundred years, legal, and consequently, social ideas about the nature of privacy have become complex and ambiguous. Today, this concept is invoked in a seemingly endless variety of cases ranging from contraception and abortion to information control. Although a number of authors have attempted to capture the exact meaning of privacy, (see for example, Shils [1966] 1970; Parker 1974; Thompson 1986; Keeton et al. 1984; Wacks 1989), these attempts have not been tremendously successful. As a result, Raymond Wacks invoked a phrase coined by Schauer and concluded that the concept of privacy has become a generalized value that—like freedom, equality, fairness, and so on—is "pervasively indeterminate" (Wacks 1989, 19).[10]

---

9. Brandeis was appointed to the U. S. Supreme Court in 1916 by President Woodrow Wilson. He served with great distinction until his retirement in 1939.

10. This notion calls to mind what W. B. Gallie earlier called "essentially contested concepts." Such concepts, as Donald Levine has explained, are "concepts whose meaning must be permanently a matter of dispute. Gallie argues that such a condition of permanent irresolution must be the fate of concepts that are internally complex, linked with changing historical circumstances, productive of disputes that cannot be easily resolved, and used in an aggressive and defensive manner by their proponents. This would certainly include, in social science, concepts like 'elite,' 'equality,' 'alienation,'

Whatever privacy's essence, the point is that what distinguishes the modern conception of privacy from the older one is the implication that one can or should expect to be let alone not just by some distant (and mistrusted) government but by one's neighbors. Until the twentieth century, the expectation of privacy did not afford protection to individuals as much as it did to *communal groups* whose members, while regarding governmental scrutiny as anathema, jealously guarded their rights to snoop into their own fellows' lives. As Georges Duby noted, the traditional difference between private and public life had little to do with an individual's right to be let alone; instead it had to do with the *source* of interference that an individual could expect in each domain: "Think of two realms in which peace and order were maintained in the name of different principles. In both realms the individual was disciplined, supervised, corrected, and punished, but correction and punishment were administered by different authorities" (1988, 7). In the civil domain, the control was legal; in the communal domain, the control was normative.

In contrast, the contemporary right to privacy affords legal remedy against informal or normative, as well as formal or legal, social control. The legal right to privacy today thus protects Persons from what might be called the perils of gemeinschaft: gossip and ridicule. Intrusions that a hundred years earlier might have been considered the upright citizen's duty—peeping into windows,[11] for example—suddenly, were not only frowned upon but remediable in court. The debate over the nature of privacy continues, but one thing seems certain: the "right to privacy" is not simply the right to be left alone; it is, instead, the right not to be held accountable—with respect to both formal and informal sanctions—for one's behavior outside of the public arena. The difference between defamation and privacy laws illustrates this distinction: On the one hand, in a defamation (slander or libel) case, the defendant can raise "truth" as a defense—a truthful statement is not a defamatory statement. The more recently invented tort of invasion of privacy, on the other hand, extends even to a truth that is given "unwarranted publicity" (Keeton et al. 1984, 862-863). A reporter

---

'anxiety,' 'secularization,' 'anomie,' 'stranger,' 'form,' 'rationality,' 'freedom,' and hundreds of others" (Levine 1985, 17).

11. Prosser and Keeton noted that "This topic gave rise to a possible nomination for the all-time prize law review title, in the Note, Crimination of Peeping Toms and Other Men of Vision [1951 5 Ark. L. Rev 388]" (Keeton et al. 1984, 855 n57).

may wrongfully invade someone's privacy by publishing the fact that she once served time in prison for auto theft. This is not defamation (since the allegation is true), but unless the reporter has lawful justification for publishing this fact, he may have committed the tort of invasion of privacy by giving unwarranted publicity to this fact.

The process in which Persons use law to redefine existing social relations goes on. More recently, the U.S. legal system has seen an increasing number of cases invoking the power of law to change existing social relationships—for example, to redefine certain kinds of "flirtation" as "sexual harassment," particular manifestations of "parental affection" and/or disciplinary techniques as "child abuse," and overly enthusiastic "seduction" as "rape" (Smart 1989, 165). These changes are not simply a result of interest groups pushing their particular points of view onto other Persons. Generally, they have come about as a result of renegotiations of social expectations (and civil ones) made possible by the ongoing dialectical process between social and legal norms and principles.

The Dialectic of Norms

Although the law can create social expectations, in most cases legal rules emerge from the social norms of some group(s) of Persons. But it does not do to imagine that the relationship between law and norms remains ever one-sided. The relationship is better thought of as a dialectical one—especially in heterogeneous civil domains. For the most part, this dialectical process proceeds simply: A statute is enacted or a legal decision rendered that clarifies or refocuses the nature of a social relation, and those participating in that relation (or ones like it) adjust their behavior accordingly. Again, because the new behavior comes to be expected (relied upon by others), it may acquire normative significance.

This is not as rare a process as one might think; often it happens without many people actually noticing.

> Say a thirty-two year old woman is diagnosed with glaucoma and ultimately she goes blind from the disease. Blindness was inevitable only because the disease hadn't been treated in time. Prior to the diagnosis she had been under the care of an ophthalmologist off and on for various complaints. Had the ophthalmologist performed a test for glaucoma (using Schiotz tonometry, commonly called the pressure test), the woman's vision might have been saved. However, because the risk of glaucoma to those under forty is only about 1 in 25,000, the

test, though inexpensive, quick and easy, is not routinely given to such patients.

The woman sues the ophthalmologist and ultimately wins a judgment of malpractice. After this case, other ophthalmologists take pains to protect themselves from similar suits, and the Schiotz tonometer comes to be routinely used during eye exams—even for young people. (See Helling v. Carey, 83 Wash.2d 514, 519 P.2d 981 [1974])

In this example, the legal decision led ophthalmologists to adjust their behavior—they began to routinely conduct the glaucoma test, and the patients then came to expect the test.

Generally, the dialectical process played out between legal and social norms is played out against the dynamic quality of ideas in the social construction of reality. Berger and Luckmann pointed out that the "original creators of the social world, can always reconstruct the circumstances under which their world and any part of it was established" but that their "children are in an altogether different situation." Conventional behaviors, customs, norms, and institutions may arise for a variety of reasons ranging from reasoned planning to accident to convenience. But, Berger and Luckmann argued, such arrangements will persist only when they can be justified in terms that seem valid to a new generation of Persons. If institutions are to persist, they must be given meanings, or what Berger and Luckmann called "legitimating formula" that make sense to the children. To make sense and to "carry conviction," these legitimating formulas "will have to be consistent and comprehensive in terms of the institutional order. . . . The same story, so to speak, must be told to all the children" (1967, 61-62).

Here it is helpful to distinguish the "meaningful" or legitimated institution from what Weber called "mere custom." Custom, he wrote, is simply an empirical uniformity "based on nothing but actual practice." Whether one follows custom depends upon convenience or self-interest; "conformity with it is not 'demanded' by anybody" (1978, 29). By way of example Weber noted, "Today it is customary every morning to eat a breakfast which, within limits, conforms to a certain pattern. But there is no obligation to do so" (1978, 29).

Like Berger and Luckmann, anthropologist Mary Douglas suggested that what elevates mere custom to social institution is the existence of a compelling legitimating formula. Moreover, she said that these legitimating formulas will be of a specific sort: "every kind of institution needs a formula that founds its rightness in reason and in nature" (1986, 45).

> Minimally, an institution is only a convention. . . . For a convention to turn into a legitimate social institution it needs a parallel cognitive convention to sustain it. . . . Here, it is assumed that most established institutions, if challenged, are able to rest their claims to legitimacy on their fit with the nature of the universe. A convention is institutionalized when, in reply to the question, "Why do you do it like this?" although the first answer may be framed in terms of mutual convenience, in response to further questioning the final answer refers to the way the planets are fixed in the sky or the way that plants or humans or animals naturally behave. (1986, 46-47)

These formulas must satisfy only the needs of *Persons;* they may, but need not, be believable to others (though the situation would be more stable if they were). Thus, for example, while the institution of slavery in the United States originally may have resulted from slave owners' self-interested pursuit of economic gain, the institution's relative durability ultimately depended on the ability of slave-owning Persons to discover or invent formulas that legitimated slavery. In other words, though slavery emerged because of economic concerns, its survival was facilitated by the ability of white Persons to legitimate slavery by grounding it in persuasive ideas about the subhuman nature of African people (see Chapters 2 and 3). As Stephanie Coontz noted, in the post-Revolutionary War era,

> There was only one way for slave-holders and those who tolerated slavery to resolve the contradiction between the principles for which they had fought a war and the property they refused to relinquish. If all human beings were created equal, but some remained slaves, the slaves must have some characteristic that rendered them less human. One sprang immediately to the eye—the color of their skin. The definition of Blacks was separated from its social basis and redrawn along racial lines. Older cultural and religious theories about Blacks gave way to a coherent theory of racism that had been largely absent in early writings on slavery. (1988, 140)

Indeed, a successful formula might well preserve an institution long past the time when the "real" reason for its existence has been extinguished. Consider, for example, the persistence of a gendered division of labor. At one time such a division of labor may have been necessary because of differences in men's and women's reproductive responsibilities, or even because of differences in the average strength of men and women. However, the notion that gendered division of labor is tied to "innate sexual differences" became elaborated way past the point (or so many would argue) of having any basis in objective reality; indeed, a gendered division of labor may have become counter-productive. This institution continues at least in part because it is grounded in larger theories about what is "natural" for men and women to do (and, because it no doubt serves the "interests" of some Persons).

Mary Douglas put it this way: "The successful formula is predatory. Sheer consistency of use endows it with might, and it will swallow up competition" (1986, 73). Yet, such a view of legitimating formulas is too narrow inasmuch as it only underscores the role they play in helping to maintain existing social or institutional arrangements. As I illustrate below in two brief case studies, the important (and certainly the more sociologically interesting) fact is that once an idea or legitimating formula is accepted, it can take on a life of its own. One possible result is that the formula may be used ultimately to extinguish an institution or to move it in ways that are counter to its authors' intentions.

Case Study #1:
African Americans and Equality

The civil domain in the United States came into being as a result of a revolution against Britain that was justified by such notions as "all men are created equal . . . and have certain inalienable rights." The exclusion of African Americans from the civil domain was long justified by claims that they lacked the ability to reason—either owing to their "situation" or to an innate lack of ability.

After the Civil War, in December of 1865, the Thirteenth Amendment to the Constitution was ratified. The Amendment was a simple one:

SECTION 1. Neither slavery nor involuntary servitude, except as punishment for crime whereof the party shall have been duly convicted, shall exist within the United States, or any place subject to their jurisdiction.

SECTION 2. Congress shall have power to enforce this article by appropriate legislation.

The abolition of slavery was not enough, however, to bring African Americans into the civil domain. Predictably, eight southern states responded by passing laws known as "black codes." These codes were attempts to shore up the traditional caste system by restricting the freedoms of African Americans. The content of the codes differed from state to state, but the overall impact was to deny the rights of full citizenship to African Americans. Especially, the black codes interfered with African Americans' rights as workers—establishing what was for most intents and purposes a new form of servitude. In Louisiana, for example, the black code stated that,

> SECTION 2. Every laborer shall have full and perfect liberty to choose his employer, but when once chosen, he shall not be allowed to leave his place of employment until the fulfillment of his contract . . . and if they do so leave, without cause or permission they shall forfeit all wages earned to the time of abandonment.

> SECTION 7. . . . Every civil officer shall, and every person may, arrest and carry back to his or her legal employer any freedman, free negro, or mulatto who shall have quit the service of his or her employer before the expiration of his or her term of service without good cause; and said officer and person shall be entitled to receive for arresting and carrying back every deserting employee aforesaid the sum of five dollars, and ten cents per mile from the place of arrest to the place of delivery; and the same shall be paid by the employer, and held as a set-off for so much against the wages of said deserting employee. (Commager 1968, 445, 453)

Congress, in turn, responded by passing the Civil Rights Act of 1866, which preempted the black codes. There was concern, however, about whether the Civil Rights Act would survive a constitutional challenge and so, a few years later, the Fourteenth and Fifteenth Amendments to the Constitution were ratified (in 1868 and 1870, respectively). Here are the relevant sections of each amendment:

> AMENDMENT XIV, SECTION 1. All persons born or naturalized in the United States and subject to the jurisdictions thereof, are citizens of the United States and of the State wherein they reside. No State shall make or enforce any law which shall abridge the privileges or immunities of citizens of the United States; nor shall any State deprive any person of life, liberty, or property, without due process of law; nor deny to any person within its jurisdiction the equal protection of the laws.

> AMENDMENT XV, SECTION 1. The right of citizens of the United States to vote shall not be denied or abridged by the United States or by any State on account of race, color, or previous condition of servitude.

Finally, Congress sought to deliver the coup de grace to southern rebellion by passing the Civil Rights Act of 1875. This act broadened civil rights to encompass jury service and public accommodations:

> *Be it enacted,* That all persons within the jurisdiction of the United States shall be entitled to the full and equal enjoyment of the

accommodations, advantages, facilities, and privileges of inns, public conveyances on land or water, theaters, and other places of public amusement; subject only to the conditions and limitations established by law, and applicable alike to citizens of every race and color, regardless of any previous condition of servitude.

As the northern states and their congressional representatives turned their attention to resolving the pressing economic matters that followed the Civil War, the U.S. Supreme Court seemed to put an end to racial progress when it heard a case that challenged Congress's ability to block segregation by private citizens who owned public accommodations and conveyances. The Supreme Court held that the Congress had exceeded its authority in the Civil Rights Act of 1875 and that the Fourteenth Amendment was valid only against the actions of government officials and not private citizens (*Civil Rights Cases*, 109 U.S. 3 [1883]).[12] Within ten years, segregation statutes were in place throughout the South that not only permitted but required segregation.

Laws that required segregation were an historical novelty. Until the slaves had been freed from bondage, force was used to keep them "in their place." After the Civil War, such force could no longer legitimately be used against African American citizens:[13]

The enactment of state segregation is a relatively recent phenomenon in the history of race relations in the United States. Of course, there have been numerous segregative practices and some segregation statutes for many years, even before the nineteenth century. But it was not until the final quarter of the nineteenth century that states began to evolve a systematic program of legally separating whites and Negros in every possible area of activity. And it was not until the twentieth century that these laws became a major apparatus for keeping the Negro "in his place." They were generally comprehensive and acceptable, because they received their inspiration from a persistent and tenacious assumption of the innate inferiority of the Negro. (Franklin 1956, 1)

---

12. This case was not reversed until 1965 when the Supreme Court decided the case of *Heart of Atlanta Motel v. United States*, 379 U.S. 241.

13. This is not to say, of course, that force was not used in the post-Civil War era to intimidate African Americans. This was, after all, the period in which the Ku Klux Klan rose to prominence. However, this force was not "legitimate" force (hence the costumes of white sheets which served not only to terrify victims but to protect perpetrators).

While the failure of post-Civil War attempts to bring African Americans into the civil domain was disappointing, these attempts did have an impact. The formula that legitimated excluding African Americans from the civil domain (i.e., the claim that they were not "reasonable" creatures) was made much more fragile once the Fourteenth Amendment declared, by fiat, that all those born in this country were citizens. Ultimately, the Fourteenth Amendment required that other legitimating formulas be invented to justify the exclusion of African Americans from the civil domain.

The most important move to relegitimate their exclusion was made in the case of *Plessy v. Ferguson* (1896). It was from the *Plessy* case that the so-called separate but equal doctrine emerged:

> A statute which implies merely a legal distinction between the white and colored races—a distinction which is founded in the color of the two races, and which must always exist so long as white men are distinguished from the other race by color—has no tendency to destroy the legal equality of the two races. . . . Laws permitting and even requiring their separation in places where they are liable to be brought in contact do not necessarily imply the inferiority of either race. (163 U.S. 537 [1896])

In *Plessy*, the justices of the Supreme Court acknowledged that any law that placed African Americans in a legally inferior position would be unconstitutional. They ruled, however, that laws that *looked as if* they were legally disabling to African Americans were not—that what looked like exclusion from the civil domain was not exclusion. According to the Court, laws requiring segregation merely implemented a benign social custom; anything more sinister was in the eye of the beholder. This was to be the law of the land for more than half a century. In 1954, when faced once again with the issue of exclusion, the Court found itself compelled to come to an altogether different conclusion:

> We conclude that in the field of public education the doctrine of "separate but equal" has no place. Separate educational facilities are inherently unequal. Therefore, we hold that the plaintiffs and others similarly situated for whom the actions have been brought are, by reason of the segregation complained of, deprived of the equal protection of the laws guaranteed by the Fourteenth Amendment. (*Brown v. Board of Education of Topeka, Kansas*, 347 U.S. 483 [1954])

Did the *Brown* Court overrule *Plessy*? Not quite. In the *Brown* case the Court did not say that "separate but equal" was unconstitutional, only that—when it came to educational opportunities—separate and *un*equal was unconstitutional. And, the problem wasn't simply the fact that segregated schools were physically unequal. The Court looked at equality in a more abstract manner: "Does segregation of children in public schools solely on the basis of race, even though the physical facilities and other 'tangible' facts may be equal, deprive children of the minority group of equal educational opportunities? We believe it does"(*Brown v. Board of Education of Topeka, Kansas*, 347 U.S. 483 [1954])

One might conclude that, during the years intervening between *Plessy* and *Brown*, "social change" had prompted a more humane and accepting view toward African Americans, and that this new attitude influenced the justices' decision. There is, however, little evidence of this. Rather, as Richard Kluger, in *Simple Justice* (1975), demonstrated, the justices who decided *Brown* believed that their finding was coerced by Court precedent. In other words, they believed that, given the way the law had developed thus far, they had no choice but to rule that school segregation was unconstitutional. Of course, as Mark Tushnet pointed out, "We should not ignore extralegal influences on the decision, such as the concern that segregation was inconsistent with the ideological posture that the United States was assuming during the Cold War. But Kluger's account makes it clear that such extralegal influences had only a small impact on the decision. *Brown* must be seen as primarily the product of the legal order's dependence upon consistency as an autonomous value" (Tushnet 1977, 103). If "equal" was the rule, and if "separate" was proved "not equal," then consistency demanded the Court find for the plaintiff in *Brown*. Further, although the *Brown* decision did not live up to expectations that it would bring about total equality, insofar as it involved a renegotiation of the civil contract, it effectively transformed resources available to African Americans. The *Brown* decision initiated that process that—as noted in Chapter 5—is colloquially referred to as "give them an inch and they'll take a mile." *Brown* established an important precedent that African Americans could draw upon in their fights for equality in other parts of society.

The usual view is that legal change comes about when legal institutions no longer fit social practices. Certainly this is frequently the case. But with respect to *Brown*, Kluger has persuasively argued that just the opposite happened: Social change was effected when existing social and legal practices no longer fit legitimating principles that guided legal practice. Similarly, Bruce Ackerman has observed that people can use law to preempt and to effect change in social/normative expectations: "To take a stark case: southern blacks of the

1950s did not deny that they were expected to sit in segregated railways and buses. They sought to challenge existing practice as unconstitutional" (1984, 36-37). In other words, law, as well as social custom and expectations about how things ought to be, dictated that African Americans and whites be segregated. During the 1950s, African Americans challenged the legitimacy of this law by asserting a lack of fit between the laws of segregation and the basic principles of equality upon which the United States ostensibly was founded, especially as these were enshrined in the Fourteenth Amendment:

Max Weber observed long ago that the Fourteenth Amendment, which guarantees equality of treatment for citizens, has been received in the United States not merely as enacted law but as natural law; not as if it owes its force to its origins from legitimate lawgivers, but as if it has an "immanent" and "teleological quality" (1978, 867, 869). As I have argued elsewhere, the Fourteenth Amendment essentially "has primary and not derivative legitimacy; it provides a standard against which derivative laws and institutions are measured" (McIntyre 1987, 23).

Thus, as Harry Kalven so aptly phrased it, in the 1950s African American activists litigators effectively invoked the constitutive principles of the Fourteenth Amendment equal protection clause as a strategy to "trap democracy in its own decencies" (1965, 67). So, although the laws in effect at the time (as well as social/normative expectations) were "against" them, African American citizens used to their advantage the same formula of equality that earlier had legitimated segregation. In time, the courts found that—by analogy— "separate but unequal" had no place in other areas of the civil domain as well (e.g., recreational facilities, occupational practices, and so on). All of this is not to say that winning in court was enough to cement civil rights gains. Far from it. However, winning in court was an important step. It gave African Americans a right to make a claim on the sovereign's power to assist them in their battle to integrate schools. Perhaps just as important was the cloak of legitimacy that the Supreme Court's rhetoric gave to the movement to integrate.

Case Study #2:
England and the Glorious Revolution

History, if not replete with similar examples, certainly provides other illustrations of situations in which the law seems to have taken on a life of its own and has, consequently, been invoked to achieve ends that were independent of (if not in conflict with) the interests of its creators.

For example, England's so-called Glorious Revolution of 1688 removed despot James II from the throne, and gave the monarchy to William III and Mary II. In gratitude, William and Mary "recognized a Bill of Rights that limited the powers of the monarchy" (Craig et al. 1986, 651). Among the more important constitutional and legal developments that came out of this era were "the Habeas Corpus Act of 1679, the *Bushel's* case in 1671, holding juries not to be accountable for their verdicts, the provisions of the Act of Settlement ensuring the independence of the judges, and the prohibitions of the maintenance of a standing army without Parliamentary authorization" (Atiyah 1979, 13).[14] Each of these provisions was instigated by the winners of the Glorious Revolution—landowning Persons (aristocrats) who had fought a war to protect themselves and their property from the ravages of the royal treasury, and wished to avoid finding themselves in similar straits again.

Although these legal innovations were lauded, in principle, for augmenting the liberties of *all* English subjects, in practice, the benefits accrued only to Persons—those individuals who owned property (a very small segment of society). Ironically, seventy-five years later, in the face of a popular challenge from radical newspaper editor John Wilkes,[15] the laws that had cemented the power of English Persons in the first place threatened to be the undoing of their control over Nonpersons.

---

14. Edward Bushel was the foreman of the jury that freed Quakers William Penn and William Mead in 1670. Penn and Mead had been charged with causing an unlawful assembly and disturbance of the peace by preaching. The jury acquitted them. This verdict displeased the judge, who reacted by fining each juror forty marks. Bushel refused to pay and was imprisoned. He then brought a writ of habeas corpus and was released after a court decided that juries were permitted to disagree with trial judges and that judges "may not punish or threaten to punish jurors for their verdicts" (Green 1985, chapter 6).

15. Wilkes (1729-1797), a journalist, published an attack on one of King George III's favorites, and the King, responding as if personally insulted, issued a general warrant for all of those involved. There ensued a number of sedition and libel trials and a power struggle between "Wilkites" (mostly men of the merchant class) and the government. At the center of dispute were the "government's foreign and domestic policies; impurities of the political process; private law, with its inequities for the small businessman; and the movement for [freedom of] speech and press" (Green 1985, 327).

No doubt traditional legal and "Whig" historians may have exaggerated the impartiality of the judges and the integrity of the rules of law, but neither was wholly mythical. There must have been many occasions when eighteenth-century Ministers regretted the independence of the judiciary and the nonaccountability of juries. If the propertied classes had fooled the people into thinking that it was *their* liberties which were at stake in 1688, the London Mob had no doubt whose liberties were involved when they shouted "Wilkes and Liberty" or when juries awarded huge damages against the secretary of state for authorizing an illegal search of Wilkes' house. (Atiyah 1979, 13-14)

The strength of precedent as both a constraint and a resource in law is something commonly (though mistakenly) attributed (mostly) to Western and Westernized systems of law and not to other types of legal systems. Even assuming that, for example, the courts in *Brown v. Board of Education* or in the Wilkes case were "coerced" by precedent, might it be that such coercion could happen in any legal system that places an emphasis on precedent and not just in Western legal systems?

The weight of precedent is not a uniquely Western phenomenon. "A legal system," argued anthropologist Michael Barkun, "contains the evolving perceptual categories through which actors structure situations." And these categories "will be passed on for future use in similar settings. . . . Beneath the surface of self-serving motives, every decision, looks to the past for guidance." Moreover, Barkun points out, the power of the past to guide the future is not limited to legal systems that are overtly "attuned to questions of precedent, [for] other systems acknowledge the role of precedent under different names." What different names? Custom, for one; tradition, for another (1968, 158).

It is certainly likely, however, that the power of precedent is stronger in those civil domains in which Persons rely on written law. Where unwritten law is relied upon, owing to the vagaries of memory, consistency is likely to be—at least in part—only an illusion. As Fritz Kern wrote, where unwritten or "customary" law is ascendant,

[it] quietly passes over obsolete laws, which sink into oblivion, and die peacefully, but the law itself remains young, always in the belief that it is old. Yet it is not old; rather it is a perpetual grafting of new onto old law, a fresh stream of contemporary law springing out of the creative wells of the sub-conscious, for the most part not canalized by the fixed limits of recorded law and charter. . . . Customary law resembles the primaeval forest which though never cut down and scarcely changing its outline, is constantly rejuvenated, and in a hundred years will be another forest altogether, though outwardly it remains the same "old"

wood, in which slow growth in one part is accompanied by an unobserved decay elsewhere. (Quoted in Berman 1983, 570*n*42)

The mere act of writing down law changes things. This is so principally because of the way that written law constrains the sovereign's powers at the same time that it acts as a resource for those subject to law. For this very reason, in many societies sovereigns have resisted writing down the law. For example, in the fifth century B.C., in response to the first ever promulgation of criminal codes in China, one "high dignitary" sent the following letter of protest to Tzu-Ch'an, the prime minister of the state of Cheng:

> Originally, sir, I had hope in you, but now that is all over. Anciently, the early kings conducted their administration by deliberating on matters [as they arose]; they did not put their punishments and penalties [into writing], fearing that this would create a contentiousness among the people which could not be checked....
>
> When people know what the penalties are, they lose their fear of authority and acquire a contentiousness which causes them to make their appeal to the written word on the chance that this will bring them success. ... *As soon as the people know the grounds on which to conduct disputation, they will reject the accepted ways of behavior and make their appeal to the written word, arguing to the last tip of an awl or knife.* Disorderly litigations will multiply. ... By the end of your era, Cheng will be ruined. (Bodde 1981, 177-178; emphasis added.)

Around that same period, Roman patrician magistrates administered the law in a similarly arbitrary manner, and "evidently even the knowledge of [law's] contents was denied to the populace at large" (Nicolas 1962, 15). Two thousand years later, the Persons who ruled the Puritan colony in Massachusetts likewise resisted putting their laws into writing, in large part "because a written code would put a bridle upon their own power and discretionary authority" (Haskins 1960, 37).

The Importance of Legitimating Formulas

It may well be that, for the sociologist, the actual rules that the law articulates are less important than the legitimating formulas that help maintain these rules. If we look at rules only, our impression of law is certain to be a static one. Yet, although rules themselves are constraints that (by definition) work against change, the legitimating formulas that gird these rules provide resources for those who wish to effect change.

The law articulates values that are important to Persons—equality; rights to life, liberty, and the pursuit of happiness; freedom of the press and of religion, and the like. Because of this, legal (and subsequently, social) change may be sparked not by challenges to the rules per se, but by assertions that social practices are out of kilter with the legitimating principles in which those rules are founded. In other words, there is an important feedback loop between law and normative expectations.

For example, the civil domain that exists in the United States came into being as a result of a revolution that was justified by such notions as "all men are created equal . . . and have certain inalienable rights." Eventually, the law (through the Fourteenth Amendment) expanded the meaning of "men" to include a wider variety of individuals. Once this expansion occurred (and even though it was largely a move simply to punish southern whites), the need for system legitimacy (tied to the need for system consistency)—in the long run—made it difficult for Persons to avoid feeling *compelled* to allow newly created Persons to claim the same inalienable rights as Persons and in the process avail themselves of the transformation of resources that is the essence of law.

Again, Persons will not necessarily comply meekly with such changes. It is more likely that they will resist challenges to existing interpretations of legitimating formulas; that they will resist allowing their legal system to be trapped "in its own decencies." Southern lawmakers tried at every turn to stop the inclusion of African Americans as Persons.

Another example of how Persons may resist making the civil domain more inclusive can be seen in Cynthia Eagle Russett's *Sexual Science: The Victorian Construction of Womanhood*, (1989), which offers a superb analysis of how nineteenth-century scientists strove with all of their might to shore up theories that justified women's exclusion from the civil domain. As Kuhn's (1970) work on scientific paradigms would lead us to predict, any evidence found to contradict prevailing [male] views on "the woman question," was immediately discounted. For example, Darwinian psychologist George John Romanes, a leading protagonist in this battle to keep women in their place and author of "Mental Differences Between Men and Women" (1887), upon "discovering in a timed reading test that women both read more and retained more than men, . . . quickly deduced that this faculty could have no relation to intelligence, 'some of my slowest readers' being 'highly distinguished men'" (Russett 1989, 46).

Taking the role of legitimating formulas into account puts a new twist on Zimring and Hawkin's assertions (discussed at the beginning of this chapter) about the law's relative impotency when it comes to changing behaviors that have acquired a "moral significance." Though social expectations (norms) about appropriate behaviors may be tied to important norms, if legal change is tied to "higher" moral beliefs, then change may be successfully effected.

Consider the situation in which a legislator (or, in the U.S. system, a litigant)[16] provokes a rethinking of how moral "oughts" are "operationalized." Say that the important "moral precept" that Persons have a right to life legitimizes the law against euthanasia. One would conclude that such a law would be close to impossible to change. The chance of changing the law is increased, however, if Persons could be persuaded to accept new definitions of "life"—if life is acknowledged to be more than simple existence, then the law may be changed to allow mercy killing for those whose existence is judged to be unendurable.

In a similar fashion, rather than challenging the meaning of specific moral values, litigants and legislators can effect legal change by appealing to "higher values." Thus, during World War II, lawmakers in the United States argued the ascendancy of "patriotism" over freedom of movement in order to persuade people to accept gas rationing. If one is to truly understand the life of the law, then it is important to examine the principles that undergird law and not just at the laws themselves. This idea was stressed by Barry Nicolas in his study of Roman law: "Principles, unlike rules are fertile," he said, for one "can by combining two or more principles create new principles and therefore new rules" (1962, 1).

It is important to emphasize that appeals to higher values, or to combinations of values, can be used not only to liberate Nonpersons from their legal disabilities but for the opposite effect as well. Potentially, then, appeals to values can be used either to keep people in their place—or to put them back in their former place. For example, although twentieth-century feminists have invoked such principles as "equal rights" with a modicum of success, toward the end of the century we are seeing a backlash; the same principle is being turned against women: If men and women are equal, why are women given so much say in matters of child rearing and custody after divorce? If men and women

---

16. In legal systems in which judges articulate law (even if it is only law that they have discovered and not invented), every litigant, potentially, is a legislator.

are equal, why is the woman the one who is allowed to decide whether to abort the fetus? What about equal rights for fathers? (See Smart and Sevenhuijsen 1989). Similarly, minorities who invoked the concept of equality to help win affirmative action programs are seeing these programs dismantled by Persons who argue that they discriminate against white males (e.g., *Regents of the University of California v. Bakke*, 438 U.S. 265 [1978]).

Another caveat is that a simple judicial or legislative pronouncement is not enough to effect social change. There must be a constituency prepared to make use of that precedent to move things forward. Hence, without the efforts of the NAACP, the *Brown v. Board of Education* decision would probably have had very little impact.

The importance of a constitutency or special-interest group does not mitigate the importance of legal principles. The principles give activists legs to stand on and often gain them at least tacit support from other Persons who are not particularly interested in the specific rule change but may be loyal to the principle that is invoked.[17]

Phrasing issues in moral term affects the dynamics involved in Persons' decision-making routines. Moral questions are often decided differently from other matters; for one thing, when people perceive the issue to be one of morality, they are more likely to eschew a simple utilitarian calculus. And such decisions are more likely to be seen as cut-and-dried: As social psychologists Irving Tallman and Louis Gray pointed out, "If the situation is framed in moral terms, there is little information that requires processing; one either behaves morally or immorally" (1990, 420).

Law in the Sociology of Knowledge

If we are to understand the nature of law's place in society, it is important to remember, as James Boyd White has argued, that "law is not merely a system of rules (or rules and principles), or reducible to policy choices or class interests." Instead, White said, "The law makes a world . . . [and] the greatest power of law lies not in particular rules or decisions, but in its language, in the coercive aspect of its rhetoric—

---

17. Of course, a simple appeal to higher values to effect social change is no guarantee of success. Sometimes such appeals are successful, but more often they are not. For example, activists seeking to legalize marijuana use have often phrased their goal in terms of personal liberty. Although liberty is an important value in the United States, the marijuana proponents have not gotten very far because they cannot persuade many Persons that using marijuana is an important personal liberty.

the way it structures sensibility and vision" (1985, xiii). Those who seek to change people's behavior and expectations can make use of the coercive aspect of law's rhetoric to accomplish change especially if they can create compelling moral formulas to legitimize their goals. A dramatic illustration of this exists in the role played by the U.S. Supreme Court. Arguably, insofar as the Court succeeds, it does so by the cogency of its rhetoric. As Justice Tom Clark acknowledged, "We don't have money at the Court for an army and we can't take ads in the newspapers, and we don't want to go out on a picket line in our robes. We have to convince the nation by the force of our opinion" (Kluger 1975, 706). In the same way, those who seek to understand people's behavior and expectations must examine the law's rhetoric and the use that is made of that rhetoric.

PART TWO

Law in Society

Many questions remain unanswered (many remain even unasked). But there is one question that seems especially obvious at this point. In the Introduction to Part One, paraphrasing Stinchcombe on social theory (1968), I said that the conception of law to be developed in this work was one that would strengthen the capacity of sociologists to invent explanations about the nature of society and social interaction. The question is this: *Does* the perspective on law developed in this work strengthen our capacity to do sociology?

In Chapters 7 and 8 I will begin to answer that question and suggest two examples of how the law-as-contract perspective indeed does augment our ability to understand society. More specifically, I will focus on two especially important social arenas: the family and the workplace.

The family, discussed in Chapter 7, is a particularly interesting case, for it illustrates dramatically the movement of relationships from the communal to the civil spheres of social life. The family presents an interesting case too because it raises issues that have plagued sociologists as well as policymakers in recent years: While most everyone agrees that the twentieth century has witnessed a dramatic transformation of "family," there is disagreement about why these changes have come about and what exactly they mean for society and for the individuals who make up society. Like politicians, sociologists in their way tend to see "the family" as a fundamental institution in society. More than fundamental, many see the family as the very *cornerstone* of society. Probably because it is believed to be fundamental, oftentimes discussions of the changes wrought in this century in the family have at least an undercurrent of unease, if not downright panic. This unease is certainly explicit in the policy arena.

A different view emerges when recent changes in the family are juxtaposed with changes in that part of the civil contract known as "family law." I would argue that advancing our knowledge of family requires us to look at the family-legal nexus. Again, law is by no means *the* central variable when it comes to explaining changes in family life and organizations. But it is an important variable.

In Chapter 8 I present another case study and examine some aspects of the civil contract that have had an important effect on life in the workplace. Although work may not have the sentimental hold on Americans that family does, there is no gainsaying that it is a fundamental part of social life. In modern society, many people spend more time at the workplace than they do with their families; indeed, what one does "for a living" competes with and may even overshadow the family in terms of conferring identity and status on individuals.

The law-as-contract idea is intended to sensitize sociologists to asking particular sorts of questions as they go about the enterprise of studying society. First, to what degree are the individuals we study fully Persons? What special legal abilities and disabilities do they have? Second, to what degree is any particular relationship a part of the civil domain? In other words, can those who are in a particular relationship avail themselves of the transformation of resources that law provides to remedy breaches of expectations? Third, what are the legal constitutive principles that undergird the law with respect to particular types of relationships? What is the rhetoric of rights, for example?

In the next two chapters I bring these questions to bear on the dynamics of social life in two important arenas. The goal is to demonstrate how asking questions about law's impact helps sociologists and others to better understand interpersonal dynamics as these are played out in the social arena.

7

The Civil Contract and Family Life in the United States

Law, family. The words evoke very different images: Law is formal, cold, and impersonal; families are informal, warm, and affectionate.[1] Ideally, legal relationships are detached, restrained, and sober; familial ones, demonstrative, effusive, and exuberant. On the surface, at least, the law and the family are antagonistic and belong to separate domains within society—the law to the civil domain and the family to the communal one. Yet law and family have a great deal to do with one another these days. It almost seems as if at every turn the family unit encounters the law.

What is easy to overlook is that the ties that exist between the family and the legal order are not uniquely modern. Looking back, one finds that the law has long been intertwined with family concerns. However, the nature of law's impact on the family has changed a great deal in the recent past. Moreover, although many have argued that the law has intruded too far into the domestic sphere, to the degree that in modern society the family remains a private institution, a sanctuary from the world of the market and the political arena, a great deal of this state of affairs is owed to the law.

The nature of law's relationship with the modern American family is best understood by looking back to the beginnings of this relationship, where it took root first in England.

---

1. Adapted from McIntyre 1993.

English Roots

In England, from the twelfth until the mid-nineteenth century, the laws respecting marriage and family life were of two principal sorts: secular, or common law, and church (or ecclesiastical law).[2] In the main, the regulation of marriage per se was left to ecclesiastical courts, which had jurisdiction over such matters as who could marry whom and under what circumstances husbands and wives could separate. Similarly, adultery, fornication, incest, as well as "any uncleanness and wickedness of life" (Ingram 1987, 239) were not crimes but spiritual offenses to be dealt with as church, not temporal, courts, dictated (Blackstone [1769] 1979, 4:64-65).

Guided, perhaps, by the biblical injunction that it is better to marry than to burn, a valid marriage was easily contracted according to early ecclesiastical law. As far as the Church and its courts were concerned, the essence of marriage was a private contract. Thus a valid union could be created simply by the man and woman consenting to marriage in words of the present tense (*sponsalia per verba de praesenti*) (Menefee 1981, 10).[3] Although church officials preached the importance of sanctified marriage and exhorted those wishing to marry to submit to a church wedding, all that was needed was the mutual consent of the couple: "Neither solemnisation in church, nor the use of specially prescribed phrases, nor even the presence of witnesses, was essential to an act of marriage" (Ingram 1987, 132). The truly private nature of such marriages, however, meant that doubt could exist about whether a valid marriage had ever been contracted. This uncertainty, in turn, led to a number of disputes about property: To the degree that there was doubt about the validity of marriage, so too was there doubt about whether widows and children could inherit. Such doubts and disputes were put to an end in 1753, when Lord Hardwicke's Marriage Act mandated that no marriage was valid unless solemnized in the

---

2. Hence, to be strictly accurate, in England there were not two but three social domains: the communal, the civil, and the ecclesiastical or religious. In this discussion, I will collapse the religious and civil domains because in the United States—after the American Revolutionary War, especially—the ecclesiastical domain never really existed. In England, the ecclesiastical courts lost their jurisdiction over family and marriage in 1857.

3. A second form of informal marriage, *sponsalia per verba de futuro*, was created when a man and woman pledged to marry and later consummated the union.

Anglican church after proper publication of banns or a license had been obtained.[4]

If creating a valid marriage was historically a relatively simple matter, ending one was not. In post-Reformation England, divorce *a vinculo matrimonii* (absolute divorce) was prohibited. Couples could win divorce *a mensa et thoro* (from bed and board)—akin to a modern legal separation—for sufficient cause (adultery or extreme cruelty), but this arrangement did not permit either spouse to remarry. Winning a decree of divorce *a mensa et thoro*, however, did allow an innocent wife to sue for alimony. For a few couples, annulment (a decree that the union had never been a valid marriage) provided an avenue for escape, but annulment required proof that specific impediments to marriage existed. The grounds for annulment were few: If it could be proved that the pair were related within a prohibited degree—either by blood (consanguinity) or marriage (affinity)—then the marriage might be annulled. A marriage might likewise be declared void if it could be proved that husband or wife was permanently incapable of consummating the union. Sexual incapacity, however, was not an easy way out, for as Martin Ingram has noted, "however common such incapacity may have been, it was extremely difficult to prove. The law demanded evidence that the condition was permanent and had prevented consummation" (Ingram 1987, 173). Such evidence was not easy to produce.[5]

In any case, annulment was not an altogether satisfactory substitute for absolute divorce. Although it allowed for remarriage, it cut off the woman's rights to support through alimony and her right to inherit a share (generally a third) of her former husband's estate (the so-called dower portion), and made bastards of any children born to the couple during the marriage.

After 1700, divorce *a vinculo matrimonii*, or absolute divorce, began to be granted—but only by a private act of Parliament. This procedure was time consuming and very expensive and hence was out of the reach of all but the very rich and influential (Stone 1977, 38). (It would not be

---

4. Lord Hardwicke's Act put an end to "irregular" or informal marriages, but the requirement that unions be solemnized in the Anglican church also invalidated the marriages of Protestant dissenters and Roman Catholics.

5. Ingram further noted that, owing to the difficulty of proving sexual incapacity, some "English courts in the fifteenth century had adopted the bizarre and apparently uncanonical practice of subjecting allegedly impotent males to the attention of a group of women, whose task it was to try to excite their passion" (1987, 173).

until the Matrimonial Clauses Act of 1857 that judicial—as opposed to Parliamentary—divorce was permitted in England even on a limited basis.)

Once a marriage had been created, the law, both ecclesiastical and temporal, for most intents and purposes, lost interest. Despite the assertion by English historians Pollock and Maitland that "to the canonist there was nothing so sacred that it might not be expressed in definite rules" (1898, 2:436), church courts tended not to concern themselves with purely personal relations within intact families. The courts, for example, "made virtually no effort to punish autoerotic activities and sexual irregularities which took place between husband and wife in the marriage bed" (Ingram 1987, 239-240). This does not mean, however, that family relations were not subject to social control. What it does mean is that infringements of conventional morality were extralegal and were left to the rude but no doubt effective justice of the communal domain. One means of informal punishment was known as "skimmington," a process in which the wrongdoer was "paraded around the village seated backwards on a donkey" (Stone 1977, 145). Martin Ingram, in his study *Church Courts, Sex and Marriage in England*, described other ways in which the community might express its disapproval: "Notorious fornicators or adulterers were sometimes visited with the discordant din of 'rough music,' made by the beating of pots and pans and other household utensils. In 1586, for example, a certain Thomas Atkyns was 'rung about the town of Purton with basins for that he did live with the wife of Robert Pearce.' Cuckolds (husbands whose wives had been unfaithful) were often savagely mocked: horns or antlers were hung up on their houses, or neighbors grimaced or made horn signs at them with their fingers." In other cases, adulterers or cuckolds would be made the subject of mocking rhymes and satire, as was the case of one sorry husband in Bremhill, England, in 1816:

> Woe to thee, Michael Robins, that ever thou wert born
> For Blancute makes thee cuckold, and thou must wear the horn.
> He fetcheth the nurse, to give the child suck,
> That he may have time, thy wife to fuck.

And so the song continued, Ingram reported, "for a further ten scurrilous verses"[6] (1987, 173).

---

6. The *Oxford English Dictionary* relates the origins of the term "cuckold" to the cuckoo's habit of laying its eggs in the nest of another bird. The idea that cuckolds wore horns on their brows dates back to the ancient practice of

This is not to say that marital matters were not litigated in the ecclesiastical courts; indeed, anticipating their American descendants, English folks proved themselves notoriously litigious in the sixteenth and seventeenth centuries. Many of these cases were not instigated to punish sexual offenders but at the behest of those informally accused of prurient misbehavior. The best way to regain one's reputation after becoming the subject of such an allegation was to bring suit for sexual slander (Ingram 1987, Chapter 10). In this fashion, ecclesiastical law could be invoked to check communal normative control; the church courts afforded some degree of protection from malevolent or overly zealous neighbors.

Notwithstanding the centrality of ecclesiastical law, the effect of *secular* law on family dynamics cannot be ignored, for it was English common law that most specifically defined men's and women's places in society. Common law made the husband and father the head of the family; he was "the Person." Although his powers were no match for those of the patriarch of ancient Rome (who, according to the doctrine of *patria potestas*, literally held the power of life and death over his wife, children and servants), the English father and husband was clearly master of the domestic domain. The conventional phrasing of the main legal effect of marriage, though not originial to him, is Blackstone's: "By marriage the husband and wife are one person in law" (Blackstone [1769] 1979, 1:430).[7] But the modern gloss on this concept is more telling: Husband and wife are one—and that one is the husband (*United States v. Yazell*, 382 U.S. 341 [1966] Black, J. *dis.*). Upon marriage the woman came under the doctrine of *coverture*; she ceased to exist as a person in her own right because her legal identity was subsumed under the cover of her husband. As a married woman, or

---

engrafting the spurs of a castrated cock on the root of the excised comb. Apparently, the spurs thus attached grew and became horns, sometimes several inches in length.

7. Writing in the late nineteenth century, Pollock and Maitland took issue with Blackstone's conception of the unity of husband and wife, calling it an "impracticable proposition." The real working principle, they argued, was that the husband was a guardian of the wife and her property (Pollock and Maitland 1898, 2: 405-406). Indeed, in many respects the wife's legal status was akin to that of a minor—if she did contract with a "stranger," she could disavow that contract but the stranger, like anyone foolish enough to contract with a legal 'infant,' could be held to the bargain. Similarly, a wife had the right to pledge her husband's money for "necessaries" if he failed to provide them to her. Minor children had the right to do the same.

feme covert, she could not be sued in her own right, nor could she bring action for suit "without her husband's concurrence" (Blackstone [1769] 1979, 1:430). Although the husband was prohibited from selling or otherwise alienating property in any way that jeopardized his wife's dower rights without her consent, under common law the married woman effectively lost control over all of her possessions; whatever property she had brought to the marriage, or might acquire during that time, was subject to her husband's control. The husband was, moreover, legally responsible for his wife's behavior—for her torts and even for any crimes she committed in his presence, excepting the most "atrocious" crimes of treason, murder or robbery (*The Laws Respecting Women*, [1777] 1974). Coupled with this responsibility, the husband had the right (or, more accurately, the duty) to moderately chastise his wife when she acted contrary to his wishes or the rules of decorum: "The husband also (by the old law) might give his wife moderate correction. For, as he is to answer for her misbehavior, the law thought it reasonable to intrust him with the power of restraining her, by domestic chastisement, in the same moderation that a man is allowed to correct his servants or children; for whom the master or parent is also liable in some cases to answer (Blackstone [1769] 1979, 1:432). As noted in Chapter 2, most telling of the political relationship between husband and wife was the law that stipulated—in early times—that the husband's murder of his wife be treated as ordinary murder, but a wife's murder of husband be treated as petite treason. The principal difference between the two acts was how they were sanctioned—murder was punishable by hanging; petite treason was punishable by burning at the stake.

To an extent, the laws of England provided some relief for wives who became the victims of gross abuses by their husbands. The common law, as Blackstone noted ([1769] 1979, 1:433), would marshal its police powers to protect wives when life and limb were in jeopardy from physically abusive husbands. When less drastic action was required, as, for example, when a woman's property rights were at issue, she might find some relief in English courts of equity.

Beginning in the fourteenth and fifteenth centuries, courts of equity developed in parallel with common-law courts and served to an extent to alleviate the defects of common law which was viewed by many as overly formalistic. Although common law courts decided cases according to the strict rules of law, cases brought before equity courts were decided according to the maxims of equity—a series of principles established to help ensure that the law was not used to unfair ends.

Such principles included the maxims that "equity will not suffer a wrong to be without a remedy" and "equity looks to the intent rather than to the form," for example. As legal historian Stanley Katz noted, in a legal system that grew up in the spirit of formalism, equity "was an attempt to make law supple enough to do substantial justice" (1977, 259). Nonpersons and Persons under various legal disabilities who had the wealth to do so, including married women, could make special appeals to equity courts to protect their rights; especially important in equity were rights established by trusts and settlements, devices intended to protect married women from the excesses of profligate spouses: "Beginning in the late sixteenth century in England a woman or her relatives and friends could arrange a contract under which she or her trustee would retain full managerial rights over her separate property. Either personal or real property placed in such a trust could not be touched by the woman's husband or his creditors. Women with separate estates gained protection under the rules of equity, and their husbands lost traditional common-law marital rights under which they had access to all their wives' property" (Salmon 1986, 7-8). Although through the use of trusts and similar devices women's property could be protected from their husbands, the women themselves did not gain control of their property. Generally, control was vested in the hands of a trustee—typically, a male relative (i.e., another "Person").

The Diversity of Common Law

The idea that England was served by a "common law" is misleading to the degree that it invokes an image of a uniform body of law that everywhere applied in England. Typically, unlike statutory law that is enacted by legislators, common law is distinguished as the "unwritten law announced by judges and only when disputes are brought before them" (Rembar 1980, 59). The actual substance of much of the common law varied throughout the numerous jurisdictions within England's borders; "rules on widows' dower rights, conveyancing [i.e., transferring lands] practices, and femme sole [i.e., single women] trader actions shifted between counties and boroughs in seventeenth- and eighteenth-century England. London had many standards of its own" (Salmon 1986, 2). Primogeniture—inheritance of land by the eldest son—"was the common-law rule," but not one observed everywhere in England. For example, in Kent, all sons inherited equally under a rule known as gavelkind tenure (Friedman 1985b, 25).

The Colonial Experience

The diversity of English common law, and its different impacts on families, was amplified in the newly founded American colonies by two important factors. In the first place, those who settled in the New World were neither lawyers nor aristocrats; hence, they were not learned in the complexities of law as it was practiced in English Royal Courts. Indeed, to many of the early colonists, the English law was a bewildering and "intricate mass" of statutes and cases written in Latin and Law French. Eschewing the "loquacity and prolixity" of English law, colonial leaders sought reform (Chapin 1983, 4). Colonial laws, then, were often simplified versions of remembered English common law coupled with a mixture of local customs and practices.

In the second place the tendency to diversity was augmented by differences in colonists' circumstances. Some colonies (notably those in New England) were settled originally by men and women seeking religious freedom; others (e.g., many southern colonies) were settled by those whose motives were primarily economic. The diversity of settlers' goals was reflected in early colonial codes. Especially noteworthy, as Marylynn Salmon in her study of property law pointed out, is the fact that "no one ever envisioned a single colonial code of laws. From the earliest days of settlement, legislative bodies in the colonies held the power to create laws suited to New World conditions. Contemporaries accepted the fact that life in America required the institution of rules unknown at home, and life everywhere in America was not the same. Chattel slavery, the need to promote clearing of wilderness lands, and the creation of a new religious leadership in New England and Pennsylvania all but demanded innovation among American lawmakers" (Salmon 1986, 3-4). As George Haskins noted, even at the end of the eighteenth century, by which time the substantial reception of much common-law doctrine had brought a degree of uniformity to the American legal scene, Thomas Jefferson, writing in Virginia, could "properly refer to the law of Massachusetts, along with that of Bermuda and Barbados, as 'Foreign law'" (Haskins 1960, 6-7).

Nonetheless, it does not do too much of a disservice to the diversity of colonial law to generalize about the law's impact on families—for the nature of that impact was fairly straightforward: the law held that the husband and father was master of the domestic domain. One master of his own domain expressed his contentment with this situation in a letter to *The Spectator*, an influential periodical in England and the colonies: "Nothing is more gratifying to the mind of man than power or dominion; and . . . as I am the father of a family . . . I am perpetually taken up in giving out orders, in prescribing duties, in hearing parties, in administering justice, and in distributing rewards and punishments. . . . In short, sir, I look upon my family as a patriarchal sovereignty in which I am myself both King and priest" (quoted in Zinn 1980, 106).

Although the southern colonial laws retained those English rules that protected a married woman's rights in her property (or at least the dower share), married women in the northern colonies tended to lose these safeguards. All of the colonies were hostile to equity courts, the traditional protectors of the rights of women wealthy enough to make use of them. As a result, there was a "virtual absence of equity" courts in seventeenth-century America (Katz 1977, 263). In the New England colonies, the husband's authority was augmented by religious precepts. The good Christian woman trusted and obeyed her husband and any technicalities that existed solely to protect her were unnecessary complications. In any case, the "central tenet of Puritanism" was "the wife's submission to her husband's will." As William Gouge asserted in *Of Domestical Duties*, the husband and wife were "yoak-fellows in mutuall familaritie, not in equall authoritie. . . . If therefore he will one thing, and she another, she must not thinke to have an equall right and power. She must give place and yeeld" (quoted in Salmon 1986, 8).

As in England, however, the day-to-day relationships within intact families were unlikely to come under the scrutiny of the courts. Again, however, this did not mean that individuals within families acted autonomously or that they were not subject to interference from outsiders. The community closely watched over courtship, husband and wife relations, child-rearing practices and other domestic matters (recall, for example, the notion of "Holy Watching" that was described in Chapter 6). In other words, there was a great deal of control exercised, but it was normative, not legal.

The Republican Family

In immediate post-Revolutionary America, the laws respecting family, like most laws, entered a period of transition. With independence came the need to rethink the entire legal system, and in the Anglophobia of Revolutionary America, continued reliance on English law seemed anathema. Yet, as the leaders of the new United States set about to create a system of laws that was distinctly American, they found they could not abandon entirely their English heritage if only because, as legal historian Grant Gilmore put it,

"English law was the only law that post-Revolutionary American lawyers knew anything about" (Gilmore 1977, 19). The same presumably was true of American judges and legislators. In the main, then, English law—without its ecclesiastical overtones—was kept as the basis of law in the new states. Yet English law was not received wholesale; even early American law contained some important novelties.

There was no thought that the new American states would adopt laws common to the entire country, particularly with respect to family law. The Tenth Amendment to the Constitution provided that "the powers not delegated to the United States. . . are reserved to the States, respectively, or to the people." Because the power to regulate domestic life was not one of the powers assigned to the federal government by the Constitution, family law was to be "a virtually exclusive province of the states" (*Sousa v. Iowa*, 419 U.S. 393 [1975]).

One important difference between English law and the laws of most American states had to do with divorce. Prior to the American Revolution, the legal codes in some New England colonies had provided for divorce—this despite the fact that absolute divorce was not generally permitted in England. Thus, as Linda Kerber has pointed out, a colony that passed laws legalizing divorce "was always vulnerable to reprisal" from England. It was not until the very eve of the Revolution, however, that England did in fact take official notice of colonial disobedience in this respect. One result was that "freedom to regulate colonial marriages, like freedom to regulate colonial taxation became a Revolutionary issue" (Kerber 1986, 160). After the Revolution, all states except South Carolina passed laws allowing absolute divorce.

The nineteenth century was a period of tremendous growth and change in the United States. Two sorts of changes were particularly relevant to the development of family law. The first of these changes was essentially ideological: The same liberal ideals used to justify the break with England remained to have an impact on the everyday lives of American citizens. In other words, the revolutionary ideals that justified independence for the new nation created new legitimating formulas. The second change had to do with shifting economic conditions. In the nineteenth century, the country's economic system moved from an agricultural to a commercial and later to a full-blown industrial base.

Ideological Change

Abigail Adams is best remembered for the letter she sent to her husband John as he toiled to draft a new legal code for the soon-to-be-created country. In that letter she invoked the language of revolutionary ideals and enjoined the future president to "remember the ladies and be more generous and favourable to them than your ancestors. Do not put such unlimited powers into the hands of Husbands. Remember all Men would be tyrants if they could. If perticular care and attention is not paid to the Laidies we are determined to foment a Rebellion." John Adams's response to his wife's suggestion that women be recognized in the new code of laws is perhaps not so well known, but it is telling: "As to your extraordinary Code of Laws," he responded, "I cannot but laugh. . . . Depend on it, We know better than to repeal our Masculine systems" (Kurland and Lerner 1987, 1:518-519).

To give Abigail Adams her due, however, in many important respects hers was the more prophetic missive. Although, true to his word, John Adams and his colleagues indeed did not "remember the ladies" in an especially kindly fashion, one of the more significant effects of the war was the degree to which it provoked a rethinking of women's roles in society and in the family. The Enlightenment ideals that had justified revolution in the face of tyranny and lack of representation did not work well as legitimating formulas to undergird a society that relegated women to subordinate status. Women had supported the war effort by making great personal sacrifices (including, in some cases, actually fighting alongside men). Republican ideals demanded that the contributions of all citizens be recognized (Norton 1984, 616). So, what was to be the woman's place in the new republic?

The resounding answer was that in the new social order women were to be given official charge of the domestic arena. In an enlightened political climate in which individualism was paramount and in an economic order in which work took men further from the domestic hearth, women were charged with maintaining the morality of the American civilization; by nurturing the children—especially their sons—so that they would grow into citizens who would preserve the republic and its high moral character.

So, as it turned out, the woman's place in the new order was not all that different from her place in the old order. A cynic might observe that all that had changed was the rhetoric justifying her station in life. But the new rhetoric, the new legitimating formula, was compelling, and it caught the imagination of the American public.

Frequent biographies of "mothers of the wise and good" in the domestic literature connoted that the chief aim of women's vocation was the rearing of moral, trustworthy, statesmanlike citizens. George Washington's mother became a favored model. The story of her training George to be "a good boy" showed in a stroke that mothers were crucial influences, that women's social and political contribution consisted purely in their domestic vocation, and that the nation could not do without their service. (Cott 1977, 94)

This rhetoric, which in time enlarged to become the basis of a "cult of domesticity" so often noted as characteristic of nineteenth-century American society, became enshrined in law. At one point, the U.S. Supreme Court delimited the place of women this way: "The civil law, as well as nature herself, has always recognized a wide difference in the respective sphere and destinies of man and woman. . . . The constitution of the family organization, which is founded in the divine ordinance, as well as the nature of things, indicates the domestic sphere as that which properly belongs to the domain and functions of womanhood" (*Bradwell v. State of Illinois*, 83 U.S. [16 Wall] 130 [1873]). The rhetoric surrounding the family actually contained not one but two important messages. The first was the idea that the woman's place was in the home; her highest ambition was to manage the domestic world and raise her children to be fit to participate in the country's life. The second one, often overlooked, was no less important: Families existed for the good of society; they were the basis of civilization and the hope for the future. This message, a reiteration of the basic Puritan notion that the family was what held society together—"the root whence church and Commonwealth Cometh" (Haskins 1960, 80)—though not entirely novel, did emphasize the idea that society had a stake in the family. These themes were to prove important in the development of American family law.

Economic Change

As the United States moved away from its agrarian roots, those facets of English laws that were better suited to a social organization based on feudal ties and stable land ownership were abandoned. The English system of primogeniture, for example, was particularly ill-suited to a country in which fortunes could be made in land speculation, and after the Revolution it was rejected everywhere in the new states.

Similarly, married women's dower rights were affected by changing economic conditions. Under the English common law, a husband had full rights to manage his wife's property. Once the couple had a child, the husband's control strengthened; he became—for his lifetime—"tenant by curtesy" of his wife's estates. Although the husband enjoyed full rights to profit from the use of his wife's estates, however, he could not sell or otherwise alienate them without her consent. Moreover, owing to the right of the wife to inherit a share of her husband's estate should he leave her a widow, the husband could not sell or convey any portion of his own estates that risked his wife's dower portion. If a husband disregarded his wife's interests and attempted to sell her property, buyers would be difficult to find, for the law allowed the widow to sue to regain her property. Hence, anyone foolish enough to purchase property pledged to dower portions could never be sure of retaining title. In short, one of the effects of coverture and dower rights was that a significant amount of property was kept "outside the normal operations of the market economy" (Kerber 1986, 144). Another effect of coverture and dower was that it gave the wife at least a nominal legally enforceable power in family decisionmaking.

After the Revolution, many states acted to mitigate the effects of such constraints. In some places, the result was to abolish dower rights almost entirely; in other places, dower rights along with wives' power remained but were watered down. In a fluid, if not downright risky economic environment, the loss of dower rights put families at risk, for it meant that an unlucky husband's creditors could reach all of the family's property. In many states, legislators responded by passing Married Women's Property Acts. Beginning in the late 1830s, states began to pass laws that, in effect, undid most of the legal constraints of coverture. In consequence, married women gained some rights to own their own property; in many cases, Married Women's Property Acts placed women's property out of the reach of their husbands' creditors.

The passing of coverture, however, was not to be the undoing of women's legal disabilities that many had hoped (or, in many cases, feared). Married women, for most intents and purposes, remained Nonpersons, mostly because judges interpreted the Married Women's Property Acts in a very narrow fashion. In court decisions, the acts were deemed not to erode the husband's right to control the family assets; nor did they provide married women the right to control their own earnings or to contract without their husband's consent.

> Statutory reforms abolishing coverture forced the judiciary to recognize women as separate, but not necessarily as equal. By viewing the disabilities of married women as "general" and the capabilities created by statute as "exceptional," courts not only stemmed the flow of marketplace Amazons, but also severely impaired women's ability to obtain economic independence. For example, statutes recognizing women's right to their separate earnings were typically interpreted to

exclude domestic tasks, such as operating a boarding house or selling home products and services. The apparent theory was that such work was performed by the male head of the household through his spouse. In addition, since the husband was entitled to determine the household's needs, his wife's separate property could be charged for his purchases, even if the items were for his exclusive use. (Rhode 1989, 25-26)

The Emergence of American Family Law

The combination of economic and ideological currents that existed in post-Revolutionary America gave rise to what was, in many respects, a new family. It was smaller and more mobile than its colonial counterpart, and at its basis was a "companionate" marriage, a partnership between man and woman—each charged with separate spheres of life. Legally this partnership was a contractual one. In some respects this sort of partnership harkened back to the early Christian ideal of marriage as contract. But, absent its religious trappings, marriage as contract took on new meanings.

The idea of marriage as contract led to official recognition of informal as well as formal marriages. This informal union, the so-called common-law marriage, was effected by the simple express agreement of a man and a woman to be married, followed by their cohabitation. (Contrary to popular myth, common-law marriages did not require a specific number of years to go into effect but could be established instantly.) Although today common-law marriages are recognized only in a minority of jurisdictions (thirteen states plus the District of Columbia), until the twentieth century they were as valid as formal marriages in most states (Wardle, Blakesley, and Parker 1988, §3:17). Recognition of common-law marriage meant that settlers on the geographic fringes of society, without access to officials, could enjoy the same protection of their property rights and their children's legitimacy as was afforded by formal marriage. In 1833, Chief Justice Gibson of Pennsylvania ruled that rigid marriage laws were "ill adapted to the habits and customs of society as it now exists." Pragmatically, the court also noted that refusing to recognize common-law marriages would "bastardize the vast majority of children which have been born within the state for half a century" (*Rodenbaugh v. Sanks*, 2 Watts 9 [1833]).

Marriage as contract, rather than sacrament, also helped law-makers in many jurisdictions to justify liberalizing divorce laws to an unprecedented extent. Although by modern standards divorce was still not all that easy to obtain, it was possible and growing easier. A few states even allowed divorce simply where the cause seemed "just and reasonable." Connecticut, for example, permitted divorce for conduct that "permanently destroys the happiness of the petitioner and defeats the purpose of the marriage relation" (Clark 1968, 283).

The laws' diffidence with respect to marriage and families left a void that could not easily be filled by either parental or communal control in an increasingly heterogeneous and mobile society. In the early nineteenth century the new American family, more so than at any point in its history, emerged as an autonomous unit that was not subject to much control either from the civil or the communal domain.

The notion of companionate marriage, insofar as it stressed marriage as a partnership between husband and wife, had some important consequences. Until the nineteenth century, the legal system had not really treated the family as a unit. "Family autonomy" heretofore had meant, for all intents and purposes, "paternal autonomy." The father was more than head of household, he was the only one with a complete legal personality; all others in the household were under his "cover" and hence had no immediate relation to the law. In effect, the wife, children, and servants were the patriarch's concern and did not come under the purview of law (unless and until the male head of household failed in his duty to control his charges).

Yet, the stress placed on the woman's role in the republican family and the growing sentimental attachment to children (particularly with respect to their status as the future of the country) caused a rethinking of the father's role in the family, and in consequence, the law's role vis à vis the family. Although historians have paid a great deal of attention to the elevation of woman to domestic saint, they have typically overlooked the concomitant demotion of man to domestic lout. As Norma Basch has shown in her study of women and property law in New York, legislators debating the need to pass Married Women's Property Acts often invoked the image of husbands as intemperate, inept, and morally degenerate, likely to squander their wives' property by "extravagant and stylish living" or in "riot, drunkenness, and other homogeneous dissipation" (Basch 1982, 115-116). Elizabeth Pleck, in her study of domestic violence, suggested that the temperance movement added fuel to the flames: For example, lecturers described "with characteristic hyperbole the husband who, under the influence of cider alone, savaged with an axe his loving wife and the baby nursing at her breast" (Pleck 1987, 50).

In the mid-nineteenth century, in response to women's claims, judges took notice of society's attachment to children and women's superiority in the domestic arena and began to rethink their expectations about the relationship of children to their parents—especially with respect to the issue of custody. Under common law, children had "belonged" to their fathers. By the mid-nineteenth century, courts in many U.S. jurisdictions began to recognize that mothers had equal rights to their children. In many cases, this reevaluation of parental roles was tied to an emphasis on the importance of children to the society as a whole. Jamil Zainaldin's study of the emergence of modern custody law traces its origin to a judicial decision handed down by Senator Paige (writing for the New York Court for the Correction of Errors). In the state of nature, said Senator Paige, the father was indeed the sovereign and supreme head of the family. But once the family entered into civil society, this sovereignty was passed to the "chief or government of the nation." Because the nation could not care for all of its children on its own, the sovereign transferred to the parents "the duty of education and maintenance and a right of guardianship." This transferral of rights, however, was limited, for sovereignty remained with the state: "The moment a child is born . . . it owes its allegiance to the government of the country of its birth, and is entitled to the protection of the government." For its part, the government is obliged to "consult the welfare, comfort and interests of such child in regulating its custody during the period of its minority." Paige concluded that there could be "no inequality between the father and mother" because the parents' rights to the child's custody were delegated to them both by the state (*Mercein v. People, ex rel. Barry*, 25 Wend. 65 [N.Y. 1840]; quoted in Zainaldin 1979, 1071).

If the parents' rights with respect to their children were equal, on what basis would the state make custody decisions? According to the "child's best interests." And, given the acceptance (both in the social and legal arenas) of the natural superiority of mothers as nurturers, this generally meant that the mother would be granted custody of the children. "Any attempt to deprive the able mother of the care of her child 'would violate the law of nature' and would not be a proper exercise of discretion'" (*Mercein v. People*, in Zainaldin 1979, 1073).

This historical novelty of granting women custody of their children was not the boon to women's status in society that it had first appeared. As Michael Grossberg noted, "the judicially inspired changes in custody and guardianship shifted the locus of patriarchal authority much more than they challenged the subordinate status of women" (1983, 246-247). Yes, married women tended to receive custody of their children, but this outcome was not automatic; whether the woman would be granted custody depended, for one thing, on whether she conformed to the judge's idea of a good mother. Thus, "the decline of paternal rights did not automatically increase maternal ones. On the contrary, the law reduced the rights of parenthood itself" (1987, 246-247). Grossberg thus concluded that the decline in paternal authority gave rise not to maternal authority but rather to a novel form of judicial patriarchy.

In most respects, this is a fair characterization. But what it glosses over is the degree to which traditional patriarchal control as exercised by fathers had been subject to the normative control of the community. In a sense, the increasing legal intervention in the mid-nineteenth century was a revival of community control. However, it was no longer members of the communal domain who exerted this control, but Persons in the civil domain whose values were represented by the law. Further, by invoking the rhetoric of domesticity and women-as-nurturers, women could make use of the law's transformation of resources to gain new power in the family arena: "Good mothers," for example, were no longer captives to intemperate husbands for fear of losing their children after a divorce or separation.[8]

The legal system would come to play an increasingly important role as the fruits of laissez-faire family law and familial autonomy came to be apparent. Most disturbing was what was seen as an appalling rise in divorce rates. Although the rate was small by modern standards, it was increasing, and "to some self-appointed guardians of national morals, it was an alarming fire bell in the night, a symptom of moral dry rot, and a cause itself of still further moral decay. President Timothy Dwight of Yale, in 1816, called the rise of divorces 'dreadful beyond conception.'" Connecticut, he prophesied, was imperiled by "stalking, barefaced, pollution" (Friedman 1985b, 206).

Divorce was not the only sign of what was seen as imminent social collapse; equally troubling to many was a declining birthrate among whites. "In 1800, a married couple had an average of slightly over seven children. A generation later, in 1825, the marital fertility rate had fallen to under six children. By the 1850s, married women were bearing on average only 5.42 children, and by 1880, only 4.24" (D'Emilio and Freeman 1988, 58).

In response to these troubles, after the Civil War there came a movement to strengthen state regulation of marriage. Many of the liberal divorce laws that had been passed early in the century were repealed. The laws that remained allowed divorce only in response to specific types of fault, usually adultery, desertion, extreme cruelty, or long-term imprisonment. States also tightened entrance to marriage. Already, most states required marriage licenses, but in antebellum

---

8. Here is another example of how legal rhetoric, or legitimating formula, may work against the intentions of its authors. The woman as domestic saint—the formula that legitimated her exclusion from the civil domain in the early nineteenth century—came to be a resource in custody battles!

America, courts had treated these licenses as a way "to register, not to restrict marriage" (Grossberg 1985, 78). By the end of the nineteenth century, however, marriage licenses had clearly become a means of social control. Because the process of acquiring a marriage license brought the couple under the scrutiny of some official Person, licensing requirements helped states to prevent marriages of people who were too young or too closely related, either through consanguinity or affinity. Official scrutiny of those seeking to wed also helped to enforce laws against bigamy and polygamy. Again, in important respects, the law provided resources for Persons to maintain social control in communities where traditional, normative-based means of communal control (shaming, ridicule, and other manifestations of disapproval) were becoming more and more ineffectual in an increasingly pluralistic and mobile society.

Legislators, encouraged by eugenicists who believed that crime, mental illness, and other social ills could be traced to hereditary biological factors, also enacted laws enumerating other kinds of forbidden marriages.[9] Some categories of Nonpersons were forbidden to

---

9. The term "eugenics" was coined by Sir Francis Galton in 1883. As explained a few decades later by a president of the American Eugenic Society, "We must endeavor to show that eugenics supplies the most effective and permanent solution to the problems that have been so ineffectively dealt with hitherto by physicians, public health officials, social workers, clergymen, and reformers—the problems of combating disease, disability, defectiveness, degeneracy, delinquency, vice and crime" (Newman 1932, 441). Two primary tactics were suggested. First, society could be cleansed by sterilizing or segregating defective individuals. This strategy would limit the amount of defective "germplasm" that was circulating in society (germplasm was "that part of the cell protoplasm which [was] believed to be the material basis of heredity and is transferred from one generation to the next"—that is, ovum and sperm). Second, society should take steps to conserve desirable germplasm. One leading eugenicist, writing in 1913, cited with approval a German proposal "for the propagation of a fixed German type of humanity—a type which will be fixed as the Jewish in its characteristics. . . . Only 'typical' couples are to be allowed. . . . Neither the man nor the woman should have dark hair. Its tint may range from blonde to auburn. The eyes of the pair should be pure blue without any tint of brown" (Walter 1913, 529).

Parenthetically, although many Americans were appalled at the way that Nazi Germany put eugenics to use in the 1930s and 1940s, this same idea had a great deal of currency in the United States as well. For example, I drew much of this information about eugenics from one of my grandmother's college textbooks. She was a schoolteacher, and knowledge of eugenic principles was required as preparation for teaching in the 1920s.

marry. For example, marriage was prohibited to those not mentally capable of contracting owing to conditions variously labeled as insanity, lunacy, idiocy, feeblemindedness, imbecility, or unsound mind (Clark 1968, 95-96). Marriage was also prohibited to those physically incapable of performing the "marriage essentials." Generally, this latter criterion involved only the capacity to have "normal" or "successful" sexual intercourse, and not necessarily the ability to procreate. As one author explained it, "Copula, not fruitfulness, is the test" (Tiffany 1921, 29).

Eugenics also scientifically justified laws that prohibited people with certain diseases (e.g., epilepsy, tuberculosis, and venereal disease) and statuses (e.g., habitual criminal, rapist, or pauper) from marrying. These individuals were appalling to Persons and therefore needed to be controlled. In most cases, such obstacles could only be overcome if the individual consented to sterilization. Many believed such statutes were necessary to "prevent the demise of civilized society" (Linn and Bowers 1978, 629). Even some of the most respected legal thinkers joined the eugenicists. Justice Oliver Wendell Holmes of the U. S. Supreme Court, for example, wrote that it would be "better for all the world, if instead of waiting to execute degenerate offspring for crimes, or to let them starve for their imbecility, society can prevent those who are manifestly unfit from continuing their kind" (*Buck v. Bell*, 274 U.S. 200 [1927]). By way of example, here is a summary of the relevant Washington State statute:

> No woman under forty-five years of age or man of any age, unless marrying a woman over forty-five shall marry or intermarry within this state who is a common drunkard, habitual criminal, epileptic, imbecile, feeble-minded, idiot, or insane person, or who has heretofore been afflicted with hereditary insanity or is afflicted with pulmonary tuberculosis in its advanced stages or any contagious venereal disease, the county auditor requiring before license issuance an affidavit, sworn to before any person authorized to administer oaths, of the male applicant showing that he is not afflicted with any contagious venereal disease, an affidavit of some disinterested credible person that neither party is a habitual criminal, and an affidavit of each applicant that he is not within the other named conditions. (May 1929, 441)

It was predicted by some scientists that if such laws were reliably enforced, "less than four generations would eliminate nine tenths of the crime, insanity and sickness of the present generation in our land. Asylums, prisons and hospitals would decrease, and the problems of the unemployed, the indigent old and the hopelessly degenerate would cease to trouble civilization" (Walter 1913, 528).

The most notorious marriage impediment was race. Prior to Emancipation, as slave Nonpersons, African Americans had no relations that were accorded positive civil recognition: "By law the slave had no brother or sister, no husband or wife, no son or daughter, no ancestors and no prosperity. This 'kinlessness' and 'natal alienation' meant that among slaves spouses had no legal obligations to one another and parents could exercise no formal responsibilities toward their children" (Oakes 1990, 4). After the Civil War in the United States, African Americans had been able to legitimate (in most cases, for the first time) their marriage and kinship relations. And during the brief Reconstruction era in which African Americans actually gained a voice in the southern political system, so-called bastardy laws were passed that provided some relief to African American women whose children had white fathers, by making these fathers provide for the offspring.

The legal abilities of African Americans proved short-lived, and bastardy laws were soon repealed. Antimiscegenation statutes assumed new prominence by the end of the nineteenth century. Such statutes had long existed in the New World (Virginia enacted such a law in 1691 to prevent "abominable mixture and spurious issue") but in the late nineteenth century, lawmakers regarded these laws with new urgency (Trosino 1993, 97). Often clothed in the pseudo-scientific justifications provided by eugenics, states used antimiscegenation laws to keep the white race pure, and African Americans "in their place."[10] In a typical case, a Georgia court had little sympathy for a defendant convicted of the *felony* of interracial marriage:

> The amalgamation of the races is not only unnatural, but is always productive of deplorable results. Our daily observation shows us, that the offspring of these unnatural connections are generally sickly and *effeminate*, and that they are inferior in physical development and strength, to the full-blood of either race. It is sometimes urged that

---

10.   Miscegenation derives from the Latin *Miscere*, to mix, and *genus*, race. Forrest Wood, in *Black Scare: The Racist Response to Emancipation and Reconstruction*, traced the origins of the term to a pamphlet published anonymously in 1864. The authors of the pamphlet, purporting to support interracial marriage by extolling its benefits, Wood suggested, were actually Democrats trying to stir up white fears of racial mixing and "mongrelization" and to thereby discredit Republican Party attempts to promote Emancipation (1968, 54).

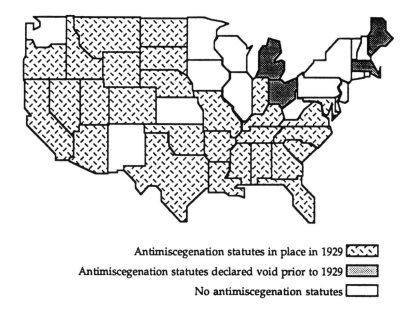

Antimiscegenation statutes in place in 1929 [▨▨▨]
Antimiscegenation statutes declared void prior to 1929 [▨▨▨]
No antimiscegenation statutes [☐]

FIGURE 7.1 Distribution of antimiscegenation laws in 1929. Compiled from Geoffrey May, *Marriage Laws and Decisions in the United States.* (New York: Russell Sage Foundation, 1929).

such marriages should be encouraged, for the purpose of elevating the inferior race. The reply is, that such connections never elevate the inferior race to the position of the superior, but they bring down the superior to that of the inferior. They are productive of evil, and evil only, without any corresponding good. *(Scott v. Georgia,* 39 Ga. 321 [1869])

By 1930, thirty states had enacted statutes prohibiting interracial marriages (see Figure 7.1)—a number that was to remain stable until after World War II.

In several cases, the prohibition of interracial marriage was extended to, for example, whites and Malays, whites and Mongolians, whites and Native Americans, and blacks and Native Americans (Kennedy 1959, 59-69). For example, Oregon law forbade "the marriage of a white person with a person of one fourth or more Negroe or mulatto blood." Further, the Oregon statutes said, "It shall be unlawful for any white person hereafter to intermarry with any person having one-fourth or more Negro, Chinese, or Kanaka blood, or any person having more than one-half Indian blood" (May 1929, 356).[11]

Early cases that challenged the constitutionality of antimiscegenation statutes in state courts failed. Those who appealed convictions under these statutes to the U.S. Supreme Court were also disappointed. In its first review of a challenge to a state antimiscegenation law in 1882, the Court ruled that such statutes did not deny rights guaranteed under the Fourteenth Amendment's equal protection clause. As Justice Stephen J. Field put it, the law "applies the same punishment to both offenders, the white and the black" and hence, offered the same protection to blacks and whites (*Pace v. Alabama*, 106 U.S. 583). Then, in 1879, the Court ruled that antimiscegenation laws did not violate the freedom of contract clause (Art. 1, §10 of the U.S. Constitution). Marriage, according to the Court, was not a "right" of U.S. citizens (*Ex parte Kinney*, 3 Hughes 9 [1879]).

Throughout the late nineteenth century and into the twentieth, judges and legislators justified the law's intrusion into the private world with references to society's (i.e., "Persons") stake in the family as the seedbed of its civilization. In *Maynard v. Hill*, for example, Justice Field of the U.S. Supreme Court put it this way: "Marriage, as creating the most important relation in life, as having more to do with the morals and civilization of the people than any other institution, has always been subject to the control of the legislature. . . . [Marriage] is an institution, in the maintenance of which in its purity the public is deeply interested, for it is the foundation of the family and of society, without which there would be neither civilization nor progress" (125 U.S. 190 [1888]). Nonetheless, with few exceptions the law's intrusion into the domestic arena was limited to regulating entry to and exit from marriage. With respect to intact families, the courts and legislators maintained a hands-off approach and the activities of and relations between husbands and wives and their children in intact marriages were generally protected from legal scrutiny.[12] This state of affairs meant, of course, that wrongs or injuries committed within the family were *truly private*.

Well into the twentieth century, the principle of nonintervention remained so strong that neither husbands nor wives *could* invoke the

---

11. "Kanaka" refers to those of Hawaiian or South Sea Islands ancestry.

12. The most notable of these exceptions was the passage of the Comstock Act in 1873, which forbade the delivery of birth control information through the mails.

law to resolve marital disputes even when they wished to. In one case, for example, the sixty-year-old wife of a well-to-do but stingy, eighty-year-old husband asked the Nebraska courts to require him to pay for indoor plumbing and provide a reasonable allowance to her. The court agreed that, given the husband's "wealth and circumstances" (he owned a farm valued at $90,000 and additional assets of $117,000) the husband's attitude "leaves little to be said in his behalf." But, said the court, "the living standards of a family are a matter of concern to the household and not for the courts to determine" (*McGuire v. McGuire,* 157 Neb. 226, 59 N.W.2d 336 [1953]).

The extent of the courts' reluctance to intervene in family matters or, as it was sometimes put, to "disrupt family harmony," was shown in the rule that spouses could not sue one another for personal torts or injuries. If, for example, a husband assaulted or battered his wife, she was enjoined from taking legal action against him in civil court (Keeton et al. 1984, 901-902).[13]

The practice of nonintervention was carried a step further around the turn of the century when the courts invented the doctrine of "parental immunity." Owing to reasons of "sound public policy, designed to subserve the repose of families and the best interests of society" (*Hewellette v. George,* 68 Miss. 703, 9 So. 885 [1891]), an unemancipated minor was barred by the Mississippi Supreme Court from suing her parents for personal injuries. The capstone of parental immunity came in *Roller v. Roller* (37 Wash. 242, 70 P. 788 [1905]). In this case, the Supreme Court of Washington State enjoined a daughter from suing for personal injuries received as a result of being raped by her father. The court ruled that society had an important interest in preserving domestic harmony, an interest not served by allowing children to sue their parents. The Washington court rejected the daughter's assertion that there was little harmony to protect when a father raped his own daughter. These cases, perhaps more than any other, proved the degree to which the family was firmly embedded in the communal domain (where might makes right).

Modern Family Law

In the twentieth century, the state has enhanced the family unit's protection against interference from both state and community with respect to marital intimacy, procreation, child-rearing, and education.

---

13. In theory, the husband could be prosecuted in criminal court, but police and criminal courts too were reluctant to interfere in domestic matters (Pleck 1987, 187).

Such protection is typically justified on the principle of "family privacy." In *Prince v. Commonwealth of Massachusetts* (321 U.S. 158 [1944]), the U.S. Supreme Court put it this way: "It is cardinal with us that the custody, care and nurture of the child reside first in the parents, whose primary function and freedom include preparation for obligations the state can neither supply nor hinder. . . . And it is in recognition of this that these decisions have respected the private realm of family life which the state cannot enter." Some twenty years later, in a case involving contraception, the Supreme Court reiterated the point: "We deal with a right of privacy older than the Bill of Rights" (*Griswold v. Connecticut*, 381 U.S. 479 [1965]).

Beginning in the 1960s, strict regulation of entrance to and exit from marriage began to unravel. In the 1967 case of *Loving v. Virginia*, the U.S. Supreme Court held antimiscegenation laws to be unconstitutional. According to the Court, the states had no right to "prevent marriages between persons solely on the basis of racial classification." Only decades after it had declared that marriage was *not* a right, the Court reversed itself: "Marriage is one of the 'basic civil rights of man,' fundamental to our very existence and survival" (388 U.S. 1 [1967]; quoting *Skinner v. Oklahoma*, 316 U.S. 535 [1942]). Since *Loving*, many other marriage restrictions have been repealed or eased. Age requirements in many states have been lowered; the mental ability needed to enter into marriage has been ruled to be less than that required for other sorts of contracts; and the necessary mental competency is presumed to be present unless there is "clear and definite" proof to the contrary. Moreover, "there is a trend in modern times to abolish affinity restrictions" (Wardle et al., 1988, § 2:09); only one state (Missouri) still prohibits epileptics to marry (Wardle, et al., 1988, §2:47); and in many states, even prison inmates are deemed to have a right to marry (*In re Carrafa*, 77 Cal. App.3d 788 [1978]). The decision to marry, according to the U.S. Supreme Court, is among "the personal decisions protected by the right to privacy" (*Zablocki v. Redhail*, 434 U.S. 374 [1978]).

Recent changes in divorce laws have been, if anything, even more dramatic than changes in marriage laws. Implicitly accepting the principle that there is a right to divorce, the Supreme Court ruled in 1971 that welfare recipients could not be denied access to divorce courts because they could not afford to pay court costs and fees (*Boddie v. Connecticut*, 401 U.S. 371 [1971]). By the mid-1980s, every state had either replaced fault-based divorce laws with no-fault laws or added no-fault grounds to existing laws (Freed and Walker 1986, 444). No longer, then, must there be a "guilty" and an "innocent" party in a divorce. Instead, one spouse simply asserts that the couple is no longer getting along or has been living apart for a certain amount of time.

Yet, notwithstanding the courts' designation of the family as a "private realm into which the state cannot enter," as regulations governing entrance to and exit from marriage and family life have decreased, there has been a concomitant *increase* in laws potentially affecting relations in ongoing families. In the late twentieth century there has been, in fact, a virtual explosion of such laws.

Today, for example, we not only speak of custody law with respect to parents, but in respect to stepparents as well; another burgeoning area of law concerns the rights of grandparents. Spousal immunity has been abrogated (or abolished) in most states (*Heino v. Harper*, 306 Or. 347, 759 P.2d 253 [1988]), and as a result there has been an increase in case law on "domestic torts"—husbands and wives suing one another for noncriminal wrongs (including intentional infliction of emotional distress, assault, battery, intentional and negligent transmission of sexually transmitted disease, etc.). Moreover, in many states the law recognizes the crime of "marital rape." Similarly, children now have rights that can be asserted against their parents. For example, minors have the right to obtain information about and use birth control without a parent's consent (*Carey v. Population Services International*, 431 U.S. 678 [1977]); to receive psychiatric care (*In re Alyne E.*, 113 Misc.2d 307, 448 N.Y.S.2d 984 [1982]); and perhaps even to separate from their parents should the parents and children prove "incompatible" (*In re Snyder*, 85 Wash.2d 182, 532 P.2d 278 [1975]). Increasingly, states are abrogating laws that afford parents immunity from being sued by their children (Beal 1984), and in many sorts of cases children may seek redress in the civil courts from intentional and negligent harms done by parents. At base, says the U.S. Supreme Court, children "are 'persons' under the Constitution" and have rights that should be protected by the state (*Tinker v. Des Moines Independent School District*, 393 U.S. 503 [1969]).

People in the United States have arrived in the late twentieth century to face a confusing situation. On the one hand, the law tends to say to outsiders, "hands off the family—families have a right to do as they see fit." On the other hand, the law now allows itself to be invoked such that wives may sue husbands and children may sue parents. Thus, while law has seemingly strengthened the family's ability to proceed as it wishes with respect to private life, more and more sorts of family squabbles are showing up in the courts.

The use of law to resolve such problems is often seen as an unnecessary burden on the courts and, more important, as a *failure* of family life in contemporary society. Former Chief Justice of the U.S.

Supreme Court Warren E. Burger sees it this way: "One reason our courts have become overburdened is that Americans are increasingly turning to the courts for relief from a range of personal distresses and anxieties. Remedies for personal wrongs that once were considered the responsibility of institutions other than the courts are now boldly asserted as 'legal entitlements.' The courts have been expected to fill the void created by the decline of church, family and neighborhood unity" (1982, 275). Burger's assessment is misleading. Why are more domestic or family issues heard in U.S. courts? For one thing, until recently courts would not hear such cases: The intact family and family matters were relegated to the communal domain. People did not litigate domestic issues at least in part because they could not litigate such issues.

The seemingly contradictory trends of offering more protection to the family from outside interference, and allowing more family disputes into the courts, actually reflect the increasing willingness of courts and legislators to protect the rights of individuals to make their own choices about marriage and related matters. Most of all, the movement of family relationships out of the communal domain and into the civil one has resulted from the extension of Personhood to a broader spectrum of individuals within society.

The idea of family autonomy and privacy, and hence, the policy of nonintervention, was traditionally based on "paternal" authority; the authority of the family patriarch. This pattern can be traced back to the Roman idea of *patria potestas.* But family autonomy and privacy based on paternal power are viable only when other members of the family are unable to invoke the power of the state against the father. Things are much different today: Although children still have many legal disabilities, they can no longer be regarded as chattel, and women have achieved at least technical legal equality.

Some people mourn the loss of near-total family autonomy; the family, they say, has lost its integrity (Peirce 1988). And there is no doubt that the notion of nonintervention served an important function. It has been "a convenient way for dealing with a problem . . . [that is] especially acute in the United States—that of devising family law which is suited to the needs and desires of persons with different ethnic and religious backgrounds, different social status, and different standards of living" (Glendon 1989, 95). At the same time, however, in many instances the policy of nonintervention that kept family disputes squarely in the communal domain created private little Hobbesian jungles in which the strong ruled and the weak could not call upon the law for help. And, to the degree that courts and legislators—as described in Chapter 5—had afforded families legal protection from communal control, the noninterventionist stance was oftentimes even more detrimental to family members—as long as the family's "privacy" is protected from normative as well as legal intervention, there was no place for abused members to turn for help.

The major impact of law on family life these days is that it provides a set of resources upon which family members may draw when they do not believe their interests are being served by other members of the family group. Thus, the transformation of resources that the law can provide is within reach of family members who believe that their expectations have been breached by other family members. Today, when the courts speak of "family privacy" it is clear that this privacy is based on family members' individual rights, existing only as long as family members are not in serious conflict about how they wish to assert those rights.

Family and Law in the Twenty-First Century

Families continue to play important roles in American society, and there can be little doubt that family relations will continue to be regarded as legally different from other relations and worthy of special protection. The big question is, To whom is the law's protection to be extended in domestic matters as the United States embarks upon the twenty-first century? Traditionally, lawmakers have extended this protection to a limited variety of relations—the two-parent household surrounded by a picket fence comes to mind here. This is the traditional family of Persons in the United States. The traditional, ideal-typical nuclear family, however, is something achieved (and perhaps aspired to) by only a small fraction of Americans. Under the auspices of promoting "family values," the courts and legislators have tended to ignore the special needs of those who attempt to create families notwithstanding the complexity of the modern world and its high divorce rate. For instance, as things presently stand, the roles of stepparents vis-à-vis their stepchildren are generally relegated to the norms of the communal domain. Thus, for example, a stepparent who has nurtured a child for years will quite likely have no claim to custody in the event that a divorce or death terminates the marriage. Moreover, the rights of a stepparent to intercede or act on a child's behalf in the civil domain (e.g., in a court of law or before officials—including school officials) are nonexistent. Simply put, the stepparent-stepchild relationship is a communal one and thus participants in "blended" families have only little or no access to the resources of the law.

I suspect that things will get worse before they get better. As individuals within society, freed from normative and legal controls to an unprecedented degree, continue to explore new ways of constituting family life, new and complex issues of law will emerge. As we move into the next century, the most serious family legal issues, I think, will evolve from situations in which people, having used their freedom from communal control to create new domestic arrangements (e.g., gay partnerships), will lobby for legal benefits heretofore denied them (e.g., legal entitlements to rent-controlled apartments, insurance rights, and so on).

The question facing lawmakers is this: Will the law continue to afford its protections mostly only to those domestic arrangements that mirror traditional family *forms,* or will it embrace and protect alternative domestic arrangements insofar as they fulfill traditional family *functions?*

8

The Civil Contract and
Working Life in the United States

In Chapter 7 I demonstrated how the law-as-contract perspective could be used to examine the law's impact on an important part of social life in the United States—the family. In the present chapter, my substantive focus moves from the family to the workplace, but my goal remains the same: to demonstrate how bringing law into the picture enhances our ability to explain the nature of relationships in an important social arena.

Consider, to begin, the constitutive employment relationship; that is, the relationship that exists between employer and employee. The basis of this relationship is the employment contract: Lee promises to work for Barbara. In return, Barbara promises to pay Lee $250 a week. Having made those mutual promises, Barbara and Lee have, in effect, entered into an employment contract. More specifically, Lee has alienated (given up) his right to do as he pleases each day and promised to do what Barbara tells him to do. In return, Barbara has promised to compensate Lee with wages.

What Barbara has acquired over Lee is "power"—that is, the ability to get Lee to do what she tells him to do. If he fails to perform to her satisfaction, she can fire him. Here's how one sociologist has characterized the nature of this power: "The foreman has power over his employees because he can always call on his superior to fire someone, the superior in turn can call on the police to eject him if he does not leave and the policeman can call on other police and ultimately on the army to reinforce him against resistance" (Collins 1975, 291).

At one time in history this was an accurate description of the employer-employee relationship in the United States. But today the employer-employee relationship carries with it a number of legally "cognizable" expectations, and so the simple "might makes right" equation is no longer an accurate description of this relationship.

It may appear that, in choosing to highlight the family and workplace, I have set out to show the impact of law in two diametrically opposed spheres of life—the private and the public; the intimate and the impersonal. These days, it is usual to think of family and work as belonging to distinct and even competing spheres of social life. However, work and family relations share some important characteristics.

In the first place, as I observed in the Introduction to Part Two, both work and family are important to the individual in terms of setting status and identity in modern society. Indeed, what one does for a living is often definitive of who one is. Consider, for example, that the first question often asked of adults in this society is, "What do you do for a living?" The answer "places" the individual in the minds of those who are listening.

In the second place, much like the modern family, the employer-employee relationship originates in a contract. The employee contracts with an employer to do a specific type of labor for a specific amount of compensation. Further, until fairly recently, the workplace was part of the domestic arena. Most people worked in their homes—on their own farms or in businesses attached to their homes. Even workers who worked away from their own homes worked in someone else's home—as a domestic servant, laborer, or apprentice. This fusion of work and domestic life was reflected in the earliest English laws touching upon employer and employee relationships which were found in the same parts of the civil contract as those laws dealing with relations between husbands and wives and parents and children. Blackstone called these the "three great relations" in private life:

> The three great relations in private life are, I. That of *master and servant;* which is founded in convenience, whereby a man is directed to call in the assistance of others, where his own skill and labor will not be sufficient to answer the cares incumbent upon him. 2. That of *husband and wife;* which is founded in nature, but modified by civil society: the one directing man to continue and multiply his species, the other prescribing the manner in which that natural impulse must be confined and regulated. 3. That of *parent and child,* which is consequential to that of marriage, being its principal end and design: and it is by virtue of this relation that infants are protected, maintained, and educated. (Blackstone [1769] 1979, 1:410]

As Blackstone himself suggested, the original meaning of "master and servant" was broad—it encompassed the relationship between any sort of employee and his or her employer. This is to say, the concept of "servant" included many "species": domestic or menial servants, apprentices, laborers, stewards, factors, and bailiffs.[1]

The law of master-servant governed the basic terms of employment in each of these cases. For example, with respect to domestic servants, Blackstone had this to say:

> The contract between them and their masters arises upon hiring. If the hiring be general without any particular time limited, the law construes it to be a hiring for a year; upon a principle of natural equity, that the servant shall serve and the master maintain him, throughout all the revolutions of the respective seasons; as well when there is work to be done, as when there is not. .... [N]o master can put away his servant, or servant leave his master, either before or at the end of his term, without a quarter's warning, unless upon reasonable cause to be allowed by a justice of the peace, but they may part by consent, or make a special bargain. (Blackstone [1769] 1979, 1:413)

The law also laid out the extent of "vicarious liability"; masters generally were vicariously responsible for what their servants did in the course of their employment.

> If a servant commit a trespass by the command or encouragement of his master, the master shall be guilty of it. .... If an innkeeper's servants rob his guests, the master is bound to restitution. .... If a servant ... by his negligence does any damage to a stranger, the master shall answer for his neglect: if a smith's servant lames a horse while he is shoeing him, an action lies against the master, not against the servant. But in these cases the damage must be done, while he is actually employed in the master's service; otherwise the servant shall answer for his own mischief. Upon this principle, by the common law, if a servant kept his master's fire negligently, so that his neighbour's house was burned down thereby, an action lay against the master, because this negligence happened in his service: otherwise, if a servant, going along the street with a torch, by negligence sets fire to a house; for there he is not in his master's immediate service, and must himself answer the damage personally. (Blackstone [1768] 1979, 1:417-419)

---

1. A *steward* is an individual appointed to represent another. Today, for example, a union steward is appointed to represent the union in each unionized workplace. In England during Blackstone's lifetime, the steward of a manor worked as a general manager of the estate. A *factor* is one who receives consignments; that is, someone who is charged with selling merchandise on behalf of another. A *bailiff* is one who is assigned to oversee or superintend another's affairs.

Here there was a significant legal parallel between master-servant and parent-child relationships. In each, the superior Person (master or parent) was responsible for the wrongs of the inferior (servant or child). So it is not surprising, that, like the parent, the master had the right to discipline or correct the servant. Any servant who presumed to strike back could receive a year in prison as well as corporal punishment (Blackstone [1769] 1979, 1:446).

The English conception of "employment law" was transplanted into the New World where it served until about the middle of the nineteenth century. For example, Tapping Reeve's (1862) treatise on the law of domestic relations in the United States followed Blackstone's format and was entitled *The Law of Baron and Femme, of Parent and Child, Guardian and Ward, Master and Servant*. Some early modifications did arise in the United States, mostly with respect to slavery. As Blackstone noted, "The law of England abhors and will not endure the existence of slavery within this nation" ([1769] 1979, 1:412). Thus, the colonists could receive no guidance from the English common law for creating slave law. The first Africans brought into the country were treated as "indentured servants"—much as white men and women who sold themselves (or were sold) into temporary servitude to pay for the costs of passage to and a stake in the colonies.[2] By 1700, as colonists became more dependent upon the labor of African slaves (especially in the South), slave laws were enacted. Without precedent in England, these laws were uniquely American.[3]

In colonial society, where labor was a scarce and valuable resource, both skilled and unskilled workers could have commanded premium wages. In many colonies, however, they were not allowed to do so: "John Winthrop reported in Massachusetts in 1638 'the scarcity of workmen had caused them to raise their wages to an excessive rate, so as a carpenter would have three shillings a day, a laborer two shillings and six pence.' As a result, commodity prices were 'sometimes double to that they cost in England.' The general court took action; they 'made an order that carpenters, masons, etc. should take but two shillings the day, and laborers but eighteen pence'" (Friedman 1985a, 81-82).

---

2. For those lucky ones who survived their period of indenture (i.e., three to five years of hard labor), servants were typically entitled to "freedom dues"—a piece of land, food, and tools or (later) money. As Richard B. Morris noted (1946), not all white indentured servants were "free-willers" (or "redemptioners" who elected to work in order to pay their way to the New World) any more than most Africans were. Many were transported against their will.

3. Slave law is discussed in Chapter 3.

This sort of regulation was justified by the colonists' belief in the economic philosophy of "mercantilism," which dictatated that government should regulate economic activity "to produce prosperity and political strength" and that the economic welfare of the community took precedence over the economic interests of individuals. Generally, "promoting the economic welfare of the community" involved subsidizing commerce and manufacturing as well as keeping wages low. "Maryland offered land to any individuals who would develop ironworks. Other colonies granted land to encourage production of potash and the construction of mills" (Ely 1992, 18-20).

The nature of the employment relationship and laws respecting work began to change with the burgeoning of industry after the Civil War. A major factor in all of this, perhaps, was simply a matter of scale: More than ever before, workers were becoming "employees." Instead of owning their own businesses or farms, workers moved into industrial occupations with the railroads and in factories and mines (Slichter 1947, 1).

The Impact of Industrialization on Work

Much has been made of the "fact" that during the nineteenth century, the United States economy operated according to principles of laissez-faire economics.[4]   Mercantilism was abandoned after the eighteenth century, and it was laissez-faire capitalism, or so the story goes, that gave birth to the modern industrial order. The philosophy of laissez-faire is typically credited to the work of Adam Smith, and especially his book *An Inquiry into the Nature and Causes of the Wealth of Nations* (1776). Laissez-faire was a radical departure from mercantilism: its principles held that public welfare is best served when law and government allow individuals and business to pursue their own interests in free competition with one another. According to the laissez-faire philosophy, when businesses are allowed to compete freely for customers, the result is lower prices and better products. In brief: free competition drives down prices and drives out businesses who produce inferior products.

---

4. Most accounts suggest this expression may have originated in a reply to a question posed to an industrialist by Colbert, French minister of finance in the late seventeenth century. When Colbert asked, "What can the government do for industry?" the answer was, *"Laissez nous faire"* (Leave us alone).

Historians have labeled laissez-faire capitalism an American myth, saying it never really existed in the United States. For one thing, the government never let business alone but continued the colonial practice of subsidizing industry. Consider the railroad industry: The Pacific Railroad Bill of 1862 gave federal lands to the Union Pacific-Central Pacific Railroads. Two years later, Congress granted lands to the Northern Pacific Railroad. Ultimately, 131 million acres of federal land were donated to the railroads, and states provided another 49 million acres. To put these figures into perspective, legal historian Kermit Hall noted that, "By 1900 the amount of land given for the purpose of subsidizing railroads was as large as the state of Texas" (1989, 191).

Like many myths, however, the idea that government let individuals sink or swim in the economic pool does contain a grain of truth. Although it is true that industry was buoyed by government largess, laissez-faire doctrines were frequently invoked to justify leaving small fry to make their own ways. For example, in 1887, when President Grover Cleveland vetoed a bill appropriating a small amount of money intended to help drought-stricken Texas farmers, he justified his action by asserting that, "Though the people support the Government, the Government should not support the people" (Hall 1989, 190).

Moreover, as the country geared up for full industrialization, labor had become anything but a scarce resource. By the end of the Civil War, in 1865, nearly 36 million people lived in the United States; that figure represented seven times the number of inhabitants counted in the census of 1800. Population growth continued and would more than double by the end of the nineteenth century—to 76 million. A great deal of this growth was owing to surges in immigration. According to census figures, during the 1880s alone, for example, close to 5 1/4 million people moved to the United States from abroad.

It is with respect to employer-employee relationships that the principles of laissez-faire economics proved especially important, for it was this philosophy that justified the doctrine of "liberty of contract." This doctrine was grounded in the contract clause of the Constitution—the clause that forbids states from passing any law "impairing the obligation of contract" (Article 1, § 10). Simply put, according to the contract clause, states were not allowed to interfere with an individual's right to enter into contractual relationships. Individuals and businesses were to be left alone so that they might freely negotiate their contracts. Of course, workers were free to refuse employment that did not pay enough or that was too risky or onerous. But, according to laissez-faire doctrines, it was not the state's place to tell workers what sorts of employment and conditions they should accept.

On the surface, this philosophy sounds appealing. Workers should be able to take whatever jobs they wish and at the best pay they can negotiate. The problem was that laissez-faire employment doctrines were grounded in the "assumption that both parties to the contract enjoyed relative equal bargaining power and should be allowed to determine freely contractual terms" of employment (Ely 1992, 90). The difficulty for the worker was exactly this assumption. In most cases, workers had very little bargaining power relative to employers.

Say that Mike is looking for work in Pennsylvania. The only jobs available involve working in the coal mines. The work is dangerous, but Mike decides to "freely contract" with the mine owner to work for very low wages. Why does Mike make such an obviously disadvantageous contract? Because he has a family to support and no money to move elsewhere. The situation that faced Mike in Pennsylvania also faced railroader Pat in Ohio and millworker (or "spinster") Ellie in Massachusetts. Each "freely contracted" with an employer to do arduous and even dangerous work for low wages. But how free was such a contract when there were no real options?[5]

Max Weber had this to say about freedom of employment contracts:

> The formal right of a worker to enter into any contract whatsoever with any employer whatsoever, does not in practice represent even the slightest freedom in the determination of his own conditions of work and does not guarantee him any influence on this process. It rather means, at least primarily, that the more powerful party in the market, i.e., normally the employer, has the possibility to set the terms, to offer the job "take it or leave it," and, given the normally more pressing economic need of the worker, to impose his terms upon him. (Weber 1978, 729-730)

Some workers attempted to equalize their bargaining position with respect to employers by forming unions (or what were then known as "combinations"). In 1794, for example, shoemakers in Philadelphia organized the Federal Society of Journeymen Cordwainers.[6] These workers demanded that master craftsmen hire only members of the

---

5. Recall the discussion of free choice versus duress in Chapter 2. Here the free choice was this: "Take this dangerous job and work for pennies a day or starve. It's your choice."

6. The term "cordwainers" makes reference to the fact that these shoemakers typically worked in cordovan leather, a fine grain leather usually made of split horsehide.

Cordwainers Society. The members of the society struck for higher wages in 1806. In response, the master craftsmen called upon Philadelphia prosecutors to arrest and prosecute the strikers for engaging in a criminal conspiracy against the liberty of contract—to wit, a conspiracy to deny individuals their right to contract to sell their labor freely—even if they did not wish to join the society.

Although law provides a transformation of resources, it can be invoked only when certain kinds of expectations have been breached. In the nineteenth-century workplace, a worker might have *expected* that his or her workplace be kept safe and that he or she be treated with respect and paid a living wage, but these expectations were no more *legally* relevant or cognizable than those of the wife who expected her husband not to strike her. Adding further insult to injury, just as the tyrannical husband or father could call upon the sovereign power to judge his children or wife incorrigible and have them punished, the employer could invoke the power of the law to prevent workers from forming combinations or unions to "level the playing field." The employer had all the power in the employment relationship. The law allowed business owners to combine their capital assets to form corporations for their mutual benefit. But workers, whose only assets were their labor, were not allowed to do the same. When owners combined their assets, the law called the result a corporation; when workers combined, they were labeled criminal conspirators (Frankfurter and Greene 1930, 1–2).

Near the middle of the nineteenth century, for a brief moment, things looked brighter. In *Commonwealth v. Hunt*, Chief Justice Lemuel Shaw of the Massachusetts Supreme Court ruled, contrary to accepted theory, that labor unions were not absolutely illegal. Shaw held that each case must be judged on its own merit in terms of the workers' motives, tactics, and intents (45 Mass. [4 Metc.] 111 [1842]). The Massachusetts decision was an influential one, and it signaled the end of using criminal conspiracy charges to fight union activity. But it was by no means a signal that the law would cease to be a weapon in the hands of businesses bent on stifling union activity.

Economic Upheaval and Legal Shenanigans

In the wild days following the Civil War, "fierce competition among maturing industries created pinched profit margins that prompted corporate managers to consolidate control over greater portions of the market" (Hall 1989, 206). This consolidation of control generally was effected through "trusts."

A trust is a legal device that allows one party to hold property for the benefit of another. A grandparent, for example, might leave her property to her young grandchildren, the property to be held "in trust" for them by a friend or a bank officer until the grandchildren reach adulthood. Business corporations took this device and made more sinister use of it. The idea was simple but powerful: Those who managed corporations realized that competition was driving down their profits and that cooperation might better serve their interests. They would agree to set prices and standards in ways that benefited them. To make this strategy work, a central board (or "interlocking directorate") would be created that would draw its members from several companies. These board members would hold stock "in trust" for stockholders, who in turn would receive "trust certificates." Ownership of trust certificates brought individuals dividends but left voting rights in the hands of the directors of the trust.

Here's how one of the first and largest trusts, Standard Oil Company, came about:

> [Corporate managers] created a board of nine trustees and persuaded all stockholders of twenty-seven competing companies to turn over their capital stock to the board and receive trust certificates in return. The trustees were now in a position to harmonize and direct the affairs of a huge aggregation of capital, for according to the Standard Oil Trust agreement, they were authorized "to hold, control, and manage the said stock and interests for the exclusive use and benefit" of all parties to the agreement. With competition thus brought under control, profits soared. (Blum et al. 1973, 427)

Within a number of industries, trusts grew to be fearsome economic entities with a great deal of power—at one point, for example, Standard Oil controlled over 90 percent of the refining capacity of the United States. They were everywhere. Although Standard Oil Company was perhaps the best known example, there was also a sugar trust, a linseed trust, a whiskey trust, and even a beef trust (created when Swift, Morris and Armour joined forces as the National Packing Company in 1902). The growth of these trusts "caused people to question the means by which such great power was accumulated, and the injurious consequences to the public of 'unfair' competition between businessmen became a major issue" (Aaron 1954, 422).[7]

---

7. Trusts were replaced by another legal device, the "holding company," by the late 1890s.

In the late nineteenth century, public unease about trusts was fueled by tumultuous economic cycles. Depressions occurred in each of the final decades of the century (1867-1868; 1873-1879; 1884-1886; 1893-1897). These were not minor dips: In 1873, for example, there were some 22,000 business failures and 500,000 unemployed workers (Martin and Gelber 1978, 477-478). In the depression of 1893-1897, "more than 18 percent of the labor force was unemployed" (Hall 1989, 200).

In response to each economic downturn, business owners sought ways to maintain their profits. One effective technique was to cut labor costs by cutting wages. Not unexpectedly, many workers resisted, but labor's attempt to do legal battle with business was constantly frustrated. No longer were unions regarded as criminal conspirators. Now, business sought protection from civil law and charged unions with being "tortfeasors." The idea was straightforward, and it developed into a powerful tactic: It is an "intentional tort" to do harm to another's property. Union strikes damage business owners' property. Ergo, unions were liable for damages (Gould 1986, 12).[8]

In a series of cases, the influential Supreme Court of Massachusetts once again took the lead. This time the court was not helpful to unions as it articulated a doctrine that allowed business to sue unions for economic harm (e.g., *Bowen v. Matheson*, 96 Mass. 499 [1867]; *Carew v. Rutherford*, 106 Mass. 499 [1867]). This series of cases culminated in 1896 when the Massachusetts court granted an injunction[9] against picketing on the theory that such conduct interfered with the freedom to contract (*Vegelahn v. Gunter*, 167 Mass. 92, 44 N.E. 1077). Without picketing, it was difficult to maintain a strike. And so, by the mid-1880s, business came more and more to rely on the use of injunctions to put down pickets. Ironically, the ultimate power to use injunctions against labor was found in a statute intended to restrain business: the Sherman Antitrust Act.

The Sherman Antitrust Act, enacted by Congress in 1890, held that "every contract, combination in the form of trust or otherwise, or

---

8. Torts as civil wrongs, as distinguished from criminal wrongs, are discussed in Chapter 4.

9. An injunction is a judicial order issued when one party to a suit persuades the court that the other party should be forced to do (or not do) something. Injunctions can be temporary or permanent.

conspiracy, in restraint of trade of commerce among the several states . . .
is hereby declared to be illegal" (26 Stat. 209 §1, 1890).[10]

Although the Sherman Act was part of civil and not criminal law, it
provided for very punitive sanctions—Section 7 held that "any person
who shall be injured in his business or property by any other persons or
corporation by reason of anything forbidden or declared to be unlawful
by this act, may sue therefor . . . and shall recover three fold the damages
by him sustained, and the costs of the suit."

The ostensible purpose of the Sherman Act was to bust trusts, but an
event in 1894 suggested the real strength of the Sherman Act was that it
could be used to bury the unions. The story actually began a year earlier
when, in the depression of 1893, a former locomotive fireman named
Eugene V. Debs organized the militant American Railway Workers. At
the time, some 3 million workers were unemployed and there had been
600 bank failures. Once again corporate managers had responded to
drops in profits by lowering wages. For a time labor acquiesced, but
recovery was slow in coming. Workers employed at the Pullman Palace
Car Company near Chicago found themselves in particularly desperate
straits. They lived in Pullman, a company town where everything was
controlled by George Mortimer Pullman.[11] Pullman workers endured
five wage cuts in one year (the final one amounting to nearly 30 percent)
but had been given no reduction in the high rents charged for company
homes. In 1894, when the Pullman Company refused an offer to arbitrate
the workers' complaints, Debs called a strike against the Pullman
Company and ultimately rallied some 60,000 railway workers,
paralyzing the railway system across some twenty-seven states and
territories.

At the behest of the railroads, President Grover Cleveland sent 2,000
troops to get the trains moving again. U. S. Attorney General Richard
Olney, a former railroad attorney, persuaded a federal court to issue an
injunction against Debs under the Sherman Act:

> You are hereby restrained, commanded, and enjoined absolutely to
> desist and refrain from in any manner interfering with, hindering or

---

10. The Sherman Antitrust Act was named for its author, John Sherman, the
senator from Ohio. Senator Sherman was the younger brother of William
Tecumseh Sherman, the famous Civil War general who succeeded Ulysses S.
Grant as commander of the U.S. Army after the Civil War.

11. George Pullman (1831-1897) began his career as a cabinetmaker. With
Ben Field he designed the first railroad car with a folding upper and lower birth.

obstructing, or stopping any of the business of any of the following named railroads. . . . As common carriers of passengers and freight between or among the states of the United States, and from in any way interfering with, hindering, obstructing, or stopping any mail trains. (*In re Debs injunction.* S. Ex. Doc. No. 7, 53rd Cong. 3d Sess. 179-189 [1894])

The union lost control of the already precarious situation when the troops arrived at the scene. Mobs of looters destroyed and stole railroad property. In early clashes, thirteen people were killed and another fifty seriously wounded. Twenty more would die before the strike was over. It required 14,000 state police and federal troops to put down the strikers. When Debs ignored the injunction, he was arrested, tried, and convicted of contempt. He was sentenced to six months in prison by a federal court.

Deb's attorney, Clarence Darrow, appealed the decision to the U.S. Supreme Court. The appeal was unsuccessful. Writing for the entire Court, Mr. Justice David Brewer held that, "the strong arm of national government may be put forth to brush away all obstructions to the freedom of interstate commerce or the transportation of the mails" (*In re Debs,* 154 U.S. 564 [1895]).

In *Debs,* the Court actually did not speak to the legitimacy of invoking the Sherman Act against union activity. However, the Supreme Court hinted that the act could be applied in this manner when it wrote that, "It must not be understood from this that we dissent from the conclusions of [the trial] court" that had found Debs guilty of violating the Sherman Act.

The Pullman strike was not the first strike to turn nasty. In 1877, a series of wage cuts by one of the nation's largest railroads, the Baltimore and Ohio, had sparked nationwide rioting that ended up destroying millions of dollars in railroad property and causing the deaths of 100 people. Nor was the Pullman strike the first (or the last) in which the federal government intervened on behalf of business. In 1877, President Rutherford B. Hayes, for example, sent 200 troops to put down a railway strike.

In 1886, there was a strike at the McCormick Harvesting Machine Company in Chicago (later known as the International Harvester Corporation). Times were tough—some 610,000 workers were unemployed and more had sustained serious wage cuts. One afternoon, as striking workers were fighting with scab laborers,[12] Chicago police fired into a crowd of strikers and spectators, killing six. That night,

---

12. The term *scab laborers* refers to workers who pass through union picket lines. Sometimes the term is also applied to nonunion workers generally.

union agitator August Spies circulated a flier, calling his fellow workers "to arms":

> Your masters sent out their bloodhounds—the police—they killed six of your brothers at McCormick's this afternoon. They killed the poor wretches, because they, like you, had the courage to disobey the supreme will of your bosses. They killed them because they dared to ask for the shortening of the hours of toil. They killed them to show you "free American citizens" that you must be satisfied and contented with whatever your bosses condescend to allow you, or you will get killed.
>
> You have for years endured the most abject humiliation; you have for years suffered immeasurable inequities; you have worked yourselves to death; you have endured the pangs of want and hunger; your children you have sacrificed to the factory lords—in short, you have been miserable and obedient slaves all these years. Why? To satisfy the insatiable greed and fill the coffers of your lazy thieving masters! When you ask him now to lessen your burden, he sends his bloodhounds out to shoot you, to kill you!
>
> If you are men, if you are the sons of your grandsires, who have shed their blood to free you, then you will rise in your might, Hercules, and destroy the hideous monster that seeks to destroy you.
>
> To arms, we call you, to arms! (David 1936, 191-192)

The next day, thousands gathered in Chicago's Haymarket Square to protest the police action. When the police arrived to break up the crowd, a bomb was thrown. The bomb killed seven police officers and wounded another fifty-nine. In response, the police fired into the crowd: The civilian toll was four dead and 200 wounded. Though there was never any proof as to who actually threw the bomb, the union received the blame for the killings.[13]

Many cities saw labor riots during the nineteenth and early twentieth centuries: Buffalo, Harrisburg, Philadelphia, Reading, Scranton, Toledo, St. Louis, Seattle and San Francisco. Even the wilds of Idaho did not escape the violence—in the mines at Coeur d'Alene, between 1892 and

---

13. Some observers have even speculated that the bomber was in the employ of the police or business owners. As one observer pointed out at the time, the bomb was "a godsend to the enemies of the labor movement. They have used it as an explosive against all the objects that the working people are bent upon accomplishing, and in defense of all the evils that capital is bent on maintaining" (David 1936, 215).

1899, there occurred what some have called a seven-year war between labor and management. Overall, the country was in a near constant state of domestic war between labor and employers; a war that was aggravated each time there was an economic downturn and business owners tried to salvage their profit margins by cutting labor costs.

What Did Labor Want?

During the 1870s and 1880s, the rhetoric of laissez-faire was invoked again and again to justify strike-breaking and union-busting. And corporate directors and business owners weren't the only "true believers" of this philosophy. Historian Richard Hofstadter observed:

> During the industrial and political conflicts of the 1870s and 1880s, the respectable opinion-making classes had given almost unqualified support to the extreme conservative position on most issues. The Protestant ministry, for instance, was "a massive almost unbroken front in its defense of the status quo." Most college professors preached the great truths of *laissez faire* and the conservative apologetics of social Darwinism, and thundered away at labor unions and social reformers. (1955, 148-149)

Industrial work in the late nineteenth and early twentieth centuries meant long hours in filthy and noisy conditions. There were no mandated "rests" except short breaks for lunch and dinner—during a twelve- to fifteen-hour workday, six days a week. Wages were low and oftentimes paid irregularly. It was not unusual for wages to be paid not in cash but in "scrip" that was redeemable only at the company store (where prices were set high enough to insure additional profits for the employer).[14] Above all, the work was dangerous. Industrial accidents were commonplace. Railroads, for example, were the sites of a tremendous amount of carnage: "between June 30, 1888, and June 30, 1889, 1972 railwaymen were killed on the job; 20,028 workers were

---

14. One of the grievances that prompted the strike at the Pullman plant involved the high prices that the company charged its workers for basic necessities. As the workers complained, "Water which Pullman buys from the city at 8 cents a thousand gallons he retails to us at 500 percent advance. . . . Gas which sells at 75 cents per thousand feet in Hyde Park, just north of us, he sells for $2.25" (Zinn 1980, 274).

injured. One worker died for every 357 employees; one in 35 was injured in this single year" (Friedman, 1985a, 479).

Railroading was perhaps an exotic industry—but it was not alone in being dangerous. Even the most mundane of industrial occupations was dangerous. Factory work was done in "cramped rooms [amid] reverberating machinery." The result was "physically a miserable experience"; "bewildering and oppressive and the work incessant and enervating. Sickness of mill fever was an almost invariable consequence of commencing work in a textile mill" (Tomlins 1988, 385). Dorothy Richardson was for a time a worker in a turn-of-the-century box factory. In that job she spent her days making elegant boxes for fancy department stores. Here's what her work involved:

> Each [box] must be given eight muslin strips, four on the box and four on its cover, two tapes, inserted with a hair-pin through awl-holes; two tissue "flies," to tuck over the bonnet soon to nestle underneath, four pieces of gay paper lace to please madame's eye when the lid is lifted; and three labels, one on the bottom, one on the top, and one bearing the name of a Fifth Avenue modiste on an escutcheon of gold and purple . . . . We worked steadily, and as the hours dragged on I began to grow dead tired. The awful noise and confusion, the terrific heat, the foul smell of glue, and the agony of breaking ankles and blistered hands seemed almost unendurable. (Richardson [1905] 1972, 69-71)

Although tedious and dull, this work hardly sounds like risky business. In fact, however, it was dangerous. Miss Richardson related what happened on her second day on the job, when she had been sent for additional "trimmings."

> During my five minutes' absence the most exciting event of the day had occurred, Adrienne . . . had just been carried away, unconscious, with two bleeding finger-stumps. In an unguarded moment the fingers had been cut off in her machine. Although their work does not allow them to stop a moment, her companions were all loud in sympathy for this misfortune, which is not rare. . . .
>
> "Did they take her away in a carriage?" Henrietta asked of Goldy Courtleigh, who had stopped a moment to rest at our table.
>
> "Well, I should say! What's the use of getting your fingers wacked off if you can't get a carriage ride out of it?" ([1905] 1972, 102)

Many business owners believed that it would be a mistake to "undermine" the competitive drive of their workers by coddling them. Thus, a carriage ride to the hospital or morgue was about the most a worker could expect in "benefits" after an injury. Workers injured on the job had to pay their own medical bills. Indeed, even when the accident was not the worker's fault, he or she would still pay the price. Although courts found that employers were liable for damages done by their servants to members of the public, in the nineteenth century the principle of vicarious responsibility stopped short of making employers liable for damages done to workers.

The common law did impose upon employers the duty to provide workers with safe workplaces, but the scope of this duty was seriously undermined by nineteenth-century judicial decisions, which crafted what Professor William Prosser called the "unholy trinity" of employer legal defenses: assumption of risk, the fellow servant rule, and the doctrine of contributory negligence (Keeton et al. 1984, 568)

The assumption of risk doctrine was the first line of defense for employers. Following from the idea of liberty of contract, the worker was seen as "an entirely free agent, under no compulsion to enter into the employment." Workers who did elect to undertake employment were therefore "expected to accept and take upon" themselves "all the usual risks of the trade . . . and to relieve the employer of any duty" to protect them.

Related to the assumption of risk doctrine was the fellow servant rule, which typically ruled that workers assumed the "risks" of having negligent coworkers. Thus, a worker whose injury resulted from the actions of a fellow servant could not hold the employer liable for injuries.

The final line of defense was the doctrine of contributory negligence. This doctrine held that any worker whose own negligence—however slight—contributed in any way to his or her injury could not obtain relief from the employer. Thus, if a worker was injured and 1 percent of the responsibility was the worker's, and 99 percent was the employer's, the worker had to bear all the costs of the injury (Keeton, et al. 1984, 568-569). Worse, injury or illness, or any reason for missing work, generally meant loss of the job; the employer simply replaced the absent worker with someone else.[15]

---

15. Because of the obvious injustices of these doctrines, toward the end of the nineteenth century and in the first years of the twentieth century courts began to carve out exceptions to these rules. For example, the fellow servant rule was modified by the "vice principal rule," which said that the employer could be held responsible for injury caused by an employee who was supervising another employee. These judicial modifications, which began to hold employers liable for their workers' injuries, were gradually superseded by the passage of workers' compensation laws in the first decades of the twentieth century. These laws were based on the idea that "the cost of the product should bear the blood of the workman" (a campaign slogan attributed to Lloyd George). As William Prosser

In retrospect, the inattention to safety measures in the workplace, the long hours, the lack of benefits, and so on, seems inhumane, but humanity is expensive. Poor working conditions and low wages were accepted by many as the price that had to be paid to make this nation a great industrial power. In the minds of many business owners, workers were not wholly Persons, but rather objects to be treated as commodities: One early business leader was quoted as saying, "I regard my employés as I do a machine, to be used to my advantage, and when they are old and of no further use I cast them in the street." This employer's perspective was seconded by a worker who testified before the U. S. Senate Committee upon the Relations Between Labor and Capital in 1885: "The employer has pretty much the same feeling toward the men that he had toward his machinery. He wants to get as much as he can out of his men at the cheapest rate. . . . That is all he cares for the man generally." A wool manufacturer "complacently observed that when workers 'get starved down to it, then they will work at just what you can afford to pay.'" Jay Gould, a prominent industrialist, noted the "axiom" that "Labor is a commodity that will in the long run be governed absolutely by the law of supply and demand" (David 1936, 7).

The "maiming or death of employees at work [was] treated as part of the social landscape—a routine, if regrettable, occurrence that was part of the price society paid for the possession and exercise of the rights and liberties, such as freedom of contract, that were the attributes of free and equal citizens" (Tomlins 1988, 421). Organized workers were loath to accept such a price, however. They wanted shorter working hours, better wages paid at regular intervals, and safer working conditions.

The Impact of Early Regulation

Any lingering doubt that the Sherman Antitrust Act could be applied to labor unions was firmly put to rest in 1908 in *Loewe v. Lawlor*, sometimes called the *Danbury Hatter's Case* (208 U.S. 274). At issue in this

---

explained it: "The human accident losses of modern industry are to be treated as a cost of production, like the breakage of tools or machinery. The financial burden is lifted from the shoulders of the employee, and placed upon the employer, who is expected to add it to his costs, and so transfer it to the consumer" (Keeton et al. 1984, 572).

case was a secondary boycott called against the suppliers and customers of the D.E. Loewe Company by the United Hatters of North America.[16] Writing for the U.S. Supreme Court, Chief Justice Melville Fuller seemed to deal a death blow to the unions.

> [The Loewe Company alleges] that defendants were members of a vast combination called The United Hatters of North America, comprising about 9,000 members and including a large number of subordinate unions, and that they were combined with some 1,400,000 others into another association known as the American Federation of Labor, . . . [and] that defendants were "engaged in a combined scheme and effort to force all manufacturers of fur hats in the United States . . . against their will . . . to organize their workmen . . . into an organization [or union]."

Having made the case that the union was a dangerous leviathan trying to do in the poor little company, the Court continued: "In our opinion, the combination is a combination 'in restraint of trade or commerce among the several States,' in the sense in which those words are used in the act, and the action can be maintained accordingly." Once again, labor had lost. And this time, labor had lost big. Pursuant to Section 7 of the Sherman Act, members of the Danbury Hatters Union were assessed treble damages. Because union members, unlike owners of a corporation, were not protected by limited liability, they were themselves held responsible for the damages, which totaled some $250,000. In order to pay the debt, the homes of 140 union members were ordered sold.[17]

---

16. An introductory text on labor law describes a secondary boycott this way: "Suppose a union has a dispute with a manufacturer; perhaps the manufacturer refuses to meet the union's demand for an increase in pay. The union strikes. The union also organizes a boycott, that is, asks the public not to buy the manufacturer's products. Both the strike and the boycott are primary activities because they are caused by a labor dispute and are aimed at the primary employer. The strike and the boycott are not successful, so the union approaches several of the primary employer's suppliers and requests that they stop selling raw materials to the primary employer. . . . [Suppose] one supplier refuses and continues to sell to the primary employer. The union then pickets the supplier. This picketing is a . . . secondary boycott" (Gold 1989, 49).

17. The case was finally settled in 1917 for slightly over $234,000. The American Federation of Labor was able to obtain $216,000 in voluntary contributions from union members, so none of the workers actually lost their homes (Gould 1986, 15).

Probably the supreme insult to unions came in the case of *United States v. E. C. Knight Company* in 1896—just a year after Debs had been jailed for contempt. The Knight Company had been charged under the Sherman Act as well, but with furthering a monopoly by selling out to the American Sugar Refining Company. Although the acquisition of the Knight Company made the American Sugar Refining Company one of the most complete monopolies in the United States, the Supreme Court saw it otherwise. The Court explained that sugar refining was not "commerce"; it was "manufacturing" and thus not subject to the restrictions contained in the Sherman Act (156 U.S. 1 [1867]). This decision demonstrated the impotency of the Sherman Act, and "literally hundreds of new [business] combinations sprung up in the next five years" (Blum et al. 1973, 428).

Another weapon used by business to dampen union activity was the "yellow dog contract." This contract was a promise extracted from a worker that, as a condition of employment, he or she would not join a union. The great appeal of the yellow dog contract to employers was not that it would allow them to sue workers who unionized. No such suit was ever reported. Rather, its value was that "the courts treated it as a property right. Consequently, efforts by a union to organize workmen who had entered into such contracts with their employer were regarded as tortious attempts to destroy his property" and thus were prohibited (Aaron 1954, 67).

Early federal and state government attempts to outlaw yellow dog contracts were found unconstitutional by the courts. As Justice John Marshall Harlan wrote for the Supreme Court in *Adair v. United States,* "The employer and the employee have equality of right and any legislation that disturbs that equality is an arbitrary interference with the liberty of contract which no government can legally justify in a free land" (208 U.S. 161 [1903]). In response to critics who argued that there was no real equality between employer and employee, the Court shrugged: "It's impossible to uphold freedom of contract and the right of property without at the same time recognizing as legitimate those inequalities of fortune that are the necessary result of the exercise of those rights" (*Coppage v. Kansas,* 236 U.S. 1 [1915]).

In the late nineteenth century, the law was working effectively to secure employers' expectations that they could hire and fire at will, and that workers could not bring collective powers to bear in their struggles for economic relief. Legally, most of the resources were on the employers' side. Even when pressure from labor stopped short of violence, it was enjoined by the courts. In 1905, for example, a federal court ruled that the mere presence of pickets was itself evidence of lawless intimidation: "There is and can be no such thing as peaceful picketing anymore than there can be chaste vulgarity, or peaceful mobbing, or lawful lynching" (*Atchison, Topeka and Sante Fe Railway v. Gee,* 1301 Fed. 582 [C.C.S.D. Iowa 1905]).

A New Century, A New Era in the Workplace

Near the turn of the century, the dynamics of the workplace began to change. In 1896, at their annual convention, the Democrats went on record against "government by injunction." They condemned the fact that the federal courts had been acting as "at once legislators, judges and executioners" (Gregory 1946, 83). Part of the change was due to the fact that big business was becoming *really big* business, and so the image of the corporation as a victim that needed protection from ruthless labor was harder to sustain. In a well-known essay, "The Working of the American Democracy," published in 1888, Charles William Eliot had shown that business had actually eclipsed government in scope. Summarizing Eliot's view, Hofstadter noted that Eliot believed "that the great corporations, as units of organization, had far outstripped the government of the states. [Eliot] remarked that a certain railroad with offices in Boston employed 18,000 persons, had gross receipts of about $40,000,000 a year, and paid its highest-salaried officers $35,000. At the same time the Commonwealth of Massachusetts employed only 6,000 persons, had gross receipts of about $7,000,000 and paid no salary higher than $6,500"(Hofstadter 1955, 231).

Alongside labor's efforts to humanize their working conditions, legislators had attempted to rein in business with respect to labor practices: "States enacted an increasing volume of protective laws. Some states forbade the blacklist. . . .[Others] outlawed the 'yellow dog' contract. . . . Other statutes made companies pay workers in cash . . . [and required companies] to pay employees weekly or fortnightly" (Friedman 1985a, 528).

Some of these laws survived—especially those regulating child labor. But many other well-meaning laws were struck down by federal courts, which ruled that such regulations were unconstitutional restrictions on liberty of contract. In *Godcharles & Company v. Wigeman* (113 Pa. 431, 6 Atl. 354 [1886]) a Pennsylvania court "threw out a statute requiring laborers to be paid at regular intervals, and in cash, as 'utterly unconstitutional and void.'" The court held that this law was an "insulting attempt to put the laborer under legislative tutelage," "degrading to his manhood," and "subversive of his rights" (quoted in Friedman 1985a, 559).

Other courts had similar responses to protective legislation. When legislators in California enacted a law requiring workers to be paid in cash at regular and frequent intervals, their courts deemed the law to be offensive: "'The working man of intelligence is treated as an imbecile. . . . He is deprived of the right to make a contract as to the time when his wages will come due.' He is not allowed to 'make an agreement with the corporation in that he will work for 60 days' and take a 'horse in payment' instead of cash. The laborer might be 'interested in the corporation, or for some reason willing to wait until the corporation could pay him'" (Friedman 1985, 560). Though, as Friedman noted, "these opinions rang false even in their day," the federal courts especially continued to invoke laissez-faire principles as justification for striking down laws aimed at protecting workers from their employers.

More Attempts to Regulate

The Sherman Antitrust Act of 1890, having proved to be an ineffective weapon when put to controlling trusts, was beefed up in 1914 by the federal Clayton Antitrust Act.[18] The Clayton Act outlawed interlocking directorates and prohibited corporations from buying into other corporations for the purpose of easing competition. This time, the authors of the legislation spoke directly to the issue of labor unions:

> Section 6: The labor of a human being is not a commodity or article of commerce. Nothing contained in the antitrust laws shall be construed to forbid the existence and operations of labor . . . operations, instituted for the purposes of mutual help . . . or to forbid or restrain individual members of such organizations from lawfully carrying out the legitimate objects thereof, nor shall such organizations or the members thereof, be held or construed to be illegal combinations in restraint of trade, under the antitrust laws.

> Section 20: [No injunction can be granted in any federal court in] any case between an employer and employees, or between employees, or between persons employed and persons seeking employment, involving, or growing out of, a dispute concerning terms of employment [absent a showing of "irreparable injury"].[19]

---

18. The Clayton Act was named after its principal author, Henry De Lamar Clayton, representative from Alabama and chair of the House Judiciary Committee.

19. "Irreparable injury" refers to injury that cannot later be remedied by money paid as compensation.

Labor leader Samuel Gompers called the Clayton Antitrust Act "labor's magna charta" and predicted it would produce "sledge hammer blows to the wrongs and injustices so long inflicted upon the workers" (1914, 971). But the long-suffering unionists were destined to be disappointed again. The U.S. Supreme Court effectively gutted the Clayton Act in *Duplex Printing Press Company v. Deering* (254 U.S. 443 [1921]). Workers had struck the Duplex Company in hopes of gaining a closed shop (i.e., a place where only union members worked). Only a few workers at the company joined the strike, and so the union decided to bring additional pressure to bear by organizing a secondary boycott. Union workers in other places who agreed to install or repair Duplex presses were threatened with the loss of their union cards. In response, Duplex sued—accusing the union of unlawful restraint of trade.

The Supreme Court said in *Duplex* that it was important to distinguish between primary and secondary boycotts. A primary boycott (that is, a strike against the workers' own employer) was lawful. But any action targeted at a broader audience was illegal: "There is nothing in the section [i.e., Section 6 of the Clayton Act] to exempt such an organization or its members from accountability where it or they depart from its normal and legitimate objects and engage in actual combination or conspiracy in restraint of trade." In an apparent attempt to finish off the unions, the Court held in another case that nothing in Section 20 of the Clayton Act legitimized "that which bears the sinister name of 'picketing'" (*American Steel Foundries v. TriCity Central Trades Council*, 257 U.S. 184 [1921]). In that case, Chief Justice William Howard Taft wrote that only a single union representative could stand at the entrance of a struck plant, "to prevent the inevitable intimidation of the presence of groups of pickets, but to allow missionaries."

Labor Relations: From the
Communal to the Civil Domain

Notwithstanding the obstacles laid down by the courts, legislators at national and state levels continued to try to bring business under control. The issue was not really sympathy for the plight of workers (although their efforts would create legal resources for workers). Of special concern to the legislators was a growing conviction that business was aggravating economic instability: When business refused to negotiate with unions, industrial conflict resulted. Congress wanted economic stability and domestic peace. Toward that end, the legislators sought to require business and labor to hammer out their differences at the bargaining table, not in the streets.

In 1932, Congress passed the Norris-LaGuardia Anti-Injunction Act. This act prohibited federal judges from issuing any restraining orders or injunctions in labor disputes. In addition, it also declared yellow dog contracts to be unenforceable in federal courts. In important respects, the Norris-LaGuardia Act was Congress's last-ditch effort to promote *real* laissez-faire capitalism: The Act required federal courts to stay out of things and to leave unions and employers to make their own deals.

The Norris-LaGuardia Act did not have the impact its authors had hoped. Although it cut off the employer's right to bring sovereign power to bear on unions, nothing in the act prohibited employers from firing or otherwise sanctioning employees who involved themselves in union activity. Moreover, management retained the right to refuse to deal with unions.

By definition, laissez-faire doctrines keep relations in the communal domain and create relationships in which participants cannot access sovereign power to remedy breaches of expectations. It did not take Congress long to realize that honest laissez-faire competition between business and labor was no real competition at all. Even without the sovereign on its side, business held too many resources relative to labor.

In 1935, Congress enacted the National Labor Relations Act, also known as the Wagner Act. In the opening section of the act, Congress conceded that "inequality of bargaining power between employees who do not possess full freedom of association or liberty of contract and employers . . . substantially burdens . . . the flow of commerce."[20] In a sense, then, the Wagner Act was a congressional confession that laissez-faire capitalism could not work, and it brought the employer-employee relation back into the civil domain.

In effect, the Norris-LaGuardia Act had given birth to a new category of Persons—unions—and the Wagner Act christened them as members of the civil domain. The Wagner Act transformed the unions' resources because it required employers to deal with labor unions, to negotiate with unions chosen by a majority of their workers, and to respect the unions' existence as members of the civil domain.

The Wagner Act was hailed as a major victory for labor—and rightly so. But it is important to take note of what the Wagner Act did not do. It

---

20. The constitutional justification for the Wagner Act was Article 1, §8, which provides that "Congress shall have Power. . . . To regulate Commerce . . . among the several states." Unlike many other federal statutes that emerged from the New Deal era, the Wagner Act survived challenges in the Supreme Court (*National Labor Relations Board v. Jones & Laughlin Steel Corporation*, 301 U.S. 1 [1937]).

did not bestow any significant rights on workers except the right to freely alienate, or give up to the union, their rights as Persons to negotiate employment contracts. Union members did not, for example, gain the right to call upon the sovereign to remedy breaches of their expectations in the workplace.

In a sense, as a result of the Wagner Act workers who joined the union were like wives in the days of coverture. Recall that a wife in coverture could not sign contracts or sue when her expectations had been breached. Instead, she could only complain to her husband. He would decide whether or not to pursue the matter and how to proceed. Similarly, if a worker had a "grievance," he or she complained to the union. If the union leadership agreed that the grievance had merit, they would take the case to the employer. Of course, it is likely that this alienation of rights did not seem to be much of a sacrifice to workers (who had not gotten very far on their own).

Recall the quotation near the beginning of this chapter describing the employer-employee relationship: "The foreman has power over his employees because he can always call on his superior to fire someone, the superior in turn can call on the police to eject him if he does not leave and the policeman can call on other police and ultimately on the army to reinforce him against resistance" (Collins 1975, 291). The legitimation of the unions changed this simple calculus: Now, if the foreman calls upon his superior to fire someone, the superior must notify the union representative of the reason why the worker is going to be fired. If the union judges the dismissal to be unjust, it will protest and possibly even call a strike.

Labor in the Post-Wagner Act Era

During World War II, the nation recovered from the economic doldrums of the Great Depression and business profits soared. For business owners, profit-making was helped along not only by wartime production orders but by patriotic no-strike clauses from unions. Wage earners, however, did not enjoy a fair share of their employers' windfall: In the textile mills of Lowell, Massachusetts, for example, workers took umbrage at the fact that while mill profits grew 600 percent between 1940 and 1946, wages grew a paltry 36 percent.

After the war, union leadership was eager to make up for lost time and the fruits of their efforts were immediately obvious: In the first six months of 1946, three million workers went on strike. During the war, the government had controlled prices and wages, but after the war all bets were off: As reconversion got underway, inflation was rampant.

Between 1946 and 1948, wholesale prices rose 50 percent and retail prices increased 30 percent. Although many factors were involved (e.g., "labor shortages, supply dislocation, depleted inventories and speculation"), labor activity supplied the most visible inflationary pressure (Tomlins 1985, 250).

When Congress moved the employer-union relationship back into the civil domain with the Wagner Act, it instituted procedures whereby unions could access sovereign power when management treated them unfairly. Apparently, Congress did not foresee that management might also need to have access to sovereign power. Postwar union activity proved otherwise and managed to stir up public sympathy for business. Ironically, many unions had begun to resort to the "take it or leave it" attitude that had formerly characterized employers' positions with respect to bargaining: "A number of unions would simply come to the bargaining table and present the area contract (the contract negotiated with most employers in the area). Where the employer was small and without economic power, the union expected no discussion or negotiation. Sometimes a union would simply throw a proposed contract on the table and tell the employer to sign it" (Gould 1986, 53).

In 1947, the relationship between employers and unions was rebalanced when the Wagner Act was amended by the Labor-Management Relations Act (also known as the Taft-Hartley Act). Among other things, the Taft-Hartley amendments *required* unions to bargain in good faith with employers (just as the Wagner Act had required employers to bargain in good faith with the unions). As such, the Taft-Hartley amendments "represented a new attitude toward unions, one which regarded them as equal or superior in power to employers, and therefore subject to the same kinds of regulations" (Aaron 1954, 71).

The Taft-Hartley amendments to the Wagner Act also spoke to union-member relations: These amendments forbade unions from coercing workers to join unions and prohibited union retaliation against workers who refused to join. This measure was the first official recognition of the fact that there might be—at least in some cases—a conflict between the interests of individual workers and union leadership. Inasmuch as the Taft Hartley Act gave workers rights against unions, it was the first step to releasing to them from coverture.

Workers' rights with respect to unions were beefed up in 1959 when Congress enacted the Labor-Management Reporting and Disclosure Act (The Landrum-Griffin Act). This act contained a "bill of rights" for workers, required unions to provide fair representation to workers for whom they bargained, and instituted formal procedures whereby workers could take legal action against unions that breached their duties.

In many states, fears that unions might take advantage of workers led to the creation of so-called right-to-work laws. In these states, workers have the right to take jobs without joining unions or paying dues. At the same time, right-to-work laws require unions to fairly represent all workers (even those who elect not to join them). Should a union discriminate against nonmember workers, they are subject to charges of "unfair labor practices."[21]

Unions made great strides in improving working conditions and wages for organized labor, but they were not a panacea for workers in the United States. Indeed, in some instances unions were more a part of the problem than a solution. Some unions, for example, vigorously supported Jim Crow laws and denied membership to African American workers. This sort of discrimination persisted well into the twentieth century. One study, published in the late 1940s, found that "discrimination against Negroes is the most important restriction on union membership. About twenty [of the approximately 190] national unions excluded Negroes by their constitutions or by their rituals. Many local unions exclude Negroes where the national do not. Some unions discriminate against Negroes by putting them in separate locals or by limiting their right to hold office" (Slichter 1947, 102).

Women too suffered discrimination at the hands of unions, even though many women had taken the lead in early organizing efforts. In their text *Women at Work* (1984), Mary Frank Fox and Sharlene Hess-Biber observed that a common union tactic was to demand equal pay for women. Although this language sounds as if it were intended to support women in the workplace, the real intent was to keep them out by not allowing employers to hire women just so they could pay them lower wages (88).

There were a number of ways that women and minorities could be excluded informally from unions. For example, trade union membership was often withheld until the individual had served a lengthy apprenticeship. Apprenticeship positions were almost nonexistent for women and minorities.

Women of color had to confront multiple biases. As a result of discrimination, the only jobs open to most African American women, for example, were in domestic service. In addition to discrimination from employers, African American women faced the prejudices of white

---

21. Twenty-one states have right-to-work laws: Alabama, Arizona, Arkansas, Florida, Georgia, Idaho, Iowa, Kansas, Louisiana, Mississippi, Nebraska, Nevada, North Carolina, North Dakota, South Carolina, South Dakota, Tennessee, Texas, Utah, Virginia, and Wyoming.

women workers who "refused to work side by side with Black women and demanded separate eating and sanitary facilities, which many small employers could not afford; in response to this demand, small businesses hired only white women. [Moreover] white customers refused to interact with Black saleswomen, secretaries, or receptionists" (Amott and Matthaei 1991, 167).

The Rise of Employment Law

Despite the exclusivity of much of organized labor, their efforts to gain higher wages and better working conditions, and their rhetoric of "workers' rights" (a legitimating formula), raised the consciousness of legislators about what workers were owed by their employers—notwithstanding their union affiliation. And so, alongside "labor law" (which deals with union-management and union-member relationships), there has grown up another section of the civil contract: employment law.

The first national entry into the field of employment law occurred in 1938 when Congress enacted the Fair Labor Standards Act (FLSA), also known as the Wages and Hours Law. The purpose of this act was to eliminate "labor conditions detrimental to the maintenance of the minimum standards of living necessary for the health, efficiency and well-being of workers." The Fair Labor Standards Act restricted the use of child labor, established a federal minimum wage and the forty-hour workweek, and required that workers be paid higher wages for "overtime."

Already the Supreme Court had legitimated a few statutes enacted by states to protect workers. But unless the work was particularly dangerous (e.g., mining) or the workers unusually vulnerable (e.g., children), such protective legislation was likely to be judged invalid. In one important case, for example, the Court ruled that it was patronizing and insulting to workers to tell them how many hours they could work each week (*Lochner v. New York*, 198 U.S. 45 [1905]).

Apparently, women (like children) could be patronized legitimately. In *Muller v. Oregon*, the Supreme Court held that it was proper for a state to limit the number of hours worked by women. Although this Court had found that protective legislation was degrading to the working*man*, such laws were no insult to working*women* for "History discloses the fact that women have always been dependent on men" for such protection (208 U.S. 412 [1908]).

Employment at Will

The employment-at-will doctrine is perhaps the last vestige of pure liberty of contract in the workplace. According to this doctrine, except for workers formally contracted for a specific period of time (including workers covered by collective bargaining agreements), the employment relationship lasts only as long as both employer and employee will it to last. Like liberty of contract, the employment-at-will doctrine treats employers and employees as equals: The employee has the right to leave any job at any time and the employer has the right to fire any worker at any time. However, the reality of the doctrine is this: For workers, employment at will means that they have no right to their jobs; for employers, employment at will means that they can hire and fire workers as they please.[22] (If a worker and an employer have a contract, the at-will doctrine has no effect and the worker can be fired only for "just cause" [e.g., incompetence, insubordination, theft, an economic downturn of the business, etc.].)

Under the doctrine of employment at will, if a factory owner (for example) believes that redheaded workers, by nature, are far superior to any others, the factory owner may elect to hire only redheaded workers. If one of these redheads dyes her hair, the employment at will doctrine allows the factory owner to terminate that worker's employment—even though she has proved herself a tremendously competent worker. If the factory is sold and the new owner has a preference for brunettes, the new owner may fire all the redheads and replace them. Employment at will held bias to be perfectly legal—not just in hiring and firing but in promotions and pay raises as well. (Of course, because workers worked "at will," they could refuse to accept a job, raise or promotion from any employer).

Well into the twentieth century, the employment-at-will doctrine was nearly sacrosanct. It was part of the common law of the nation and several states even enacted statutes that formally articulated it (California, Georgia, Kansas, Louisiana, Mississippi, Montana, North

---

22. According to Tisman (1987), the employment-at-will doctrine was first articulated by British commentator Horace Wood. In 1877 Wood published "A Treatise on the Law of Master and Servant." As Tisman explained it, Wood asserted that there was "an evidentiary presumption that a general or indefinite hiring was prima facie at will" (Tisman 1987, 20). In the United States, this principle was first used as a decision rule in the case of *Payne v. Western &Atlantic Railroad* (81 Tenn. 507 [1894]). In that case, the court held that employers did not need a reason (let alone a good reason) for hiring or firing workers.

Dakota, South Dakota). However, during the final decades of the twentieth century, lawmakers began to erode this doctrine by creating exceptions to it. Two of the most important exceptions to employment at will are tied to the ideas of *public policy* and *implied contract*.

Public Policy Exceptions

Federal law prohibits discrimination in employment decisions owing to the worker's race, color, religious beliefs, national origin, gender, age, physical handicap, or pregnancy.[23] These exceptions to the employment-at-will doctrine are justified because such discrimination is now widely viewed as contrary to important public policies. As the Supreme Court of Vermont ruled in an age discrimination case: "Discharge of an employee solely on the basis of age is a practice so contrary to our society's concern for providing equity and fairness that there is a clear and compelling public policy against it" (*Payne v. Rozendale*, 520 A.2d 586 [1986]).

In addition to these federal statutes, most states have laws that protect workers from discrimination; in many cases these state laws offer more protection to workers than do federal laws. For example, four states (Connecticut, Hawaii, Massachusetts, and Wisconsin) and the District of Columbia prohibit workplace discrimination on the basis of workers' sexual orientation. Four states (Arizona, California, Florida, and Louisiana) and the District of Columbia prohibit workplace discrimination on the basis of workers' political activity. Michigan forbids discrimination against a worker solely because of his or her weight or height, and Minnesota protects recipients of public welfare from job discrimination.

---

23. The most significant federal laws in this respect are the following: the Equal Pay Act of 1963 (requires men and women to be paid equally); Title VII of the Civil Rights Act of 1964 (prohibits discrimination on the basis of race, color, religion, national origin, or gender); the Age Discrimination in Employment Act of 1967 and the Older Workers Benefit Protection Act (1990) (protect workers over forty years of age); the Pregnancy Discrimination Act (1978) (prohibits discrimination against pregnant women); and the Americans with Disabilities Act of 1990 (prohibits discrimination against workers with physical handicaps).

Implied Contract Exceptions

In the absence of a contract, employment at will is supposed to last only as long as both parties will it. An exception to this rule discovered by the courts occurs when the nature of the employment relationship is such that an expectation arises on the part of the employee that the employment relationship is an enduring one. Say, for example, that an employee survives his or her probationary period and receives good work evaluations, pay raises, and even promotions from an employer. These things are likely to create an expectation in the mind of the worker that his or her employment contract will not be terminated without "just cause." Because of this expectation, the worker invests himself or herself in the job and may forgo other employment opportunities. Under these circumstances, the courts have held that, in effect, an employment contract—albeit an implicit or quasi-contract—is created. Therefore, the employer cannot fire the worker at will but only for just cause (*Kelly v. Georgia Pacific Corporation*, 46 Ohio St.3d 134 [1984]).

Protection in the Workplace: Physical Harm and Beyond

Laws in the late nineteenth and early twentieth centuries went some distance toward protecting workers from hazardous working conditions, but the effect left much to be desired. Overall, state-by-state legislation was piecemeal and gaps left many workers unprotected. In 1970, Congress took steps to fill those gaps when it enacted the Occupational Safety and Health Act. This act applies to virtually all employers and places a general duty upon them to create workplaces free from "recognized hazards" of the sort that are likely to cause physical harm.

More recently, courts and legislators have enlarged the protection offered workers to allow them remedy for injuries that may not be physical. The most visible of these sorts of protections offer recourse for verbal harassment. This protection has its roots in Title VII of the Civil Rights Act, which, as mentioned above, forbids employers to discriminate against workers on the basis of their race, color, religion, sex or national origin.

Title VII does not prohibit harassment in and of itself; rather, it targets specific types of harassment. Simply put, when harassment is differentially applied to workers on the basis of their membership in a protected group, harassment is treated as illegal discrimination.

The link between harassment and discrimination was not immediately obvious. Because harassment tends to be verbal, and often does not result in *obvious* physical or even economic injury, the courts were loath to recognize it as causing a civil injury. For example, a federal court in one case refused to find that the use of racial epithets in the workplace was affecting the workers' workplace environment or "condition of employment."

> The language of the factory and the language of the street have long included words such as "Greaser," "Dago," and "Spick," and "Kike" and "Chink" as well as "Nigger." In the past three years we have even adopted as part of our national folk lore a character who is prejudiced and biased against all persons other than of his own neighborhood, religion and nationality. We refer to such people now as "Archie Bunkers." The Archie Bunkers of this world, within limitations, still may assert their biased view. We have not yet reached the point where we have taken from individuals their right to be prejudiced, so long as such prejudice did not evidence itself in discrimination. This Court will secure plaintiff against discrimination; no court can secure him against prejudice. (*Howard v. National Cash Register*, 388 F. Supp. 603 (S.D. Ohio 1975)

In distinguishing between discriminatory *conduct* and prejudicial *speech*, this judge likely had in mind the well-entrenched legal principle that mere words cannot create harm (or, at least, legally cognizable harm). The leading case here was an English court's ruling that "mental pain or anxiety the law cannot value and does not pretend to redress, when the unlawful act complained of causes that alone" (*Lynch v. Knight*, 9 H.L.C. 577 [1861]). In the United States, traditionally it has been held that speech alone "however violent, threatening or insulting . . . afforded no grounds for redress" (Keeton et al. 1984, 60). Exceptions are made, but only when the conduct is "outrageous," that is, "exceeding all bounds usually tolerated by decent society, of a nature which is especially calculated to cause, and does cause, mental distress of a very serious kind" (Keeton et al. 1984, 61). The kicker is that generally the behavior must be of the sort that a "reasonable man" finds outrageous. The law is not set up to redress perceived harms to unduly sensitive individuals who are victims of mere insults.

Fairly quickly, however, many courts lowered their thresholds for judging behavior to be outrageous when it came to race. Most courts now find that verbal insults directed toward Persons because of their race are *prima facie*—or on the face of it—outrageous and have a significant impact on the conditions of employment by creating a hostile work environment. A leading case in this respect was *Alcorn v. Anbro Enbro Engineering* (2 Cal. 3d 493, 468 P.2d 216 [1970]. After several racial epithets were directed at Alcorn by his supervisor, Alcorn was fired.

Alcorn brought suit. The California Supreme Court ruled that Alcorn could recover damages for "emotional distress" given the "extreme and outrageous intentional invasions" of his "mental and emotional tranquillity." The court emphasized that Alcorn's employer owed him more than it owed a stranger in this respect because employees have a "particular susceptibility to emotional distress"—after all, employees are essentially a captive audience. Later, the Washington State Supreme Court came to the same conclusion in a similar case: "Racial epithets which were once part of common usage may not now be looked upon as 'mere insulting language'" (*Contreras v. Crown Zellerbach Inc.*, 88 Wash. 2d 735, 565 P.2d 1173 [1977]). A federal court in New York State likewise declared that police and fire supervisors acted improperly by not taking action when coworkers referred to an African American as an "Uncle Tom" and displayed posters proclaiming "The KKK is still alive" (*United States v. City of Buffalo*, 457 F. Supp. 612 [W.D. N.Y. 1978]).

Courts have proved less willing to provide relief to workers who claim that sexual harassment has a negative impact on their work life. Judges frequently explain this reluctance by noting their suspicion that sexual harassment claims might reflect nothing more than the courtship process gone awry. For example, in the first sexual harassment case to be heard in a federal court, the plaintiff complained that she had been fired when she refused to have a sexual affair with her supervisor. Was this sort of harassment a form of sex discrimination? According to the court, it wasn't. Instead, the court claimed that "this is a controversy underpinned by the subtleties of an inharmonious personal relationship. Regardless of how inexcusable the conduct of the plaintiff's supervisor might have been, it does not evidence an arbitrary barrier to continued employment based on plaintiff's sex" (*Barnes v. Train*, 13 Fair Employment Practice Cases, 123 [D. D.C. 1974]). A year later, in *Corne v. Bausch and Lomb, Inc.*, another federal court ruled that sexual harassment was not sexual discrimination but a matter of "personal proclivity, peculiarity or mannerism" of the offending supervisor. The court concluded that nothing in federal law prohibited verbal or physical sexual advances when these have "no relation to the nature of employment" (390 F. Supp. 161 [D.C. Ariz. 1975]).

In *Tompkins v. Public Service Electric and Gas Company*, a woman claimed that her supervisor had gotten her demoted after she refused to go along with his suggestion that she have sex with him. After her demotion, she received poor job evaluations and was fired. Was this illegal discrimination? Again, the court said no. This was not sex discrimination in the first place because it could have happened to a man. The court also said it was loath to rule that such behaviors constituted sexual discrimination because such a precedent might put a damper on normal sexual relationships: "If the plaintiff's view were to prevail, no superior could prudently attempt to open a social dialogue with a subordinate of either sex. An invitation to dinner could become an invitation to a federal lawsuit if a once harmonious relationship turned sour at some later time" (422 F. Supp. 553 [D.C. N. J. 1976]).

Things began to change in 1976 when a federal court in the District of Columbia heard the case of *Williams v. Saxbe* (413 F. Supp. 654 D. D.C. [1976]). The facts of this case were similar to those heard in earlier cases: The plaintiff claimed that she had been fired when she refused the sexual advances of her supervisor. This time, the court judged the supervisor's conduct to be sexual discrimination; it was no defense (said the court) to assert that if a behavior could be targeted at men as well as women it wasn't discriminatory. Either way, sexual harassment was sexual discrimination. As the U.S. Supreme Court would later rule, "Without question, when a supervisor sexually harasses a subordinate because of a subordinate's sex, that supervisor discriminates on the basis of sex" (*Meritor Savings Bank v. Vinson*, 477 U.S. 57 [1986]).

In 1980, the Equal Employment Opportunity Commission issued a series of guidelines defining sexual harassment:

> Harassment on the basis of sex is a violation of Sec 703 of Title VII. Unwelcome sexual advances, requests for sexual favors, and other verbal or physical conduct of a sexual nature constitute sexual harassment when
>
> (1) submission to such conduct is made explicitly or implicitly a term or condition of an individual's employment,
>
> (2) submission to or rejection of such conduct by an individual is used as the basis for employment decisions affecting such individual, or
>
> (3) such conduct has the purpose or effect of unreasonably interfering with an individual's work performance or creating an intimidating, hostile or offensive working environment. (EEOC, *Guidelines for Discrimination Because of Sex*, 29 C.F. R. §1604.11)

Scholars have focused primarily on two forms of sexual harassment: The most blatant form was labeled by law professor Catharine A. MacKinnon as "quid pro quo" harassment (1979). As one court explained, "The classic example of sexual harassment is the situation in which sexual demands are made by a supervisor to a subordinate in exchange for career advantages or under threat of adverse job consequences" (*Downes v. F.A.A.*, 775 F.2d 288 [1985]). The second form involves behavior that creates a hostile work environment. In these cases, the plaintiff may not actually suffer tangible consequences (e.g., loss of job, pay raise, or promotion) but is forced to endure an antagonistic environment (*Meritor Savings Bank v. Vinson*, 477 U.S. 57 [1986]).

For years it proved difficult to win a hostile environment case when the behavior complained of was sexual harassment (as opposed to racial harassment). Although even fairly mild racial harassment is prima facie outrageous, in sexual harassment cases the plaintiff must prove that the unwelcomed sexual behavior constituted an "unreasonable interference" within the workplace. (Apparently, then, not all unwelcomed sexual harassment is unreasonable.) The court's objective is to determine whether a reasonable person would find the behavior complained of offensive to the degree that it would interfere with his or her ability to do the job. As one court explained it, "in the absence of conduct which would interfere with that hypothetical reasonable individual's work performance and affect seriously the psychological well-being of that reasonable person under like circumstances, a plaintiff will not prevail on . . . charges . . . of a hostile . . . work environment regardless of whether the plaintiff was actually offended by the defendant's conduct" (*Rabidue v. Osceola Refining Company*, 805 F.2d 611 [6th Cir. 1986]).

The reasonable person standard is frequently invoked in the Anglo-American legal tradition. This is the standard by which, for example, conduct is judged in tort cases. Let's say that I unintentionally drive into a parked car. My reason for doing so, I claim, was to avoid hitting a small child who had darted out into the street. In deciding whether I am liable for the damages, the jury will consider whether a reasonable person in the same situation would have acted as I did. The reasonable person standard is also invoked in cases in which one person who has injured another claims to have acted in self-defense. If someone accosts me on the street and I shoot him, I will claim that I shot him in self-defense. The validity of my claim will be judged on the basis of whether a reasonable person would have felt himself or herself to be in mortal danger under the same circumstances.

The reasonable person standard has several virtues. Principal among them is the fact that it holds people accountable to meeting an external standard of behavior the community judges is reasonable. Thus, when someone injures someone else, it is not enough for her to say that she did her best to avoid the harm. The law requires that she act with a reasonable amount of care and diligence. If her best is not up to that standard, then she (not her victim) should bear the costs.

The chief defect of the reasonable person standard is that what is reasonable to one group of Persons may not be reasonable to another group. To some extent, the law already recognizes this: Children are generally not held to the same standard of reasonableness as adults; individuals with special abilities or lack thereof are held to higher or lower standards. That the courts may not have gone far enough to recognize such differences, however, was demonstrated in *Rabidue v. Osceola Refining Company.* In that case, Vivienne Rabidue claimed that she had been subjected to a hostile work environment.

> For seven years plaintiff [Rabidue] worked at Osceola as the sole woman in a salaried management position. In common work areas plaintiff and other female employees were exposed daily to displays of nude or partially clad women belonging to a number of male employees at Osceola. One poster, which remained on the wall for eight years, showed a prone woman who had a golfball on her breasts with a man standing over her, golf club in hand, yelling "Fore." . . .
>
> In addition, Computer Division Supervisor Doug Henry regularly spewed anti-female obscenity. Henry routinely referred to women as "whores," "cunt," "pussy," and "tits." (*Rabidue v. Osceola Refining Company*, 805 F.2d 611 [6th Cir. 1986])

Again, racial epithets seemed to have more power than sexual ones; or at least judges tended to find them more offensive. In this case, plaintiff Rabidue did not prevail. According to the court, the offensive language, "although annoying," was not "so startling as to have affected seriously the psyches of the plaintiff or other female employees." Likewise, the sexually oriented posters, said the court, "had a de minimis effect on the plaintiff's work environment when considered in the context of a society that condones and publicly features and commercially exploits open displays of written and pictorial erotica at the newsstands, on prime-time television, at the cinema and in other public places."

In essence, the majority of the court held that Rabidue was being unduly sensitive and that the behaviors to which she objected were not unreasonable interferences in her worklife. One member of the three-judge panel that decided this case, Judge Keith, dissented from the majority. In his analysis, Judge Keith pinpointed what many have come to see as a weakness of the "reasonable person" standard as it is currently used: It ignores the degree to which there may be a "wide divergence between most women's views of appropriate sexual conduct and those of men." Furthermore, "Unless the outlook of the reasonable woman is adopted, the defendants as well as the courts are permitted to sustain ingrained notions of reasonable behaviors fashioned by the offenders, in this case, men."

What Judge Keith was suggesting, in a sense, was that applying male notions of "reasonable behavior" in sexual harassment cases is tantamount to applying the standards of demolition derby drivers in auto negligence cases. Keith's view, however, remains the minority one.[24]

The Impact of Law on the
Workplace in the Late Twentieth Century

Mary is an executive administrative assistant. Her boss invites her to dinner to discuss her job performance. Over dinner, Mr. Boss says that Mary would certainly rise faster in the company if she had more education. He suggests that her education should begin by accompanying him to a three-day convention. Of course, to save money, they should share a room.

John is an African-American police officer. Many of his coworkers are displeased that he has joined the force. They paint a white cross on his locker door and hang a poster in the bathroom that says: "Join the KKK."

Josephine is an attorney who works for a large law firm. Her mentor advises her that the leaders of the firm, although very pleased with her work, are on the verge of denying her application to become a partner because she is "too aggressive" and "not feminine enough" in her appearance. The mentor suggests that Josephine visit a beauty spa to be "made over" and then just hope for the best.

Peter is a fifty-nine-year-old factory worker. His employers, seeking to save money in bad economic times, decide to lay off some workers. They choose to lay off the most senior workers—thus saving the higher salaries and more frequent claims made on health benefits.

---

24. As this book was going to press, things seemed about to change. For the first time since its 1986 decision in *Meritor*, the Supreme Court had agreed to hear a case involving sexual harassment. In *Harris v. Forklift Systems, Inc.* a lower court had held that Harris, the plaintiff, could not prevail in her allegations of sexual harassment, because the harassing behavior, although clearly disruptive, had not caused her actual psychological harm. In its ruling in *Harris*, the Supreme Court reaffirmed that sexual harassment is a violation of federal laws that forbid discrimination in employment. Further, writing for the unanimous Court, Justice Sandra Day O'Connor declared that a "hostile" and "abusive" workplace does not have to cause severe mental or psychological harm in order to constitute harassment: "So long as the environment would reasonably be perceived, and is perceived, as hostile or abusive, there is no need for it also to be psychologically injurious" (92-1168).

Twenty years ago, none of the workers mentioned in these scenarios would have had any recourse. No doubt they would have felt wronged, but the injuries they suffered were extralegal ones. Today, they probably have redressible grievances.

This brief look at the impact of law on working life in the United States, while overlooking many of the complexities of labor and employment law, has made clear that changes in law have brought about significant changes in the relationship between employer and employee (between employees). In retrospect, many of the changes have been as well as similar in effect to changes in marriage and family law. The nineteenth-century theory of employment law was that the employer-employee relationship was based on a contract—a contract that, in essence, placed the relationship outside of the civil domain. The worker alienated his or her rights to the employer during the period of employment, just as the wife alienated her rights to her husband. The law would not interfere with the employment relationship except to maintain the superiority of the employer.

The legal doctrines that applied to the employment relationship—liberty of contract and employment at will, for example—mostly worked to the benefit of the employer inasmuch as they kept the relationship in the civil domain where might makes right.

In the twentieth century, the Wagner Act gave workers access to the power of the collective; subsequent acts and employment laws gave workers direct access to sovereign powers. These legal developments brought the employment relationship back into the civil domain—where workers have gained more and more access to sovereign powers to transform their resources in disputes with their employers. At present, we seem to be in flux; new norms are emerging with respect to what is and what is not appropriate workplace behavior between men and women, for example, and the limits of these new norms are being occasionally tested in lawsuits.

9

Final Words

It is impossible to deny (at least with any conviction) the fact that law has come to play an increasingly obvious and important role in our society (*cf.* Taylor 1986). Lawrence Friedman summed it up this way:

> One of the most striking aspects of American society, to natives and foreigners alike, is the way law and the legal system seem to dominate public life—and, apparently, much private life as well. There [is] . . . an extraordinary number of lawyers in this country; and they seem to be multiplying like rabbits. In general, law appears to be growing at an alarming pace. If an outside observer took the daily newspaper as a rough guide to events and situations that worry or excite Americans, he would conclude that sports and law are the two main topics of interest in the country. And law has even been creeping into the sports pages, with stories about contracts for basketball players, court struggles over team franchises, and so on. Any reader can make the test for herself, picking up at random any copy of any newspaper, any day. Almost every domestic story has a legal angle. Almost every story mentions a judge, a court, a rule, the police, the state legislature, Congress, some administrative agency, somebody suing somebody— *some* aspect of law, some rule or regulation. (Friedman 1985b, 3)

Yet, as I noted at the beginning of this book, concern with law has come to be less and less important in the field of sociology. What we needed as sociologists, I thought, was a vocabulary that allowed us to use law in our investigations of and discussions about society and a framework that would help us direct and conduct those investigations and discussions. Providing that vocabulary and that framework has been the goal of this book.

I have suggested that we look at law as if it were a contract writ large; a contract that specifies, with more or less precision, expectations about minimally acceptable behaviors. Most of the time the power of law stays in the background. But when expectations about how people ought to behave are breached, and this breach creates an injury, then the injured Persons can call upon the resources of the sovereign or sovereign entity to attempt to remedy that breach.

Not all people have equal access to the law. Using the civil contract perspective, I distinguished between Persons, who are parties to the contract, and Nonpersons, who are not. The most important difference is that Persons have access to the potential transformation of resources that the law provides and Nonpersons do not.

In addition, I distinguished between two social domains: civil and communal. Within the civil domain reside Persons and some of their relationships; in communal domains one finds Nonpersons and their relationships as well as some relationships between Persons. Within the civil domain, Persons whose expectations are breached may use the law to effect a remedy; within the civil domain, then, right makes might.

In contrast, law does not intrude into the communal domain and cannot be invoked there. Social relations in the communal domain involve different dynamics than social relations in the civil domain. Simply put: ultimately, in the civil domain right makes might; in the communal domain, the opposite holds and might makes right.

Parenthetically, I must acknowledge that sociologists have long been known for their reliance on dichotomies. This is so even though most of us depreciate the value of simple dualisms and insist (as I have insisted) that *our concepts* be regarded as laying at opposite ends of a continuum. A question that begs to be asked is this: What does the Person/Nonperson distinction contribute to our understanding of social relationships over and above the contributions of such typologies as haves/have nots, insiders/outsiders, capitalists/proletariat, and the like? Relatedly, what does the distinction between the civil and communal domains add to a landscape already cluttered with mechanical/organic, Gemeinschaft/Gesellschaft, folk/urban, center/periphery and even simple/complex?

Unlike my predecessors (Durkheim, Tönnies, Redfield, Shils, and others), who claimed at least implicitly that their typologies explained vast portions of social life, I would argue that the distinctions I have made in and of themselves probably add little to our understanding of social things.[1] After all, at this point in time it

---

1. I do suggest, however, that the Person/Nonperson distinction has an advantage over economic-based typologies insofar as it allows us to make better sense of the social position of individuals who, economically, may be apparently advantaged but who have no real power to affect their relationships.

hardly comes as a surprise to discover that some people are better off than others or that contemporary society is different from society as it used to be. Although in many places throughout this book I have offered a number of hypotheses about the nature of law and its relation to society, I have not attempted to create a theory of society (nor a theory of law). Instead, I have sought a way to augment our capacity for using "law as data" in sociology. Thus, the distinctions between Person and Nonperson and between civil and communal domains are valuable only insofar as they succeed in strengthening our ability to use law to understand social phenomena. I have mapped out a way to treat law as a resource that is accessible to some ("Persons") and not others ("Nonpersons"), and available in some relations (those in the "civil domain") and not others (those in the "communal domain").

* * * * * * * *

Although the discussion of the family and workplace presented in previous chapters hardly does justice to the law/society nexus, I hope that it begins to demonstrate the value of explicitly using law in sociological analyses. Law—both as a constraint and a resource—has had, and continues to have, important effects on life in this society. A full understanding of social institutions and processes in modern society is predicated on having an understanding of law's role in these institutions and processes. It is not true in all societies, but increasingly, life in Western society has become law-related as the civil domain has expanded.

If the family, long isolated from law's influence, has been brought into the civil domain, how can we doubt the impact of law in other, traditionally more public spheres of social life? Contrary to Justice Warren Burger's assessment, an increase in litigation need not mean a decline in the efficacy of communal institutions—which, within their respective spheres, may continue to function effectively. An increase in litigation might simply mean an increase in access to legal institutions or in the efficacy of these institutions. Professor Friedman offers this example:

> Take the upsurge of claims by Native Americans—claims for ancient fishing rights, for autonomy, or *re*claims for whole empires stolen or wheedled away in the nineteenth century. The militance may be new, but the grievances are not, and there is now a sense (or a hope) that

---

Thus, class-based (and certainly caste-based) theories are hard pressed to explain the relative powerlessness of women and children.

> courts may set things right. . . . In 1850 or 1900, Indian claims would be
> laughed out of court—not that the grounds were illogical, or the cause
> unjust, but simply . . . because. (1980, 671)

As Friedman has argued, "The real architect of judicial review is
American society, the world outside the court door" (1980, 671). Still, it
cannot be ignored that once that courtroom door was opened to Native
Americans, African Americans, women, and children (even to Little
League baseball players dissatisfied with their places in the batting
order or more likely, to girls displeased by having no place in the
batting order), things changed.

An increase in litigation over certain issues almost certainly
signals, as well, a renegotiation of social expectations and the civil
contract. Forty years ago, job discrimination was a "fact" of life: A
woman would likely be denied membership in the carpenters' union; an
African American did not have much of a chance of finding employment
as a university professor. Of course, discrimination persists, but the
dynamics have changed: those who face discrimination today have
some new avenues of recourse. Recourse to law is not a sufficient remedy,
but—absent revolution—it does seem to be a necessary one.

Changes in law both reflect changing attitudes *and* require
changing behaviors. Hence, the fact that individuals who have been
discriminated against have legal recourse will make even the most
ruthless employer think twice before harassing an employee.

The impact of law is not limited, of course, to family and work
relationships. The civil domain in the United States today includes
expectations about behavior on the football field, in the physician's
office, and in virtually every other arena of social life. At one time, for
example, the courts would not allow the law to be invoked to punish
intentional injuries incurred in professional sports; the games of
professional athletes were played only in the fields of the civil
domain. Today the law handles these things differently and allows
legal rememdy to victims of unfairly earned injuries. As one judge put
it, it is no longer the case that "the only possible remedy for the person
who has been the victim of an unlawful blow is retaliation" (*Hackbart
v. Cincinnati Bengals,* 601 F.2d 516 [10th Cir.] [1979]). At one time, a
patient with questions about surgical procedures and medications could
be told, "Just you never mind; it will be okay," or "Here is your
prescription, just take it." Today, the law of informed consent gives

patients the power to ask questions and physicians the duty to answer them.[2]

Some have argued, and will continue to argue, that the increasing intrusion of law into society (i.e., the increasing size of the civil domain) is changing the character of society for the worse—that the intrusion of law takes away too much from interpersonal relationships. Legal scholar Grant Gilmore summed up this attitude at the conclusion of his book *The Ages of American Law*: "The worse the society, the more law there will be. In Hell there will be nothing but law, and due process will be meticulously observed" (1977, 111).

"Evidence" in support of Gilmore's point can be found quite easily. Pick up a newspaper and there is apt to be a story similar to this one, which ran under the headline "Harassment Claims Vex Teachers; Teachers Back Away From Teens":

> . . . Some teachers are apprehensive of working closely with students for fear their motives might be misinterpreted.
>
> "In the old days you could, in a motherly way, put an arm around a child if he was disturbed or upset for some reason. Now you can't do that," said Christine Nowak, who retired this year from teaching English in Buffalo, N.Y.
>
> "It does affect the teaching atmosphere in the room. It's not as warm," she said.
>
> Nowak and other teachers attending the National Education Association convention in San Francisco agreed that children should be more aware of and willing to report cases of sexual harassment involving teachers because such incidents do occur.
>
> . . . Still, some teachers said they fear being falsely accused by angry, street-savvy kids. (*Spokesman Review*, 4 July 1993, A8)

---

2. Many, of course, suggest that the litigiousness of disappointed patients and the fear of lawsuits on the part of physicians has had a terribly negative impact on the physician-patient relationship. Yet giving patients more legal power has had important positive effects. For example, since physicians have been required (by the legal doctrine of informed consent) to explain the various alternatives to women with breast cancer (radiation, lumpectomy, partial mastectomy, or radical mastectomy), the rate of radical mastectomies has decreased without having a negative impact on women's survival rates. In any case, if there was a malpractice litigation explosion (and some doubt this), it appears to be over. It seems, then, that doctors and patients have survived this renegotiation of mutual expectations.

Seventy years ago, similar sorts of concerns were voiced by those who said that family members should not be allowed to sue or take other legal action against one another. Children would be suing their parents for sending them to bed too early!

Yet, as others pointed out, the possibility of fraudulent claims and charges is no reason to deny remedy to the true victims: the children who are physically and emotionally abused by their parents; the husbands or wives who live in mortal fear of their spouses. Children who are sexually or otherwise abused by their teachers deserve legal protection.

My sense of the meaning of law's intrusion into society, or the broadening of the civil domain, is different from Professor Gilmore's: It's not "The *worse* the society, the more law there will be," but "the more *diverse* the society, the more law there will be." I suspect that the more pluralistic a civil domain is, the more law there will be. Litigation will increase periodically as Persons within society attempt to define the limits of norms and expectations about how each ought to be treated.

In any case, whether positive or negative, the law has an important impact on life in society and this impact is something we need to take into account in our studies of social life. The message, I hope, is a persuasive one. Sociologists need to attend to law, and the idea of the civil contract provides means to do so.

Bibliography

Aaron, Benjamin. 1954. Changing legal concepts and industrial conflict. In *Industrial Conflict*, edited by Arthur Kornhouser, Robert Dubin, and Arthur Ross, 418-427. New York: McGraw Hill.

Ackerman, Bruce A. 1984. *Reconstructing American Law*. Cambridge, MA: Harvard University Press.

————. 1977. The structure of Subchapter C: An anthropological comment. *Yale Law Review* 87:436-446.

Amott, Teresa L., and Julie A. Matthaei. 1991. *Race, Gender, and Work: A Multicultural Economic History of Women in the United States*. Boston, MA: South End Press.

Atiyah, P. S. 1981. *Promises, Morals, and Law*. New York: Oxford University Press.

————. 1979. *The Rise and Fall of Freedom of Contract*. Oxford: Clarendon Press.

Aubert, Vilhelm. 1989. *Continuity and Development in Law and Society*. Universitetsforlaget, AS: Norwegian University Press.

————. 1969. Introduction to case studies of law in Western societies. In *Law in Culture and Society*, edited by Laura Nader, 273-281. Chicago: Aldine.

Barber, Bernard. 1983. *The Logic and Limits of Trust*. New Brunswick, NJ: Rutgers University Press.

Barkun, Michael. 1968. *Law Without Sanctions: Order in Primitive Societies and the World Community*. New Haven, CT: Yale University Press.

Basch, Norma. 1982. *In the Eyes of the Law: Marriage and Property in Nineteenth-Century New York*. Ithaca, NY: Cornell University Press.

Baxi, Upendra. 1974. Durkheim and legal evolution. *Law & Society Review* 8:645-651.

Beal, R. 1984. "Can I sue mommy?" An analysis of a woman's tort liability for prenatal injuries to her child born alive. *San Diego Law Review* 21:325-370.

Beccaria, Cesare. 1764 [1963]. *On Crimes and Punishments*. New York: Bobbs-Merrill.

Beck, J. M. 1930. *May It Please the Court*. New York: Macmillan.

Berger, Peter, and Thomas Luckmann. 1967. *The Social Construction of Reality*. New York: Anchor Books.

Berman, Harold. 1983. *Law and Revolution: The Formation of the Western Legal Tradition*. Cambridge, MA: Harvard University Press.

Black, Donald J. 1989. *Sociological Justice*. New York: Oxford University Press.

————. 1976. *The Behavior of Law*. New York: Academic Press.

Blackstone, William. 1769 [1979]. *Commentaries on the Laws of England*, 4 vols. Chicago: University of Chicago Press.

Blau, Peter M. 1955. *The Dynamics of Bureaucracy.* Chicago: University of Chicago Press.

Blauner, Robert. 1964. *Alienation and Freedom: The Factory Worker and His Industry.* Chicago: The University of Chicago Press.

Blum, John M., Edmund S. Morgan, Willis L. Rose, Arthur M. Schlesinger, Jr., Kenneth M. Stamp, and C. Vann Woodward. 1973. *The National Experience: A History of the United States since 1865,* 3rd ed. New York: Harcourt, Brace Jovanovich, Inc.

Blumberg, Abraham. 1967. The practice of law as a confidence game. *Law & Society Review.* 1:15-39.

Bodde, Derk. 1981. *Essays on Chinese Civilization.* Princeton, NJ: Princeton University Press.

Bohannan, Paul. 1971. *Law and Warfare.* Austin: University of Texas Press.

———. 1968. Law and legal systems. In *International Encyclopedia of the Social Sciences,* edited by D. Sills, 9:73-77. New York: Macmillan and Free Press.

Bredemeier, Harry C. 1962. Law as an integrative mechanism. In *Law and Sociology,* edited by William M. Evan, 73-90. New York: Free Press of Glencoe.

Brown, E. L. 1938. *Lawyers and the Promotion of Justice.* New York: Russell Sage Foundation.

Burger, Warren. 1982. Isn't there a better way? Annual report on the state of the judiciary. *American Bar Association Journal* 68:274-277.

Cardozo, Benjamin N. 1924. *The Growth of Law.* New Haven, CT: Yale University Press.

Carroll, Chas. 1900. *The Negro a Beast.* Reprinted in 1991. Salem, NH: Ayer Co.

Chambers, Julius L. 1990. Black Americans and the courts: Has the law been turned back permanently? In *The State of Black America 1990,* edited by Janet DeWart, 9-25. New York: National Urban League.

Chapin, B. 1983. *Criminal Justice in Colonial America, 1606-1660.* Athens, GA: University of Georgia Press.

Chestnut, Mary Boykin. 1980. *A Diary from Dixie.* Edited by Ben Ames Williams. Cambridge, MA: Harvard University Press.

Chevillard, Nicole, and Sébastien Leconte. 1986. Slavery and women. In *Women's Work, Men's Property: The Origins of Gender and Class,* edited by Stephanie Coontz and Peta Henderson, 156-169. New York: Verso.

Clark, Homer H., Jr. 1968. *Law of Domestic Relations.* St. Paul, MN: West Publishing Company.

Cochran, Thomas C. 1953. *Railroad Leaders, 1845-1890: The Business Mind in Action.* Cambridge, MA: Harvard University Press.

Colby, James F., ed. 1915. The earliest Anglo-Saxon Laws. In *A Sketch of English Legal History,* by Frederic W. Maitland and Francis C. Montague, 193-199. New York: G. P. Putnam's Sons.

Coleman, James S. 1990. *Foundations of Social Theory.* Cambridge, MA: Harvard University Press.

———. 1988. Social capital in the creation of human capital. *American Journal of Sociology* 94[Supplement]:95-120.

————. 1986. Social theory, social research, and a theory of action. *American Journal of Sociology* 91:1309-1335.

————. 1974. *Power and the Structure of Society.* New York: W. W. Norton.

Collins, Randall. 1975. *Conflict Sociology.* New York: Academic Press.

Commager, Henry Steele. 1968. *Documents of American History,* 8th ed. New York: Appleton-Century-Crofts.

Cooley, Thomas M. 1880. *A Treatise on the Law of Torts Which Arise Independent of Contract.* Chicago: Callaghan and Company.

Coontz, Stephanie. 1988. *The Social Origins of Private Life: A History of American Families, 1600-1900.* New York: Verso.

Cott, Nancy. 1977. *The Bonds of Womanhood: "Women's Sphere" in New England, 1780-1835.* New Haven, CT: Yale University Press.

————. 1976. Eighteenth-century family and social life revealed in Massachusetts divorce records. *Journal of Social History* 10:20-43.

Craig, Albert M., William A. Graham, Donald Kagan, Steven Ozment, and Frank M. Turner. 1986. *The Heritage of World Civilizations,* Vol. 2, *Since 1500.* New York: Macmillan.

Dalzell, John. 1942 [1979]. Duress by economic pressure. In *The Economics of Contract Law,* edited by Anthony T. Kronman and Richard A. Posner, 67-71. Boston: Little, Brown & Co.

David, Henry. 1936. *The History of the Haymarket Affair.* New York: Russell & Russell

Davis, F. James. 1962. The sociological study of law. In *Society and the Law,* F. James Davis et al., 3-37. New York: Free Press.

Davis, James F. 1991. *Who Is Black? One Nation's Definition.* University Park: The Pennsylvania State University Press.

Davis, Samuel M., and Mortimer D. Schwartz. 1987. *Children's Rights and the Law.* Lexington, MA: Lexington Books.

Dawson, John P. 1947. Economic duress—an essay in perspective. *Michigan Law Review* 45:253-290.

D'Emilio, J. and E. B. Freeman. 1988. *Intimate Matters: A History of Sexuality in America.* New York: Harper and Row.

Diamond, A. S. 1971. *Primitive Law Past and Present.* London: Methuen.

Douglas, Mary. 1986. *How Institutions Think.* Syracuse, NY: Syracuse University Press.

Duby, Georges. 1988. Private power, public power. In *A History of Private Life.,* Vol. 2, *Revelations of the Medieval World,* edited by Philippe Ariès and Georges Duby, 3-31. Cambridge, MA: Belknap Press of Harvard University Press.

Duff, Johnelle, and George G. Truitt. 1991. *The Spousal Equivalent Handbook.* Houston, TX: Sunny Beach.

Durkheim, Emile. 1904 [1983]. Review of E. Kulischer's "Untersuchungen über das primitive Strafrecht," *L'Anée Sociologique* 8:460-463. Reprinted in *Durkheim and the Law,* edited by Steven Lukes and Andrew Scull, 154-156. London: Basil Blackwell.

————. 1901 [1978]. Two laws of penal evolution. In *Emile Durkheim on Institutional Analysis,* edited and translated by Mark Traugott, 153-180. Chicago: University of Chicago Press.

————. 1938. *The Rules of Sociological Method.* Glencoe, IL: The Free Press.

————. 1933. *The Division of Labor in Society.* New York: Free Press.

Ely, James W., Jr. 1992. *The Guardian of Every Other Right: A Constitutional History of Property Rights.* New York: Oxford University Press.

Empey, LaMar T. and Mark C. Stafford 1991. *American Delinquency,* 3d ed. Belmont, CA: Wadsworth.

Faludi, Susan. 1991. *Backlash: The Undeclared War Against American Women.* New York: Crown Books.

Faris, E. 1934. Emile Durkheim on the division of labour in society. *American Journal of Sociology* 40:376-377.

Favre, David S., and Murray Loring. 1983. *Animal Law.* Westport, CT: Quorum Books.

Feeley, Malcolm F. 1976. The concept of laws in social science: A critique and notes on an expanded view. *Law & Society Review* 10:497-523.

Fitzhugh, George. 1854. *Sociology for the South: Or, the Failure of Free Society.* New York: Burt Franklin.

Flaherty, David. 1978. Law and enforcement of morals in early America. In *American Law and the Constitutional Order,* edited by Lawrence M. Friedman and Harry N. Scheiber, 53-68. Cambridge, MA: Harvard University Press.

Fotiades, John M. 1989. *You're the Judge! How to Understand Sports, Torts and Courts.* Worchester, MA: Edgeworth and North Books.

Foucault, Michel. 1979. *Discipline and Punish: The Birth of the Prison.* New York: Vantage.

Fox, Mary Frank, and Sharlene Hess-Biber. 1984. *Women at Work.* Palo Alto, CA: Mayfield Publishing Company.

Frankfurter, Felix, and Nathan Greene. 1930. *The Labor Injunction.* New York: Macmillan.

Franklin, J. H. 1956. History of racial segregation in the United States. *Annals* 304:1-9.

Freed, Doris J. and Timothy B. Walker. 1986. Family law in the fifty states: An overview. *Family Law Quarterly.* 20:439-587.

Friedman, Lawrence M. 1985a. *A History of American Law,* 2d ed. New York: Simon & Schuster.

————. 1985b. *Total Justice: What Americans Want from the Legal System and Why.* Boston: Beacon Press.

————. 1984. Rights of passage: Divorce law in historical perspective. *Oregon Law Review* 63:649-669.

————. 1980. The six million dollar man: Litigation and rights consciousness in modern America. *Maryland Law Review* 39:661-677.

Fuller, Lon L., and Melvin A. Eisenberg. 1981. *Basic Contract Law,* 4th ed. St. Paul, MN: West Publishing Company.

Galanter, Marc. 1983. Reading the landscape of disputes: What we know (and think we know) about our allegedly contentious and litigious society. *UCLA Law Review* 31:4-71.

Geertz, Clifford. 1983. *Local Knowledge*. New York: Basic Books.

Gervais, Karen Grandstrand. 1986. *Redefining Death*. New Haven, CT: Yale University Press.

Gilkes, Cheryl Townsend. 1985. "Together and in harness": Women's traditions in the Sanctified Church. *Signs* 10:678-699.

Gilmore, Grant. 1977. *The Ages of American Law*. New Haven, CT: Yale University Press.

————. 1974. *The Death of Contract*. Columbus: Ohio University Press.

Glendon, Mary A. 1989. *The Transformation of Family Law: State, Law and Family in the United States and Western Europe*. Chicago: University of Chicago Press.

Goffman, Erving. 1961. *Asylums: Essays on the Social Situation of Mental Patients and Other Inmates*. Garden City, NY: Doubleday Anchor.

Gold, Michael Evan. 1989. *An Introduction to Labor Law*. Ithaca, NY: Cornell University Press.

Gompers, Samuel. 1914. The charter of industrial freedom: Labor provisions of the Clayton anti-trust law. *Federationist* 21:971.

Gordon, Colin, ed. 1980. *Power/Knowledge: Selected Interviews and Other Writings, 1972-1977, by Michael Foucault*. New York: Pantheon Books.

Gordon, Robert M. 1984. Critical legal histories. *Stanford Law Review* 36:57-125.

Gordon, W. M. 1988. Property and succession rights. In *The Legal Relevance of Gender*, edited by Sheila McLean and Noreen Burrows, 61-79. Atlantic Highlands, NJ: Humanities Press International.

Gould, William B. IV. 1986. *A Primer on Labor Law*, 2d ed. Cambridge, MA: MIT Press.

Grace, Clive, and Philip Wilkinson. 1978. *Sociological Inquiry and Legal Phenomena*. New York: St. Martin's Press.

Grant, Walter M., John LeCornu, John A. Pickens, Dean H. Rivkin and C. Roger Vinson. 1970. The collateral consequences of a criminal conviction. *Vanderbilt Law Review* 23:929-1241.

Green, Stuart P. 1988. Private challenges to prosecutorial inaction: A model declaratory judgment statute. *Yale Law Journal* 97:488-507.

Green, Thomas A. 1985. *Verdict According to Conscience: Perspectives on the English Criminal Trial, 1200-1800*. Chicago: University of Chicago Press.

Gregory, Charles O. 1946. *Labor and the Law*. New York: Norton.

Gregory, Jeanne. 1987. *Sex, Race and the Law: Legislating for Equality*. Beverly Hills, CA: Sage.

Grossberg, Michael. 1985. *Governing the Hearth: Law and Family in Nineteenth Century America*. Chapel Hill: University of North Carolina Press.

————. 1983. Who gets the child? Custody, guardianship, and the rise of a judicial patriarchy in nineteenth-century America." *Feminist Studies* 9:235-260.

Gulliver, Philip H. 1969a. Introduction to case studies of law in non-Western societies. In *Law in Culture and Society*, edited by Laura Nader, 11-23. Chicago: Aldine.

———. 1969b. Dispute settlements without courts: The Ndendeuli of Southern Tanzania. In *Law in Culture and Society*, edited by Laura Nader, 24-68. Chicago: Aldine.

Gwaltney, John Langston. 1980. *Drylongso: A Self-Portrait of Black America*. New York: Random House.

Haley, John O. 1982. Sheathing the sword of justice in Japan: An essay on law without sanctions. *Journal of Japanese Studies* 8:265-281.

———. 1978. The myth of the reluctant litigant. *Journal of Japanese Studies* 4:359-390.

Hall, Kermit L. 1989. *The Magic Mirror: Law in American History*. New York: Oxford University Press.

Hane, Mikiso. 1982. *Peasants, Rebels, & Outcastes: The Underside of Modern Japan*. New York: Pantheon Books.

Hart, H.L.A. 1961. *The Concept of Law*. Oxford: Oxford University Press.

Haskins, George L. 1960. *Law and Authority in Early Massachusetts: A Study in Tradition and Design*. New York: Macmillan.

Hast, Adele. 1969. The legal status of the Negro in Virginia, 1705-1765. *Journal of Negro History* 56:217-229.

Herzog, Don. 1989. *Happy Slaves, A Critique of Consent Theory*. Chicago: University of Chicago Press.

Higginbotham, A. Leon, Jr. 1978. *In the Matter of Color: Race and the American Legal Process: The Colonial Period*. New York: Oxford University Press.

Hirschman, Albert O. 1970. *Exit, Voice and Loyalty*. Cambridge, MA: Harvard University Press.

Hobbes, Thomas. 1651 [1962]. *Leviathan, Or the Matter, Forme, and Power of Commonwealth Ecclesiastical and Civill*. Edited by Michael Oakeshott. New York: Collier Books.

Hoebel, E. Adamson. 1954. *The Law of Primitive Man*. Cambridge, MA: Harvard University Press.

Hofstadter, Richard. 1955. *The Age of Reform*. New York: Vintage.

Hohfeld, Wesley Newcomb. 1923. *Fundamental Legal Conceptions as Applied in Judicial Reasoning*. New Haven, CT: Yale University Press.

Holmes, Oliver Wendell. 1963. *The Common Law*. Edited by Mark DeWolfe Howe. Cambridge, MA: Harvard University Press.

———. 1921. *Collected Legal Papers*. New York: Harcourt, Brace.

———. 1897. The path of the law. *Harvard Law Review* 10:457-478.

Hume, David. 1748 [1965]. Of the original contract. In *Hume's Ethical Writings*, edited by Alasdair MacIntyre, 255-273. New York: Collier Macmillan.

Ingram, Martin. 1987. *Church Courts, Sex and Marriage in England, 1570-1640*. New York: Cambridge University Press.

James, Simon, and Chantal Stebbings. 1987. *A Dictionary of Legal Quotations*. New York: Macmillan.

Kalven, Harry, Jr. 1965. *The Negro and the First Amendment.* Columbus: Ohio State University Press.

Katz, Stanley N. 1977. The politics of law in colonial America: Controversies over chancery courts and equity law in the eighteenth century. *Perspectives in American History* 5:257-284.

Kawashima Takeyoski. 1973. Dispute settlement in Japan. In *The Social Organization of Law,* edited by Donald Black and Maureen Mileski, 59-74. New York: Seminar Press.

Keeton, W. Page, Dan B. Dobbs, Robert E. Keeton, and David G. Owen. 1984. *Prosser and Keeton on the Law of Torts.* St. Paul, MN: West Publishing Company.

Kennedy, Stetson. 1959. *Jim Crow Guide to the USA.* London: Lawrence and Wishart.

Kerber, Linda K. 1986. *Women of the Republic: Intellect and Ideology in Revolutionary America.* New York: W. W. Norton.

Kidder, Robert L., and John A. Hostetler. 1990. Managing ideologies: Harmony as ideology in Amish and Japanese Societies. *Law & Society Review* 24:895-922.

Kirp, David L., Mark G. Yudof, and Marlene Strong Franks. 1986. *Gender Justice.* Chicago: University of Chicago Press.

Kluger, Richard. 1975. *Simple Justice.* New York: Vintage Books.

Kronman, Anthony T., and Richard A. Posner. 1979. *The Economics of Contract Law.* New York: Little, Brown & Co.

Kuhn, Thomas S. 1970. *The Structure of Scientific Revolutions,* 2d ed. Chicago: University of Chicago Press.

Kurland, Philip B. 1970. *Politics, the Constitution, and the Warren Court.* Chicago: University of Chicago Press.

Kurland, Philip B., and Ralph Lerner. 1987. *The Founders' Constitution,* 5 vols. Chicago: University of Chicago Press.

The Laws Respecting Women, 1777. [1974]. London: J. Johnson Edition. Reprinted, Dobbs Ferry, NY: Oceana Publications.

Levine, Donald N. 1985. *The Flight From Ambiguity: Essays in Social and Cultural Theory.* Chicago: University of Chicago Press.

Lieberman, Jethro K. 1981. *The Litigious Society.* New York: Basic Books.

Linn, Brian J., and Lesly A. Bowers. 1978. The historical fallacies behind legal prohibitions of marriages involving mentally retarded persons—the eternal child grows up. *Gonzaga Law Review* 13:625-690.

Locke, John. 1678 [1963]. *Two Treatises of Government.* Edited by Peter Laslett. Cambridge: Cambridge University Press.

Lofgren, Charles H. 1987. *The Plessy Case: A Legal Historical Interpretation.* New York: Oxford University Press.

Long, Joseph R. 1905. *A Treatise on the Law of Domestic Relations.* St. Paul, MN: Keefe-Davidson.

Macaulay, Stewart. 1963. Non-contractual relations in business: A preliminary study. *American Sociological Review* 28:55-67.

MacKinnon, Catharine A. 1979. *Sexual Harassment of Working Women: A Case of Sex Discrimination.* New Haven, CT: Yale University Press.

Maine, Henry S. 1861 [1986]. *Ancient Law: Its Connection with the Early History of Society and Its Relation to Modern Ideas.* New York: Dorset Press.

Martin, Michael, and Leonard Gelber. 1978. *The Dictionary of American History.* New York: Dorset Press.

May, Geoffrey. 1929. *Marriage Laws and Decisions in the United States.* New York: Russell Sage Foundation.

McAdam, Doug, John D. McCarthy, and Mayer N. Zald. 1988. Social movements, in *Handbook of Sociology,* edited by Neil Smelser, 695-737. Beverly Hills, CA: Sage.

McIntyre, Lisa J. 1994. American family law: Issues and antecedents. *Marriage and Family Review* (forthcoming).

———. 1989. A sociological perspective on bankruptcy. *Indiana Law Journal* 65:123-139.

———. 1987. *The Public Defender: The Practice of Law in the Shadows of Repute.* Chicago: University of Chicago Press.

Meier, Robert F. 1987. Deviance and differentiation. Presented for a conference on Theoretical Integration in the Study of Deviance and Crime. State University of New York at Albany.

———. 1981. Norms and the study of deviance: A proposed research strategy. *Deviant Behavior: An Interdisciplinary Journal* 3:1-25.

Menefee, S. P. 1981. *Wives for Sale: An Ethnographic Study of British Popular Divorce.* New York: St. Martin's Press.

Mill, John Stuart. 1869 [1912]. The subjection of women. In *On Liberty, Representative Government, The Subjection of Women: Three Essays,* edited by Millicent Garrett Fawcett, 427-548. London: Oxford University Press.

Mohr, Richard D. 1988. *Gays/Justice: A Study of Ethics, Society, and Law.* New York: Columbia University Press.

Morris, Richard B. 1946. *Government and Labor in Early America.* New York: Columbia University Press.

Nader, Laura, and Harry F. Todd Jr. 1978. *The Disputing Process—Law in Ten Societies.* New York: Columbia University Press.

Nelson, Robert L. 1988. Ideology, scholarship, and sociolegal change: Lessons from Galanter and the "litigation crisis." *Law & Society Review* 21:677-693.

Nelson, William E. 1975. *Americanization of the Common Law: The Impact of Legal Change on Massachusetts Society, 1760-1830.* Cambridge, MA: Harvard University Press.

Newman, Horatio Hackett. 1932. *Evolution, Genetics, and Eugenics.* 3d ed. Chicago: University of Chicago Press.

Nicolas, Barry. 1962. *An Introduction to Roman Law.* Oxford: Clarendon.

Noonan, John. 1984. The root and branch of *Roe v. Wade. Nebraska Law Review* 63:668-679.

Norton, Mary B. (1984) The evolution of white women's experience in early America. *The American Historical Review* 89:593-619.

Oakes, James. 1990. *Slavery and Freedom.* New York: Vintage Books.

Park, R. E. 1950. *Race and Culture.* Glencoe, IL: The Free Press.

Parker, Richard. 1974. A definition of privacy. *Rutger's Law Review* 27:275-296.

Patterson, Orlando. 1982. *Slavery and Social Death, A Comparative Study.* Cambridge, MA: Harvard University Press.

Payne, A. T. 1977/1978. The law and the problem parent: Custody and parental rights of homosexual, mentally retarded, mentally ill, and incarcerated parents. *Journal of Family Law* 16:797-818.

Peirce, Dorothy S. 1988. *BRI v. Leonard:* The role of the courts in preserving family integrity. *New England Law Review* 23:185-219.

Pleck, Elizabeth. 1987. *Domestic Tyranny: The Making of Social Policy Against Family Violence from Colonial Times to the Present.* New York: Oxford.

Pollock, Frederick, and Frederic William Maitland. 1898. *The History of English Law: Before the Time of Edward I,* 2d ed. 2 vols. Cambridge: Cambridge University Press.

Pound, Roscoe. 1940. The economic interpretation and the law of torts. *Harvard Law Review* 53:365-385.

———. 1930. *Criminal Justice in America.* New York: Da Capo.

———. 1910. Law in books and law in action. *American Law Review* 44:12-36.

———. 1908. Common law and legislation. *Harvard Law Review* 22:383-407.

Prosser, William L. 1960. Privacy. *California Law Review* 48:383-423.

Purcell, Edward A., Jr. 1973. *The Crisis of Democratic Theory: Scientific Naturalism and the Problem of Value.* Lexington: University Press of Kentucky.

Quinney, Richard. 1972 [1978]. The ideology of law: Notes for a radical alternative to legal oppression. *Issues in Criminology* 7:1-35. Reprinted in *The Sociology of Law: A Conflict Perspective,* edited by Charles E. Reasons and Robert M. Rich, 39-71. Toronto: Butterworths.

Rawls, John. 1971. *A Theory of Justice.* Cambridge, MA: Harvard University Press.

Redfield, Robert. 1964 [1967]. Primitive law. *University of Cincinnati Law Review.* 33:1-22. Reprinted in *Law and Warfare: Studies in the Anthropology of Conflict,* edited by Paul Bohannan. Austin: University of Texas Press.

Reeve, Tapping. 1862. *The Law of Baron and Femme,* 3d ed. Albany, NY: William Gould.

Reiner, Robert. 1984. Crime, law and deviance: The Durkheim legacy. In *Durkheim and Modern Sociology,* edited by Steve Fenton, 175-201. Cambridge: Cambridge University Press.

Rembar, Charles. (1980). *The Law of the Land.* New York: Simon and Schuster.

Reuschemeyer, D. 1973. *Lawyers and Their Society.* Cambridge, MA: Harvard University Press.

Rhode, D. L. 1989. *Justice and Gender.* Cambridge, MA: Harvard University Press.

Richardson, Dorothy. 1905 [1972]. *The Long Day: The Story of a New York Working Girl.* Reprinted in *Women at Work,* edited by William O'Neill, 3-303. New York: New York Times Press.

Richardson, J. 1912. *Supplement to the Messages and Papers of the Presidents Covering the Administration of W. H. Taft.* New York: Bureau of National Literature.

Ringer, Benjamin. 1983. *We the People and Others: Duality and America's Treatment of its Racial Minorities*. New York: Tavistock Publications.

Rivera, Rhonda. 1985. Queer law: Sexual orientation in the mid-1980s, part one. *University of Dayton Law Review* 10:459-540.

Rodman, Hyman, Susan H. Lewis, and Saralyn B. Griffith. 1984. *The Sexual Rights of Adolescents*. New York: Columbia University Press.

Rosenblum, Victor G. 1971. A place for social science along the judiciary's constitutional law frontier. *Northwestern University Law Review* 66:455-470.

Ross, Edward A. 1901. *Social Control*. New York: Macmillan.

Rousseau, Jean Jacques. 1762 [1954]. *The Social Contract*. Chicago: Regnery Gateway, Inc.

Russett, Cynthia Eagle. 1989. *Sexual Science: The Victorian Construction of Womanhood*. Cambridge, MA: Harvard University Press.

Sachs, Albie, and Joan Hoff Wilson. 1979. *Sexism and the Law: A Study of Male Beliefs and Legal Bias in Britain and the United States*. New York: The Free Press.

Salmon, M. 1986. *Women and the Law of Property in Early America*. Chapel Hill: University of North Carolina Press.

Schaber, Gordon, and Claude Rohwer. 1984. *Contracts*. St. Paul, MN: West Publishing Company.

Schlegel, John H. 1979. American legal realism and empirical social science: From the Yale experience. *Buffalo Law Review* 28:459-586.

Scotch, Richard K. 1984. *From Good Will to Civil Rights: Transforming Federal Disability Policy*. Philadelphia, PA: Temple University Press.

Schwartz, Gary T. 1981. Tort law and the economy in nineteenth-century America: A reinterpretation. *Yale Law Journal* 90:1717-1775.

Schwartz, Mildred A. 1978. Human rights in war and peace: The case of the Japanese in Canada and the U.S. panel on human rights: The problems of minorities from an international and domestic perspective. *International Studies Association Annual Meeting*, Washington D.C., February 23.

Schwartz, Richard D., and James C. Miller. 1964. Legal evolution and societal complexity. *American Journal of Sociology* 70:159-169.

Scruton, Roger. 1982. *A Dictionary of Political Thought*. New York: Harper and Row.

Seabury, Samuel. 1861. *American Slavery Distinguished from the Slavery of English Theorists, and Justified by the Law of Nature*. New York: Mason Brothers.

Selznick, Philip. 1968. The sociology of law. In *International Encyclopedia of the Social Sciences*, edited by David Sills, 9:50-59. New York: Macmillan and Free Press.

———. 1959. The sociology of law. In *Sociology Today*, edited by R. K. Merton and L. S. Cottrell, 115-127. New York: Basic Books.

Shapiro, Susan. 1987. The social control of impersonal trust. *American Journal of Sociology* 93:623-658.

Shils, Edward. 1966 [1970]. Privacy: Its constitution and vicissitudes. *Law and Contemporary Problems*, 31. Reprinted in *Selected Essays by Edward*

Shils, Student Edition, 73-98. Chicago: Center for Organization Studies, Department of Sociology, The University of Chicago.

Short, James F. 1990. Hazards, risks, and enterprise: Approaches to science, law, and social policy. *Law & Society Review* 24:179-198.

Simmel, Georg. 1978. *The Philosophy of Money.* London: Routledge and Kegan Paul.

———. 1955. Conflict. In *Conflict and the Web of Group-Affiliations,* 111-124. New York: Free Press.

———. 1950. Superordination and subordination. In *The Sociology of George Simmel,* edited and translated by Kurt H. Wolff, 181-304. New York: Free Press.

Simon, Rita J., and James P. Lynch. 1989. The sociology of law: Where we have been and where we might be going. *Law & Society* Review 23:825-847.

Singer, Peter. 1975. *Animal Liberation: A New Ethics for Our Treatment of Animals.* New York: Avon Books.

Slichter, Sumner. 1947. *The Challenge of Industrial Relations.* Ithaca, NY: Cornell University Press.

Smart, Carol. 1989. *Feminism and the Power of Law.* New York: Routledge.

Smart, Carol and Selma Sevenhuijsen (eds.). 1989. *Child Custody and the Politics of Gender.* New York: Routledge

Smelser, Neil J. 1963. *A Theory of Collective Behavior.* New York: The Free Press of Glencoe.

Smith, Adam. 1776 [1970] *An Inquiry into the Nature and Causes of the Wealth of Nations.* Middlesex, England: Penquin Books.

Spitzer, Steven. 1975. Punishment and social organization: A study of Durkheim's theory. *Law & Society Review* 9:613-637.

Stannard, Una. 1977. *Mrs. Man.* San Francisco: Germain Books.

Stinchcombe, Arthur L. 1968. *Constructing Social Theories.* New York: Harcourt, Brace and World, Inc.

Stone, Christopher. 1987. *Earth and Other Ethics.* New York: Harper and Row.

———. 1974. *Should Trees Have Standing? Toward Legal Rights for Natural Objects.* Los Altos, CA: William Kaufman.

Stone, Lawrence. 1977. *The Family, Sex and Marriage in England, 1500-1800.* New York: Harper and Row.

Stowe, Harriet Beecher. 1965. *Uncle Tom's Cabin; or, Life Among the Lowly.* New York: Harper and Row.

Stroud, George M. 1856. *A Sketch of the Laws Relating to Slavery in the Several States of the United States of America,* 2d ed. Philadelphia: Henry Longstreth.

Sudnow, David. 1965. Normal crimes: Sociological features of the penal code in the public defender's office. *Social Problems* 12:255-277.

Sullivan, Teresa, Elizabeth Warren, and Jay Westbrook. 1989. *As We Forgive Our Debtors.* New York: Oxford University Press.

Sumner, William G. 1906. *Folkways: A Study of the Sociological Importance of Usages, Manners, Customs, Mores, and Morals.* Boston: Ginn and Company.

Tallman, Irving, and Louis N. Gray. 1990. Choices, decisions and problem solving. *Annual Review of Sociology* 16:405-433.

Taylor, Charles. 1986. Foucault on freedom and truth. In *Foucault: A Critical Reader.* Edited by David Couzens Hoy, 69-102. New York: Basil Blackwell.

tenBroek, Jacobus. 1964. *Family Law and the Poor.* Westport, CT: Greenwood.

Thompson, Judith Jarvis. 1986. Privacy. In *Rights, Restitution, and Risk,* 117-134. Cambridge, MA: Harvard University Press.

Tiffany, Walter C. 1921. *Handbook on the Law of Personal and Domestic Relations,* 3rd ed. St. Paul, MN: West Publishing Company.

Tisman, Russell G. 1987. How to prevent employee suits for unjust dismissal. *National Law Journal* May 11, page 20.

Tocqueville, Alexis de. 1845. *Democracy in America.* New York: Vintage Books.

Tomlins, Christopher L. 1988. A mysterious power: Industrial accidents and the legal construction of employment relations in Massachusetts, 1800-1850. *Law and History Review* 6:375-438.

———. 1985. *The State and the Unions: Labor Relations, Law and the Organized Labor Movement, 1880-1960.* Cambridge, MA: Cambridge University Press.

Trattner, Walter I. 1974. *From Poor Law to Welfare State: A History of Social Welfare in America.* New York: The Free Press.

Trosino, James. 1993. American Wedding: Same-Sex Marriage and the Miscegenation Analogy. *Boston University Law Review* 79:93-120.

Tushnet, Mark. 1977. Perspectives on the development of American law: A critical review of Friedman's *A History of American Law. Wisconsin Law Review* 1977:81-109.

———. 1975. The American law of slavery, 1810-1860: A study of the persistence of legal autonomy. *Law & Society Review* 10:119-184.

Vago, Steven. 1988. *Law and Society.* Englewood Cliffs, NJ: Prentice Hall.

Voegeli, V. Jacque. 1967. *Free But Not Equal: The Midwest and the Negro During the Civil War.* Chicago: University of Chicago Press.

Vogel, Ursula. 1988. "Under permanent guardianship": Women's condition under modern civil law. In *The Political Interests of Gender,* edited by Kathleen B. Jones and Anna Go Jónasdóttir, 135-159. Newbury Park, CA: Sage.

Vrba, Rudolf, and Alan Bestic. 1964. *I Cannot Forgive.* London: The Byron Press.

Wacks, Raymond. 1989. *Personal Information: Privacy and the Law.* Oxford: Clarendon Press.

Waldon, Jeremy. 1988. When justice replaces affection: The need for rights. *Harvard Journal of Law and Public Policy* 11:625-647.

Walter, Herbert E. 1913 [1932]. *Genetics.* New York: Macmillan. Excerpted in *Evolution, Genetics and Eugenics,* edited by H. H. Newman, 521-531. Chicago: University of Chicago Press.

Wardle, Lynn D., Christopher L. Blakesley, and Jacqueline Y. Parker. 1988. *Contemporary Family Law: Principles, Policy and Practice.* 4 vols. Deerfield, IL: Callaghan.

Warren, Samuel D., and Louis D. Brandeis. 1890. The right to privacy. *Harvard Law Review* 4:193-220

Weber, Max. 1978. *Economy and Society.* Berkeley, CA: University of California Press.

————. 1946. *From Max Weber: Essays in Sociology.* Edited by H. Girth and C. W. Mills. New York: Oxford University Press.

Weitzman, Lenore. 1985. *The Divorce Revolution.* New York: Free Press.

Wheeler, G. R., and C. L. Wheeler. 1980. Reflections on legal representation of the economically disadvantaged: Beyond assembly line justice. *Crime and Delinquency* 26:319-332.

White, G. Edward. 1985. *Tort Law in America: An Intellectual History.* New York: Oxford University Press.

White, James Boyd. 1985. *The Legal Imagination,* abridged ed. Chicago: University of Chicago Press.

Wice, Paul B. 1983. Private criminal defense: Reassessing an endangered species. In *The Defense Counsel,* edited by W. F. McDonald, 39-64. Beverly Hills, CA: Sage.

Williams, Raymond. 1983. *Keywords: A Vocabulary of Culture and Society,* rev. ed. New York: Oxford University Press.

Winch, Peter. 1963. *The Idea of Social Science and Its Relation to Philosophy.* London: Routledge and Kegan Paul.

Wood, F. G. (1968). *Black Scare: The Racist Response to Emancipation and Reconstruction.* Berkeley: University of California Press.

Woodward, C. Vann. 1966. *The Strange Career of Jim Crow,* 2d ed. Oxford: Oxford University Press.

Yoshiyuki, Noda. 1976. *Introduction to Japanese Law.* Tokyo: University of Tokyo Press.

Zainaldin, J. S. 1979. The emergence of a modern American family law: Child custody, adoption, and the courts, 1796-1851. *Northwestern University Law Review* 73:1038-1089.

Zellinke, Georg. 1878. *Die socialetische Bedeutung von Recht, Unrecht und Strafe.* Vienna: Alfred Holder.

Zimring, Franklin, and Gordon Hawkins. 1971. The legal threat as an instrument of social change. *Journal of Social Issues* 27:33-48.

Zinn, Howard. 1980. *A People's History of the United States.* New York: Harper.

Cases Cited

Adair v. United States, 208 U.S. 161 (1903)

Alcorn v. Anbro Enbro Engineering, 2 Cal. 3d 493, 468 P.2d 216 (1970)

American Steel Foundaries v. TriCity Central Trades Council, 257 U.S. 184 (1921)

Atchison, Topeka and Santa Fe Railway v. Gee, 1301 Fed. 582 (C.C.S.D. Iowa [1905])

Barnes v. Train, 13 Fair Employment Practice Cases, 123 [D. D.C. (1974)]

Betts v. Brady, 316 U.S. 255 (1942)

Boddie v. Connecticut, 401 U.S. 371 (1971)

Bowen v. Matheson, 96 Mass. 499 (1867)

Boyd v. United States, 116 U.S. 616 (1886)

Bradwell v. State of Illinois, 83 U.S. (16 Wall.) 130 (1873)

Brown v. Board of Education of Topeka, Kansas, 347 U.S. 483 (1954)

Buck v. Bell, 274 U.S. 200 (1927)

Carew v. Rutherford, 106 Mass. 499 (1867)

Carey v. Population Services International, 431 U.S. 678 (1977)

Chapman v. Phoenix National Bank, 85 N.Y. 437 (1881)

Civil Rights Cases, 109 U.S. 3 (1883)

Commonwealth v. Hunt, 45 Mass. (4 Metc.) 111 (1842)

Connecticut General Life Insurance Company v. Johnson, 303 U.S. 77 (1938)

Contreras v. Crown Zellerbach, Inc., 88 Wash.2d 735, 565 P.2d 1173 (1977)

Coppage v. Kansas, 236 U.S. 1 (1915)

Corne v. Bausch and Lomb, Inc. 390 F. Supp. 161 (D.C. Ariz. 1975)

Dartmouth College v. Woodward, 4 Wheaton 518 (1819)

Downes v. F.A.A., 775 F.2d 288 (1985)

Duplex Printing Press Company v. Deering, 254 U.S. 443 (1921)

Ex parte Kinney, 3 Hughes 9 (1879)

Gideon v. Wainwright, 372 U.S. 335 (1963)

Godcharles & Company v. Wigeman, 113 Pa. 431, 6 Atl. 354 (1886)

Griswold v. Connecticut, 381 U.S. 479 (1965)

A Brief Guide to Case Citations

For the uninitiated, case citations are decoded this way: *Adair v. United States*, 208 U.S. 161 (1903):

Adair v. United States—This title says that *Adair* is suing the United States. (The plaintiff, or the one who instigates the suit, is listed first. Then the defendant's name is given.)

208 U.S. 161 (1903)—The U.S. Supreme Court decided the case in 1903 and the opinion begins at page 161 of volume 208 of the *United States Reports* (the official record of the Supreme Court's decisions since 1875). (Very early cases were reported in volumes that sometimes were named for their compilers.)

State Courts: Citations to state appellate court decisions tend to look more complex, but that is only because alternate sources for the decisions are generally included in the citation. Most (though not all) state appellate court decisions are published in volumes called "case reporters." The largest publisher of these is West Publishing Company. Each published opinion will appear in one of seven regional reporters, depending upon which state's court decided the case: *North Eastern* (N.E.), *Atlantic* (A.), *Pacific* (P.), *South Eastern* (S.E.), *South Western* (S.W.), *North Western* (N.W.), and *Southern* (So.) More recent citations will refer to the second series of a reporter. This is indicated by the initials "2d."

So, for example, *McGuire v. McGuire*, 157 Neb. 226, 59 N.W. 2d 336 (1953), may be decoded as follows: The first set of numbers (157 Neb. 226) refers to the version of the decision that is published in the official Nebraska reports, volume 157, starting at page 226. The second series of numbers (59 N.W. 2d 336) refers to the opinion's location in the *North Western Reporter*, second series. The decision may be found in volume 59 at page 336.

About the Book and Author

Few would dispute the notion that law has a tremendous impact on modern life. But social scientists who study the dynamics of family, work, and other important social institutions often ignore the pervasive influence of law. This introduction to the legal world and the sociology of law shows how social scientists can better account for the influences of legal issues in a wide range of social settings.

Incorporating historical and cross-cultural research into her book, Lisa J. McIntyre explains the general effects of law on interpersonal relations, the concept of the civil contract, and the relationship between law and social norms. She discusses why some societies and domains within societies have more law than others and shows that, contrary to popular wisdom, law is not only a reflection of social values but also fundamental to the formation of those values.

Lisa J. McIntyre is associate professor of sociology at Washington State University.

Author Index

Subject Index

DATE DUE